# Prehistoric Painting

*To Michel Leiris*

# History of Painting

Illustration on title page:

**Gargas,** Haute-Garonne
Hand "*in reserve*" Gravettian

Illustration on cover:

**Tassili n'Ajjer,** Sahara
*Group of bovids*

Pre-historic Painting
Egyptian and Ancient Eastern Painting
Greek and Etruscan Painting
Roman and Palæochristian Painting
Byzantine and Russian Painting
Roman Painting
Gothic Painting I
Gothic Painting II
The Renaissance I
The Renaissance II
The Renaissance III
Baroque Painting I
Baroque Painting II
Eighteenth Century
Romanticism
Impressionism
Expressionism
Post Impressionism
Cubism
Futurism and Dadaism
Surrealism
The Great Masters in Modern Painting
Abstract Painting
Chinese Painting
Japanese Painting
Islamic and Indian Painting
American Painting

# Prehistoric Painting

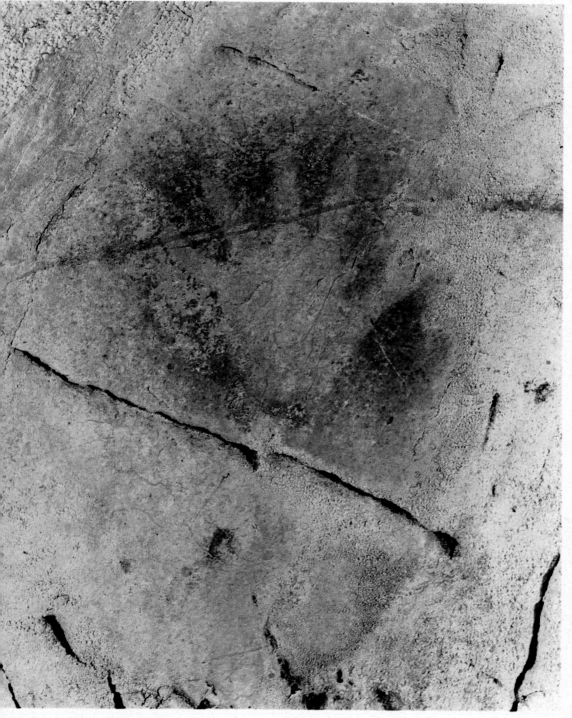

Raoul-Jean Moulin

*Translated by Anthony Rhodes*                    *Funk & Wagnalls, New York*

Series edited by Claude Schaeffner
Artistic advisor: Jean-Clarence Lambert
Illustrations chosen by André Held
Assistant: Martine Caputo

Library of Congress Catalog Card Number:
68-27363

Published by Funk & Wagnalls,
A Division of Reader's Digest Books, Inc.
by arrangement with Editions Rencontre
Printed in Italy

The coloured illustrations on pages 3, 6, 12, 15, 18,
21, 23, 24, 25, 26, 34, 35, 36, 39, 41, 42, 43, 44, 45,
52, 53, 54, 60, 61, 63, 65, 66, 67, 70, 74, 79, 80, 85,
87, 91, 92 and 93 are published by permission of
André Held Lausanne;
Prof. E. Ripoll-Perello, Barcelona: page 47;
Jean-Dominique Lajoux: pages 49 and 51;
The illustrations on pages 29, 30 and 31 are published with the permission of la Caisse nationale
des monuments historiques et des sites, Paris.

The black and white illustrations in the dictionary
are published with the permission of:
Andre Held: pages 154, 162 right, 171, 175 right,
177, 182, 183, 187, 193, 197 and 199;
Musee de l'Homme, Paris: pages 146, 148, 150,
151, 152, 153, 157, 158 left, 160, 162, 163, 166,
172, 175 left, 178, 180, 189, 190, 191, 194, 195,
198, 201 and 202;
Raoul-Jean Moulin: pages 165, 168 left, 185, 188
and 203;
Muller: pages 159 and 169;
Information service of the Ivory Coast: pages 158
right and 168 right;
Musee d'Aquitaine: page 172 right.

# Table of contents

The story of man represents the sum of his conquests over nature and man's own nature. It has taken millions of years of ceaseless effort for man to change himself from an animal, through the progressive differentiation of the hand from the foot and its adaptation as a tool; that is to say the use and appropriation of nature and its transformation through a certain social form. The freer the hand became, the more it loosened and became perfected, the more man developed; triumphing over difficulty, mastering the physical world in which he lived. Through the hand's modifying action he strengthened his power over things. The more that man dominates the world the more he is aware of it. Thus the faculty of thinking and reasoning, the forming of the senses and his creative force and articulate language are born of work. This vital premeditated activity makes him forever distinct from the animal.

All the art of the world begins with the first stone sharpened by a Paleolithic hunter, with these first attempts of man at testing matter and its quality. Though the appearance of art is confused with that of technique, art very quickly requires an important qualification and soon stands out within the design of the diveristy of work. If it were only for intellectual enjoyment or for pleasure, art would be nothing more than a game when in fact it is the projection of a real life experience. Whatever archaic or modern civilization he belongs to, the artist, each time he begins to work, stands aside from the arguments of his time, overcomes the doubts and anguish which strew his path and primarily rediscovers that moment of privilege when there is reason in humanity's conflict.

Art expresses the innate life of man in his wish to regain possession of his own nature, the fact of his power to create. Art humanizes man. It transforms him.

If indeed, artistic activity is conditioned by the development of techniques and existing social relationships, it does not reflect their limitations, it is not their prisoner. Art survives the societies which create it, the mythologies which inspire it: statues do not die, only men and their myths. Authentic art materializes the spiritual potential of a culture or civilization inexhaustibly, always ahead of its time: no one can interpret it once and for all, its meanings are not immutable, it reveals our feelings to us.

Also, we must guard against segregating the prehistoric art and peoples which we call "primitive" because they did not have as well developed a material life as ours. To see in theirs only magic, religious or utilitarian art would be to hint at an inferior state of artistic activity, an under-development of spirit, when, in fact, they participate by their form as much as by their function in the process of human evolution. In the same way, while we recognise the originality of their vision through our inability, clumsiness or instinct, we falsify the meaning, we do not see the obstinate and impassioned work through which man has conquered his animal nature, in order to make concrete his conception of the world and to once again overcome the social or natural objects which menace its realization.

This understanding the art of the past, this recognition of the work of people of all civilizations implies a radical revolution which cannot be accomplished without a complete and irreversible revolution of all mankind.

*By his work the artist develops that which is richest in man. Art cannot be made more perfect and denies all ideas of progress but it has never ceased to work towards an ever closer approximation with humanity. Whatever social or religious taboos he by his art more or less consciously transgresses, it delivers man from original darkness, shatters his solitude and permits him to communicate with his equals.*

*Art is a social act, an action of man on nature, an action of man on men. Whichever period or civilization it belongs to, art builds man, it expresses a certain moment of his experience, it is the interrogation through which he poses problems which experience and knowledge cannot yet resolve.*

R.-J. Moulin

# Introduction

*Whether drawing preceded painting or whether the two from the beginning were closely bound together, it is certain that prehistoric painting is very much older than is generally believed.*

*Perhaps man first began using colour to decorate the human skin. In a very old East African site fragments of red ochre were discovered which were obviously used for this purpose. For thousands of years ochre was sprinkled on the bodies of the dead and the custom of painting the living body    for magic or religious ritual purposes    still exists today. Tattooing, furthermore, is only a permanent form of body painting and it may be supposed that the men who took part in ritual ceremonies in the caves which they had decorated also had painted skin.*

*Prehistoric painting probably has a long history spread over the thousands of years which preceded the epoch of cave wall paintings in Europe, which are not more than twelve thousand or so, years old. It is to men like ourselves, 'homo sapiens', that we owe this pictorial art.*

*About 40,000 years ago these men appeared in Europe, probably coming from South West Asia. Gradually they eliminated or absorbed Neandertal Man who from the beginning of the last Ice Age, about 70,000 years gao, had occupied our Continent. Neandertal men were of various types, sometimes quite similar to us physically. They have left in certain parts where they lived, fragments of coloured objects, little plaques carrying traces of painting, perforated bones and geometrically engraved horns. It is thus very probable that a certain number of them painted and engraved. It is also known that they celebrated rites in the caves and that they buried their dead with objects that probably had a religious significance.*

*While we may assume that pictorial art was created by men of our species, in many of the regions where Upper Paleolithic 'homo sapiens' was fixed, he left no trace of either paintings or engravings.*

*It is evident that cave art is the work of many generations. It can be established that wall painting arose at the final period of the last Ice Age, after which the climate of western Europe, still very different from ours, improved. But during the course of thousands of years of prehistoric art there were numerous changes in climate; during the last 20,000 years western Europe has undergone six principal climatic phases.*

*Prehistoric artists lived in a Europe dominated by the Steppe, where forests were not widespread, where the winters were rigorous, and the summers relatively mild, that is to say in a climate analogous to certain parts of Siberia today.*

*Herds of great mammals wandered the plains and valleys and were the means of life for men living in small scattered groups. These species also changed considerably. Some became rarer — thus the mammoth, the cave bear and the long haired rhinoceros disappeared before the end of Paleolithic art.*

*A hundred years ago, paintings were known to exist in the Grotto of Niaux but at the time of their discovery did not raise much curiosity. It was the same with those in the Grotto at Rouffignac and until the beginning of this century such confused and contradictory ideas about prehistoric art were held that even the idea of pictorial art*

9

going back thousands of years seemed absurd. The history of the discovery of Altamira is a good example.

In 1868 a hunter having seen his dog disappear into a hole brought to light a passage leading to a grotto: Altamira! He hardly went any further once his dog had reappeared. But he told his adventure to anyone who would listen. With no result. Ten years later a land owner of the district, M. de Sautuola, visiting the Paris Exhibition, admired a collection of prehistoric objects — sharpened stones, engravings on bone, painted shields, female statuettes, etc., moveable prehistoric art was in fact recognised already as such. On returning to Spain Sautuola remembered the story of the hunter and wondered if the Grotto of Altamira might not yield similar treasures. He, therefore, began to dig at the front and there found traces of human occupation, but it did not occur to him to examine the walls. It was his grand-daughter who drew his attention to them. She had in fact discovered the famous polychrome ceiling of bison and other animals in a composition of extraordinary movement and life: a masterpiece of Magdalenian art.

Sautuola made several sketches to send to Vilanova of Madrid University. Vilanova came to Altamira. He thought the paintings very old. In 1880 in a letter to the Archeological Congress taking place in Lisbon he proposed, in vain, an exploration of the site, but in the face of the general lack of interest he did not press the matter.

However, during the last years of the XIXth century discoveries in the grottos of south west France gave rise to new controversies about prehistoric art. The sceptics were numerous and their objections only slowly dispelled. It was necessary to wait till Breuil and Cartailhac had extensively explored the Grotto of Altamira in 1906 for the existence of prehistoric wall painting to begin to be accepted.

Which are the areas where paleolithic paintings and engravings are found in Europe? First of all, the Franco-Cantabrian region: the basin of the Dordogne and its neighbourhood, part of the Charentes, a sub-Pyreneen zone which extends into the Cantabrian chain of northern Spain, and the southern site of Arcy-sur-Cure in the Yonne. Then there is the region which runs from Escoural in south Portugal to Nerja in eastern Malaga. One must also add, in the Castilles, two or three sites with decorated walls. Elsewhere in Europe there is little wall painting: traces in central Europe and Belgium, whilst in Italy there are a few decorated caves — Addaura, Levanzo and the Romanelli grotto in Otranto.

One must expect that with so many manifestations of art spreading over thousands of years, the aesthetic quality of the painting and engraving although within one tradition contains great inequalities.

In general, it is believed that prehistoric pictorial art was firstly a naturalistic art growing out of a visual realism which evolved afterwards into a more and more simplified and symbolic art. . . . But in truth, 'symbols' are found throughout the evolution of prehistoric painting and it is very likely that pictorial art looked for abstract or at least symbolic representation from the beginning.

Among the oldest traces left by man in the caves one sees marks made by a finger, a sort of streak on the clay surface. Certain scholars have been able to interpret them as being copies of cave bears' claw marks. Scribbles, interlacings, 'macaronis' are also found — with sometimes superimposed drawings of animals, nearly always represented in profile without the eye.

The imprints of hands, coated with colour used for body painting and placed on the rocky walls, appear to be the first pictorial attempts in the grottos. These hand prints are found moreover in all the periods of wall painting and it is curious to note that they often have a finger or phalanx missing. It is known to-day that among certain peoples there exists the custom of cutting off a phalanx or finger to denote mourning or as a propitiatory sacrifice. But one can also interpret the hand prints as one of the first attempts at drawing.

The paintings and engravings are conditioned by the rock relief. In the irregularities, the cracks of the walls, the artist found forms which he tried to modify. Relief is thus one of the main elements in prehistoric rock art. It is with the Magdalenian art that wall painting reached its summit. In the subterranean sanctuaries rites took place of which we can only guess at the nature and import. They were very probably of a religious character in the sense of a supposed relationship between man and the universe whose order it was necessary to maintain by ceremonies.

Magdalenian art was not long in disappearing as a consequence of drastic changes of climate. The glaciers of the north began to disappear while vast forests covered the steppes. A milder more humid temperature succeeded the rigorous cold. The great mammals on which man lived emigrated or disappeared. The Mesolithic succeeded the Paleolithic. Man lived by preference on the shores of lakes, rivers and the sea, bringing his dwelling places more and more out into the open. He made new tools for fishing and sea hunting. His artistic work was limited to drawings, to 'Alphabetiform' signs on shields. Probably his beliefs and rites changed with his art.

It is probable that the Magdalenian traditions were not perpetuated and it is assumed that paleolithic painting disappeared without trace.

Apart from any documentary side it may have, this painting belongs in a world where thought and feeling are mixed. At the beginning of the human adventure it is already, in the strongest sense an art, the urgent voice addressing us all.

Alan Houghton Broderick

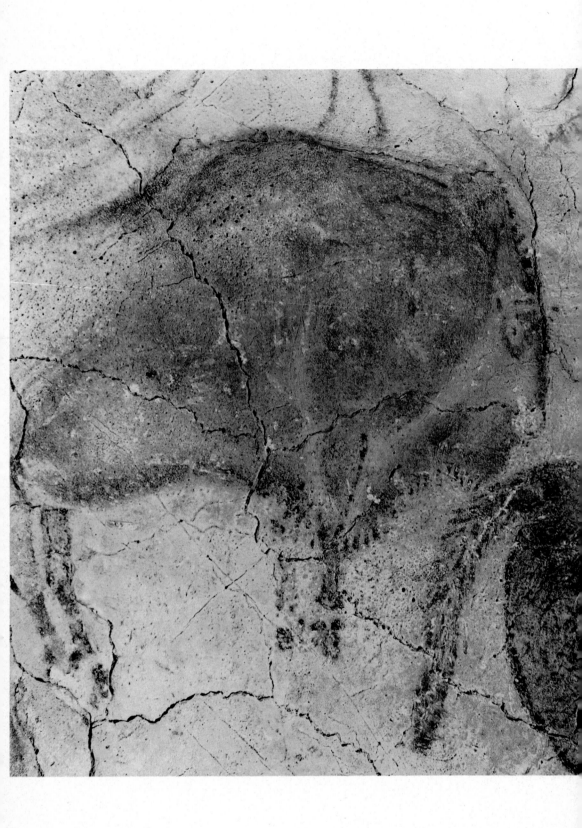

**Altamira,** province of Santander, Spain
*Bison.* Middle Magdalenian

# Prehistoric painting

Because of our ignorance of prehistoric peoples' social structure, we can date* the principal periods of evolution only by accepting a classification system based on techniques of which we have material proof.

Apart from various types of tools and arms which have come down to us (valuable indications of how humanity lived at the time), certain kinds of transport, beliefs and the first signs of artistic activity help us to distinguish the different primitive humanities. We learn about them more from their economic conditions than from the way they handled tools.

A first group, the "predatory" peoples, lived by hunting, berry-picking and fishing — nomads who gradually improved their arms and tools; and developed a highly expressive and skilled art. They belonged to Paleolithic humanity. A second group, the "producers", invented agriculture; they reared and domesticated animals, built and settled in villages, developed institutions, beliefs and techniques. They belonged to Neolithic* humanity.

As time passes, we tend to draw our conclusions more from the evidence of cultural activities than from the morphological evolution of tools. However, we still lack data on certain phenomena, and cannot entirely disregard the first chronologies established at the beginning of the century. On the other hand, we know know that the history of humanity is not continuous, that a uniform development of technique throughout the world did not exist; and that classification systems used for the prehistory of western Europe cannot be systematically applied to other continents. For the European Upper Paleolithic, the most recent chronology extends from Chatelperronian* to Magdelenian*, via Aurignacian*, Gravettian*, Solutrean* and a number of sub-divisions; it is concerned with Spain and France, above all with the Franco-Cantabrian* area. At present, owing to the richness of the sites, the high aesthetic quality of the finds in them, and their excellent state of preservation, these places alone can provide material for a synthetic sketch. Eleswhere, the chronologies are different.

The shape of a Levalloisian* flake, an Acheulean* hand-axe, the shape of an Aurignacian blade, or the flaking of the Solutrean period cannot reveal the foundations of a society; while the study of painted sanctuaries enables us to glimpse an entire elaborated system of thought, the social relationships implied and the existence of a culture.

Before painting or expressing himself through the medium of mineral colouring, man left his traces and printed his mark — the only indications he has left of intellectual activity. The tools of the early hominids* bear witness to constant efforts both formal and functional. Later, the "stone figures", flint nodules formed by natural causes, as well as shells, perforated teeth or fragments of bone, objects of veneration or ornament, reveal magical activity, as if they indicated an obscure need for creation. Lastly, it may be that, owing to pieces of red ochre found in many sites, we have evidence that they dyed their arms and tools, and painted their bodies*.

13

# Engraving and its experimental field

We know that during the Upper Paleolithic period, about 35,000 years before our era, during the last glaciation *, when homo sapiens succeeded Neandertal * man, revolutionizing tools and arms by the use of flint blades (scrapers, knives, awls), the first collections of cuttings appear on bones and plaques. Whether they were of a practical nature, magical or simply decorative, these repeated incisions reveal through the Chatelperronian period — however imprecise they may be — evidence of conscious artistic activity. When man engraved them, he was no doubt trying to recapture and deliberately recreate the traces of an animal sharpening its claws on stone, or those of his hand on the clay walls of the caves. Whether through imitation or mimicry, he produced in these fragments of bone which are cut, crenellated or in dotted design, apart from experiment in the technique of engraving, the outline of a still unformulated decoration, above all, the objective desire to achieve a form of visual expression.

Although this manner of portrayal was rough and imprecise, it succeeded in achieving, during the Aurignacian period, towards 30,000 B.C., the schematic line of the heads or the front parts of animals. The blocks, slabs of stone, which were found at La Ferrassie *, Isturitz *, and in the Bernous Cave * reveal some of the most ancient engraved and painted figurative compositions we know. One should note at the outset that a certain number have a purely symbolic character; in particular, the presence of the vulva (vagina) adjacent to pictures of animals emphasizes the sexual aspect of this symbolism, connected doubtless with some fecundity cult. This association of the female element with the animal, implying probably the early beginnings of religion, appears often during the Paleolithic period in wall painting * art *.

Painting and engraving are found simultaneously, sometimes on the same site. We should therefore study them with equal attention, not only because many incised figures have been painted, and still bear the traces of colour; but also because engraving (essentially graphical before becoming, through the relief and bas-relief, a form of extended sculpture) starts in a space and area similar to that of painting. They arose and developed together, but engraving, by exploiting the possibilities of a material, broke new ground, with a means of expression later to be adopted by painting. But the first is more than a mere laboratory, more than a sketch made with a graven, for the second. In engraving, lie the sources of painting.

While colour at the outset is frequently confined to blobs or patches, to uncertain finger tracings as if in soft clay, engraving in stone, bone or reindeer-antler reveals a greater technical assurance, combined with a desire to dominate and explain the nature of the world by employing its materials. According to the Abbé Breuil *, "For reasons we still do not know, man collected clay on the walls of the caves . . . he noted with curiosity the traces left by his fingers, which he repeated for the pleasure of seeing evidence of his own activity; he arranged them in volutes, winding lines, and

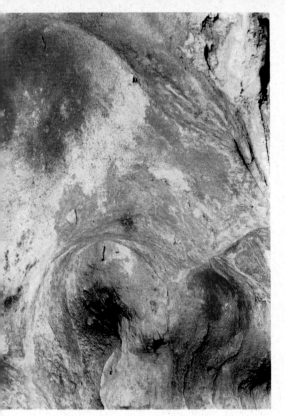

criss-cross designs; with these, he modified the natural relief into forms suggestive of figures, then he began interpreting his tracings, finding a meaning in them . . . in this way the first design was born, engraved on clay with a finger, then with any piece of handy wood or bone, finally with flints on the rock." [1] We cannot tell with certainty if painting and engraving were regarded as two separate kinds of activity; nevertheless it appears probable that engraving on an object, or on a wall, continually stimulated wall painting, but without ever achieving its fullness or lyrical quality.

This stimulatory quality of engraving beginning with the Gravettian period (about 25,000 B.C.) yields many and varied results. It is found on a piece of shale in the Pechialet cave*, in the simplicity of the line depicting a bear standing between two men, as well as in the linear entanglement of superposed animal figures which cover the pebbles of the Colombière shelter. In another domain, the same experimental and expressive intensity is to be found in a pebble in Laugerie-Haute*. Here the gradations of scratches, the sharpness and firmness with which the surface is attacked, cannot be explained as decorative in intention, but by a determination to enliven the surface, to alter the appearance of the material, to create a rhythm, a certain "colour", all due exclusively to the act of engraving.

## The first appearance of colour

It was during this period, in the first sanctuaries near the light of day, that the hand of man is found on the rocks. "His hand, dirtied with ochre or sweat was placed on a flat wall — and he saw it" wrote Breuil [2]. "This was the first wall painting. He varied it, used it as a kind of negative which he imitated by tracing it with some coloured

15

[1] Henri Breuil and Raymond Lantier, *Les Hommes de la Pierre ancienne*, Payot 1959.
[2] Ibid.

matter . . . As on silhouette designs in clay, the line was traced three times with the finger, then simplified into one line, and coloured design was discovered."

An amusement, an experiment, a magical operation or a ritual one — these coloured prints delight us, as much as they mystify us; the more they touch us directly, the more they seem fleeting, meaningless as engravings. We understand neither their uncertain shape nor their meaning; they are no more than vaguely anthropometric evidence, at the most signatures. They must not be confused with hands "in reserve", in black or red — formed by mineral earths diluted in the human mouth, which man would spit out forcibly around his hand placed upon the wall, after the manner of the contemporary Australian aborigines. In the cave of Gargas, the hands reveal rudimentary colours between the fingers spread open.

As distinct from this kind of impression, no more than a tracing or mark, the delineation of an uncertain shape by the hand "in reserve" (as at Gargas, and later at Pech-Merle *), man also acquired the illusion that he could create. His recognition of colour was no longer passive, as when he placed his clay-stained fingers on the rock to trace involuted and winding designs, but active and, to a certain degree, consciously directed. He increased the colour, placing it carefully and no longer confining it to the outlines of the hand but to the rocky material of the stone; he even drew an image of some kind. If he had not yet reached through colour a form of expression as rich as that of engraving, he appears to have discovered an original new language.

By varying the traceries of his own hand, by imprinting its shape "in reserve", he gradually began to outline figures, drawing a picture of the world around him. His awkwardness seems less important to us today than the freshness of this first impression; the figures he drew delight us less on account of his only partially successful attempt at depicting reality, but for his conscious intention of expressing himself in terms of that reality. The animals painted on the stone blocks of Parpallo * are clumsy daubs, if we judge them by the normal criteria of "beauty" In fact, they possess a certain freedom in their awkwardness, allowing us to follow the variations of line, less concerned with modelling a shape than with enclosing a space. Another painting on a block of stone, the deer spreading his antlers in the Labatut * shelter, gives an even greater feeling of this conquest of space; this is primarily due to the drawing, which is bursting with life.

Repetition is already rare, due entirely it appears to chance or a particular difficulty. In spite of the problems of the surface, of which the artist attempted to take advantage, he felt the need of a greater graphic continuity. Finger tracings or scratchings were no longer enough for him. Engraving once again shows its experimental nature; apart from certain heavy incisions in the rock, such as those at Belcayre *, it is less hesitating than painting, and seldom abandons the course it has set itself. In the bison of La Grèze *, for example, the deeply incised line is precise and powerful, drawn in one movement with no attempt at hiding its artificiality. Nothing appears to hinder

16

or distract the artist when he attempts the stronger, more varied engraving of the delicate dorsal line in the Pair-non-Pair Cave *, and which henceforth enlivens most of the animal figures in the Franco-Cantabrian world.

The horse, the ox, the ibex, the mammoth, the feline, the bison, are never the subject of a description or an anecdote, but the movement of their bodies are graphically seized, as if to symbolise their whole lives. Man knows that he wants. He deliberately sacrifices the details of his subject, having no intention of copying from nature. From each subject he elaborates his own vision, his own way of expressing himself and depicting the world.

It was at first believed that most of these creations, isolated or simply juxtaposed, had no organic link; but recent research has shown that they are connected, and should be regarded as a whole. The engravings disposed at intervals along the corridor of the Croze-à-Gontran, at the Eyzies *, influence one another as they unfold. The set of engravings opens and closes with signs, or rather with a set of delicate rapid incisions, haphazardly placed. Apart from certain indeterminate animals, they include a central group of horses and bovids placed between a mammoth and an ibex. It is perhaps too early to speak of composition; but it is true to say that, from the later Gravettian, we are aware of a definite theme running through the work.

## The elaboration of a natural material

The intrinsic qualities of engraving tell us towards what goal that art was aspiring. While engraving on bone or reindeer-antler, is exclusively graphic, incisive, dominated by a constant desire for a diagram, wall-engraving is notable from the outset for its attempt to discover the gradations between the actual incision and the form of the rock. The artist, addressing himself to the wall surface, is aware that he is working in a tangible, a living material; he therefore takes advantage of the slightest flaws, of the hollows, embossments, influences whose effect cannot be foreseen. He attempts less to outline a figure, to set down its contours, than to let the form or shape flourish on its own flush with the surface of the rock. This invention of natural "passages", this altering of the surface by the act of engraving, is the forerunner of an essentially pictorial technique.

Our estimate of Paleolithic art would therefore be wrong if we attempted to associate most of the reliefs and bas-reliefs created directly by engraving, by following the surface of the walls, to sculpture. Interpretation of this work, which is both self-confident and skilled, is difficult in the blocks of stone at Laussel *, particularly in that of the woman with horns. Here it appears that the artist, through the act of engraving, confident in his use of material, suddenly began to hollow out the stone, thereby producing shapes.

**Cougnac,** Lot
*Composition of Cervids and Ibexes*
Ancient Magdalenian

**Cougnac,** Lot
*Composition with Cervids, human figure
and Ibexes (detail of preceding illustration)*
Ancient Magdalenian

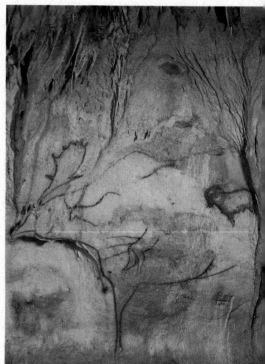

The means employed, although based on engraving, are not necessarily sculptural — in the same way that certain light tracings of red ochre do not mean that the artist was attempting to paint a picture. We must go beyond conventional analysis, or aesthetic dogmatism attached to this extraordinary evidence of man's desire to create, and approach him from a more modern angle. What impresses us most, apart from the crudity of this feminine figure holding what appears to be a bison's horn in an allegorical gesture, is the feeling of space. The figure is not detached from the rock, but is an intimate part of it; and it is this which gives it life. The deep and varied incision altering the surface of the stone, gives it a life of its own. The stone accentuates the broad flanks of the woman, and she stands out sharply from the rock surface.

In the same way, any comparison between the relief of Laussel and the many feminine statuettes, generally called "Aurignacian Venuses", appears unjustified. Although they are no longer considered Aurignacian (most of them are Gravettian, Solutrean, or even Magdalenian), the fact that their female characteristics are exaggerated alone justifies any connection with a fertility symbol. On the other hand, the space connected with the embossment has nothing to do with the relief, nor with an

18

act of creation common to both. The statuettes of Lespugue* and Willendorf* escape from their material, and become part of a space we understand, their emotional content being governed by the angle from which we regard them; but the Laussel relief is unconnected with sculpture, the result of an expressive use of the material in which it is bedded and its formation. The result is that the space is exclusively visual, hollowed out like a colour under the action of the engraving.

During the Solutrean period (about 18,000 B.C.) engraving became more precise. The spearheads and perforated bones* are now covered with geometrical designs; this graphic character is finally seen in the stylisation of the feminine body in the mammoth ivory of Prédmost* which is even schematic. But this composition of scratchings, chevrons, triangles, concentric curves and ovals could still be the transcription of tattooings* or corporal painting. In any case engraving on blocks or walls now stopped being only graphic, taking advantage of the configuration of the rock to shape its own space and produce its own light and shadow.

The blocks of stone of Roc-de-Sers*, and those of Bourdeilles* reveal this clearly. The first, which marked perhaps a sanctuary (some are overturned or buried) reveal a remarkable band of moving animals — a bull charging a small man, pregnant mares, a mythical creature with a bison's body and the groins of a wild boar, two ibex charging one another. The latter reveal skilful composition in the alternating curves of the horns, which prolong not only the rhythm of the dorsal line, but emphasise the ferocity of the clash. The block of stone at Fourneau-du-Diable, Bourdeilles, is equally imposing, although its impact is less due to the violent movement, but to the intense animation of the heavy static masses which communicate the internal power of its composition. Flush on the rock, a bull and a cow are superposed, becoming a part of the space, which they immediately transform. The space becomes a landscape of coarse stone, open to the play of light.

Rock is never neutral; as the artist works it, he uses its collaboration. He accepts it as it is, hard or soft, smooth or rough, taking advantage of its defects as well as its help, causing its expressive possibilities to work for him. Nor is this transformation of the material without its effect on the artist. His creative impulse increases as he discovers, re-invents, the natural shapes. The more we examine the reliefs of Roc-de-Sers, Bourdeilles, and Laussel, the more we understand the feelings of the painter, his chromatic treatment of material, his organic sense of space.

Wall painting did not evolve in the same definite way. For long dominated by finger tracings and hand imprints, it took time to modulate its own line, before rendering its shapes more subtle, reproducing movement and using the rich experience of engraving. Colour played only a secondary or subjective role, confining itself to the delimitation of contours. Not until the Early Magdalenian period did it take possession of the stone in the caves, developing its own language, in conformity with its own technique and requirements.

## Pictorial creation

After about 15,000 B.C., the caves of Las Chimeneas *, Gabillou * and Ebbou * reveal this slow movement towards pictorial creation, of which Cougnac * and Pèch-Merle are a definite stage. At Cougnac, the distribution of the great red figures follows the lay-out of the surroundings, using the whitened and irregular surface of the stalactite halls. The deer, moose, and mammoths enclose within their profile ibex, and men transfixed by spears whose mythical character is undoubted. But this symbolism is not limited to any given figure; its influence is spread to different compositions on the site, in association with the signs, and figures. In any given group, it is still hard to determine the exact meaning.

One of the designs of Pèch-Merle is more decipherable. It combines in a small room on the same panel figures deriving from a bison, a mammoth and a woman. There is no attempt at decoration, and they are closely associated by a double movement at once both graphic and symbolic. They both share the same supple, precise, continuous line and reveal an identical thought. In fact, it is this common line shared by all of them which makes the shape of the bisons and the women if not similar, at least closely related. Nothing could be simpler, yet at the same time more elaborate, than the self-possessed profile of this female leaning forward, the movement of whose breasts is superimposed in a manner as graphic as it is sensuous.

At Pèch-Merle, with its animated hands "in reserve" in black and red ochre, painting has become an act of incantation, by which man inaugurates the series of great theatrical sanctuaries, in a gesture celebrating the Universe. Powerful mammoths stand along the walls, traced with a firm hand in black; but they are not depicted by simple contours enclosed in silhouettes; the line is hachured, brief, rhythmical. With a few rapid lines he seizes the outline of a cow, but he uses complicated hachuring in his portraits of the mammoths, widening the gap between them, or closing it in order to illuminate or obscure them. Although the line seems to be pencilled, it already contains colour. What delights us most is the speed of his composition, the energy in a hand determined to create.

The man who achieves this is never made prisoner by reality. We recognise today that a certain clumsiness in the hypothetical "naturalism" of Paleolithic art is the expression of a reality which is more complex than we suppose. The mammoths of Pèch-Merle are not described; nor are they sketches for a more elaborate work, even less "put down as notes" to jog his memory. Their deliberate simplicity, their terrifying, ghostly appearance, is a part of their nature as mythical creatures; they are the projection of man's thought. In the same way, in the imposing allegory of two speckled horses, there is no "realism" in the strict sense of the term, but the invocation of a myth. Partly superposed and turned, one to the right, the other to the left, the two horses are powerfully drawn, their bodies speckled with great black points which

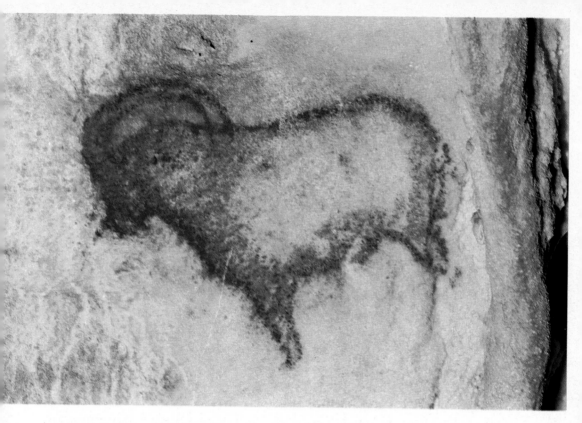

reverberate irregularly around them. The mane and the withers, painted in black, blend together, while the hands "in reserve" frame them, "freezing" them in space. Everything tends to intensify the conventional quality of the composition, and the esoteric nature of the subject, which is emphasised by a big fish painted in red on the right-hand horse, and which is only just visible.

For the man of the Ice Age *, as for us today, the act of painting appears to be essentially a refusal of pretence. Reality takes form through the myths, as does an active participation in creation.

## The conquests of human gesture or movement

Lascaux *, one of the great sites in the history of humanity, reveals the measureless creative power of man faced by nature. Of all the painted caves yet known, Lascaux possesses undoubtedly the richest collection of works of art. Here we are aware of that great privileged moment when colour founds its expression, accentuating and diversifying its melodic line, without however reaching polychromy. Supporting the engraving or modifying the drawing of the shapes, it passes from black to brown, from ochre to yellow, turning sometimes to violet red or mauve with the influence of time and natural phenomena.

The impressive movement which gave life to the vast rock compositions of Lascaux was determined by the shape of the rooms, galleries and alcoves. There was never any question of decoration, of arbitrary occupation of available emplacements, but rather of extolling the places — and this confirms a religious intention. As soon as we enter the hall of the Bulls, we are struck by the headlong movement of these animals. About a hundred animal figures, whose dimensions vary from nine inches to fifteen feet, unfold in precipitous flight. The smallest, probably the oldest, are no more

21

than shadows, spots of colour on the wall; the others are full of lustre and vigour in their gallop. They are dominated by four enormous bulls, of which the biggest measures five metres fifty; although we are conscious of their enormous bulk, the general unity remains. Freed of their weight, their trembling masses seem impelled into the air, in a continuous conquest of space, revealing the impulsive force of man's first truly pictorial gesture.

The bulls of Lascaux have a monumental grandeur which is not only due to their scale, exceeding that of all other examples of Paleolithic art. Through their impulsive movement, they seem to inhabit the wall, the texture of the stone; they are superposed on several moving figures, in varying proportions, which absorb them into their own space. Between the two bulls facing one another a group of stags can be distinguished, leaping and flaunting their horns, the dark red becoming indistinct in a background where a dark horse can be seen. Elsewhere, other horses with flowing manes, gallop about with brown cows, introducing new rhythms into the composition

In the neighbouring halls and corridors are other painted or engraved figures of deer, ibex, bovids, horses, coloured with black, ochre or dark brown by the finger of man, his brush or expectoration. There are bisons whose heavy mass seem to stand out from the wall; but in no other place is the lyrical inspiration which gives the hall of the Bulls its great majesty to be found. If the meaning of this highly coloured troop of animals is still uncertain, we should not underestimate the fantastic creature with long pointed horns in front, a figure considered by some to be a masked man, by others a unicorn. It is more likely a mythical incarnation, which is at the base of the whole composition.

There is a strange painting in the lower gallery at Lascaux. It shows a man with the head of a bird, his sex emphasised, lying on the floor in front of a bison; the animal has been transfixed by a spear and has lost its entrails. In the foreground, a bird is perched on a stick planted in the ground, while a two-horned rhinocerous is leaving the group. This has been interpreted as a hunting drama, the man being identified as a hunter wearing the mask of a bird, a totem sign found again in a stick signifying a funeral post. Other commentators have seen in this no more than a human stylisation beside a wounded bison; they regard the stick as a simple spear-thrower *, carved in the form of a bird, of which there are many examples.

## The presence of the myth

Ridding ourselves of all picturesque notions, it appears difficult not to admit here, even more than in the case of the female bisons of Pèch-Merle, the intervention of mythical creatures in the midst of symbolical themes. We must free ourselves as soon as possible from any notion limiting the significance of these pictures, regarding them to

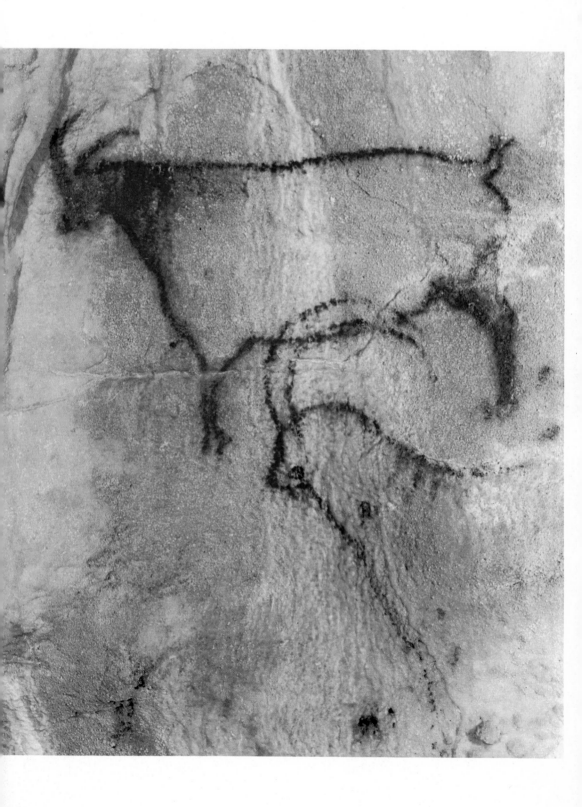

be no more than exercises in magic, "a sort of hunting notebook in which the Paleo-lithic artist, by drawing a bison with eviscerated entrails, is giving a command" (Leroi-Gourhan)[1]. The fertile body of the woman of Laussel, the feminine figures of Pèch-Merle, whose graphical variations are interwoven with those of the bisons, the fabulous animal in the hall of the Bulls, the wounded bison of Lascaux, like that of Lougerie-Basse*, accompanied by a climbing man, belong to a conception of the world in keeping with the cultures which have created them. The themes of the artists in the reindeer age reflect less the anecdotes of their daily life, than their system of thought, less their habitual beliefs than the cultural basis of their spiritual feelings, and of the society in which they live. Their creations are not the remains of magical and ultilitarian operations; they regard hunting as no more than the means of social communication; on the contrary, they tend, by using this common language, to increase the presence of the myth by conferring an aspect of reality on it, the moral visage of what humanity confusedly is aware that it is not. Thus, as Annette Laming-Emperaire* suggests, "the association of the horse, the bison and the woman appears

[1] André Leroi-Gourhan, *Histoire de l'Art*, Vol. I, Encyclopédie de la Pléiade, Gallimard 1961.

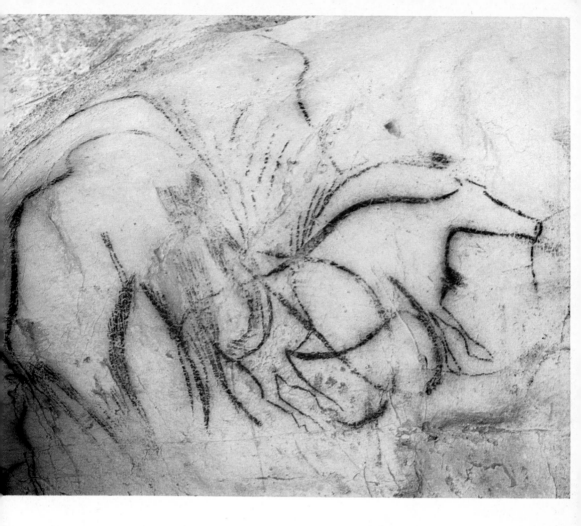

to go deeply into Paleolithic beliefs. It appears that the persistent exaggeration of the sexual character of the woman gives a sexual sense to that association . . . we can gradually distinguish the broad lines of a theme by which woman, the universal principle of fertility, occupies a central place. The male principle would then be represented by the bison which is regarded by man as a mortal enemy. In this group, the horse would correspond to a feminine element"[1].

Most of the themes dealt with are not therefore derived from the magic of the hunt, or very rarely, but from the opposition between destruction and fertility. On this subject, André Leroi-Gourhan rightly says that "fecundity and destruction are not incompatible; a metaphysical conception of birth and death are to be found behind every figurative group — something so common to all religions as to appear banal. However, we must consider that the proof of the existence, in the upper Paleolithic period, not of a magic in hunting, but of a metaphysical connotation, is a notable acquisition"[2]. From this point of view, a vast composition as complex and many-sided as that of the hall of the Bulls takes on all its symbolical sense, and reveals the sacred nature of the cave.

At Lascaux, as in all the caves containing paintings and engravings, we have as yet found no trace of religious ceremonies which the Paeolithic hunters could have celebrated here. Only the systematic excavations at the foot of the wall revealed

[1] Annette Laming-Emperaire, *La Signification de l'Art rupestre paléolithique*, Editions Picard 1962.

[2] André Leroi-Gourhan, «Le symbolisme des grands signes dans l'art pariétal paléolithique. *Bulletin de la Société préhistorique française*, October 1958.

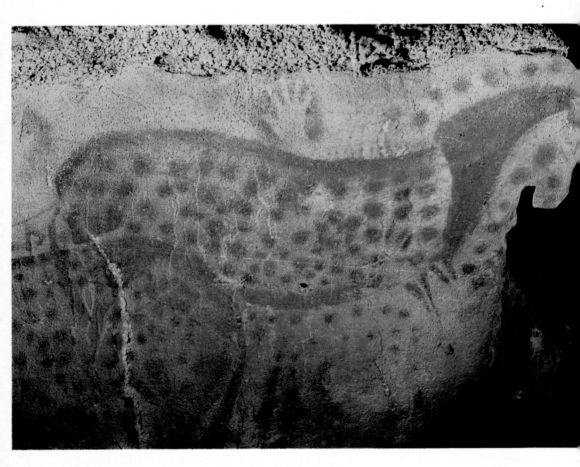

material evidence of these rites, of which up to now we possess only intuitive knowledge. On the other hand we know that these caves were never occupied and, if we judge by the foot-imprints in the earth, nothing would indicate these places for cults had been regularly visited by numbers of people.

The paintings and engravings are neither passive nor commemorative, but have a social significance, part of group life, on which they comment while possessing their own intrinsic qualities. We should not consider the walls of these sanctuaries as hunting notebooks, nor as logbooks for men of the Old Stone Age.

All interpretations proposed since the beginning of the century — of the ritual image of magical ceremonies, or totemic * initiations, or attempts to relate the savages living today with them morphologically or culturally — are singularly lacking in daring. They are generally confined to conceding some magical activity to Paleolithic man, even a religious activity, by carefully emphasising the "savage" aspect of his behaviour; but they refuse him an essential factor, the ability to think and to act which he had conquered from nature, to develop his powers and make his presence felt.

# The function and symbolism of the sign

We must first learn to look at the painted or engraved rocks of the sanctuaries of prehistory properly, then to decipher their figures and compositions one by one, before being able to interpret their melodic line in all its meaning. It is at this point that the signs intervene, still considered today as a phase of evolution leading to the supposed "realism" of the archaic figures, towards an increasing schematisation, ending in the alphabet signs of the Azilian pebbles*. In fact, Paleolithic art did not evolve from realism to abstraction as certain people like to think, but from a period of research and experiment to a period in which man's desire for self-expression is seen, before he declines into decadence, to gradually disappear as the culture which created him disappears. The painted signs of Mas-d'Azil do not mark the "degeneration" of art in the Ice Age, but with their original symbolism, they inaugurate a new kind of art.

During the Upper Paleolithic period, these signs are continually appearing, notable for their graphic variety. From the Aurignacian vulvas, the hands "in reserve", or applied on the walls after the Gravettian period, up to the "abstract" signs and the wounds of the Magdalenian, the sign is extremely common in the sanctuaries. It is probably connected with an extremely complex system of punctuation, introducing and putting an end to a group of figures, either associating itself with them, or isolating them. The signs known as "abstract" are those which, paradoxically, have given rise to the greatest number of ingenious interpretations, inspired by the desire of finding an anecdotic sense in the paintings. They have been classed as tectiforms*, pectiniforms, scaleriforms*, and claviforms, and their commentators have discovered in them snares, hunting nets, weapons, enclosures, huts, even coats of arms.

Deriving largely from masculine and feminine paintings, these signs are part of a sexual symbolism; they are sometimes found coupled together, more often with animal figures. At first sight their role does not seem essential, but a more thorough analysis enables them to be situated in the evolution of the compositions, and enables us to understand why they are there. Thus, Leroi-Gourhan states "there is a relationship between the assagai and the male sign, between the female sign and the wound, in such a way that wounded animals sometimes replace animals accompanied by signs"[1]. This relationship implies a complete revision of our ideas about wall painting in the Paleolithic period; it removes all notion of the voodoo of wild game depicted by "magic" figures, and confirms the mythical nature of the works, their extremely elaborated form of expression.

[1] André Leroi-Gourhan, *Histoire de l'Art*, Vol. I, Encyclopédie de la Pléiade, Gallimard 1961.

# Small art and its decoration

The artist's mastery becomes evident towards 12,000 B.C., in the decoration of objects of household art — an invention which flourished during the Middle Magdalenian period. The spearheads are covered with a geometrical décor, the harpoons with one or two rows of spikes, the hunting spears are made of reindeer or red horn, as are the spatulae, and pendants are made of stone or bony matter. In this abundant production a place apart must be reserved for the perforated bones *, and for the spear-throwers which, without losing their functional qualities, reveal the creative ability of the artist-hunter.

Considered at first as a sceptre of rank, the perforated bone (in which some people today see a phallic allusion) was probably used after the manner of the modern straightener for arrows of the Eskimos, in a movement similar to that of a screw-spanner. Combining animal figures with geometrical decoration, which is often champlevé * over the entire surface of the instrument, these perforated bones discovered in the caves of Laugerie-Basse *, Arudy *, Gourdan *, la Madeleine *, Brunique *, Portes *, Isturitz, El Castillo *, are delicately engraved in a most imaginative way. We may sometimes be tempted to associate the spear-throwers found in the same places with sculpture because they seem to have such a sculptural shape ; but a careful examination reveals that many are not rounded. We then observe a flattening of the animal's volume, a graphical translation of his shape and posture, relating him closely to figures with well cut contours. The bison turning his head from the cave of La Madeleine is an example, the incision shallow, the muzzle depicted in light relief, giving an effect of depth without destroying the unity of the whole. For the same reason, the artist is careful to depict only one side of the head.

While these perforated bones and spearthrowers are covered with motifs which can be related directly to wall painting, the strange semi-round wands have a very individual form of decor. We still do not know if the pronounced scratches which cover their flat face have a purely mechanical purpose, but the geometric decoration which enlivens their convex face, and particularly the subtle curvilinear relief of the wands from Lourdes * and D'Arudy, are evidence of a real desire to create something.

We again see animal figures, combined sometimes with human figures, on engraved or painted plaques, pebbles, fragments of bone or stone found at the foot of the sanctuary walls. The entanglement of their lines, making them frequently difficult to decipher, the more scratched than incised appearance of their engraving, have been interpreted in the most fanciful ways. Some people claim that these small plaques are "sketching pages" of some kind, for use with vast rock compositions, even the exercises of students under the direction of a master. Some authors have even claimed that at Limeuil *, as at Parpallo (as elsewhere), there were real "studios of prehistoric art". Bearing in mind the importance given to graphic research, there may well be "studios" ;

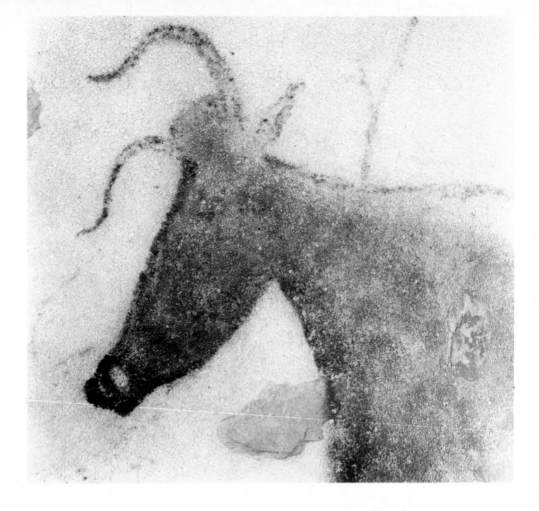

for there are remarkable similarities of theme between most of these small plaques and the great wall painting groups, in particular those associating the horse and the bison. If these are "studies", then they were undertaken by the artists themselves. But their great freedom in draughtsmanship, their repeated superpositions (even to the point of becoming inextricably confused), indicates that they were not produced gratuitiously, but with a specific intention, implying a desire for repetition rather than obliteration. It would seem therefore that because of the quantity and variety of these figures, the small plaques have an essential votive purpose.

## Stone modulation

This dazzling technique, displayed in objects of household art, appeared in all sections of artistic production during the Middle Magdalenian period; paintings, engravings and reliefs reached their highest development.

Thus, the great monumental freize of the Cap-Blanc * shelter with its seven horses, accompanied by three bovids and two bisons, unrolling in a magnificent relief on a dozen metres of wall, is a repetition of the stone modulation, and the space used at Roc-de-Ser, Bourdeilles. The two feminine figures of the La Madeleine * cave which stand out slightly from the rock are equally significant. Nude, half-reclining, the upper part of the body supported on an arm, they are symmetrically disposed, one on the right, the other on the left; the shapes are supple and lively, well illuminated, and still after the passage of the millennia, full of sensuality. But it is undoubtedly the many reliefs of Angles-sur-l'Anglin* which confirm the expressive maturity of this art. Combined with bisons, the feminine silhouettes, representing half the body, nude, upright, slender as at La Madeleine, emerge from the stone, with emphasis on the belly, the sex, and the sensually treated thighs. With superb technical assurance, the horses, bisons, and ibex move along the whole extent of the stone, becoming part of its material, even surpassing the splendours of the Solutrean period. Moreover, the traces of colours which they retain prove that relief, by its modelling of surfaces, its use of gaps caused directly by the engraving, is the proper experimental field for pictorial purposes. One of the reliefs at Angles-sur-l'Anglin, a human bust, gives an effect of polychrome, thanks to the subtleties of the black and ochre. If we rely on these painted reliefs, the various spots found on those of Laussel, Roc-de-Sers, Bourdeilles, Cap-Blanc and on the wild horses of Mouthiers* appear less enigmatic.

As for engraving, the extreme graphic complexity of the innumerable small Magdalenian plaques is on a different scale; they invade the walls of the Combarelles

cave, with even more incisions, a greater variety of figures, and reveal free artistic activity. Among several hundred figures, nearly three hundred have been identified, including oxen, ibex, reindeer, bears, deer, mammoths, lions, does, rhinoceri and above all, many kinds of horses, bisons and anthropomorphic figures. At first sight, they were considered as sketches, and their confused scratchings as proof of a clumsiness in dominating the subject; but a detailed examination reveals that several engraving techniques were used at Combarelles, and never in an arbitrary or haphazard way. The fine rock abrasions are followed by more pronounced scratches; the line becomes more distinct in the remoter parts of the gallery, although making no attempt to encircle the figures. On the contrary, it remains free, open, vital, thereby preserving all its liberty. Far from attempting to enclose a shape, it allows the shape to follow the close rhythms of the passages — a characteristic of the Parietal engravings in Paleolithic sanctuaries — at the same time recreating the richly varied "colour", the expression of painters rather than sculptors.

## Realism and paleolithic compositions

The question raised by the anthropomorphic figures is still answered in a variety of ways. Many authors, dominated by a naturalist conception of Paleolithic art, are led astray by these figures, which seem to them the product of pure fantasy, or the anecdotic portrayal of an event or a cult. They too class them as hunters, dancers, or masked and disguised magicians, when they are in reality no more than "grotesques". But the reality of the reindeer áge presupposes another kind of realism, permitting the artist to define for his fellows the system of thought on which the activity of the social group was founded and directed.

The interpretation of this realism has proved as difficult as that of the walls in Combarelles; but it would be superficial to deduce from it any disordered or instinctive expression, connected with the many needs and demands of hunting magic. Combarelles would then be no more than a huge stock of "voodoo" game, which would conceal the essential qualities of a sanctuary. In fact after the recent researches of Laming-Emperaire and Leroi-Gourhan, we see at Combarelles, and elsewhere, that most of the superpositions of the engravings are due to a need for artistic expression, and are not intended to obliterate the earlier figures. They were carried out deliberately, simultaneously, with various techniques, in order to vary the effect of the incision. These engravings are distributed in an orderly manner; their confusion is only apparent. They are not only a part of the rock, deeply penetrating it while conforming to its idiosyncrasies — but the freeze unrolls according to the shape of the gallery, using the turnings as a full stop, or hiatus in the general disorder of the composition, grouping together the associated figures at the centre of a troop.

There are sanctuaries where themes follow one another, repeated according to a well determined programme. At Marsoulas * where the colour hachuring attempts to translate the shape of certain animals by a graphic effect similar to that of engraving, the figures and signs increase; their relationship becomes more complicated as they get farther from the entrance, then become simplified and further apart as they approach the end of the cave. A similar phenomenon is found at Arcy-sur-Cure *, where the big mammoths of the central compositions emphasise the evolutionary character of this system of symbolic figures. The signs reappear frequently in the picture; rapid, closely massed, sometimes even obscure, they add expression to the picture.

In the same region, the caves of Labastide * and of Portel possess series of figures which are equally ordered; in particular the second, which with the exception of some archaic figures, appears to observe a rule in the distribution of bisons and horses, assembled respectively in different galleries. In other caves, the general plan is to separate two varieties of animals; here we may note the extremely symbolical juxtaposition, which is exceptional, of a bison and a horse wounded by an arrow. Lastly, it is not by chance, nor the result of some decorative fantasy, that at Portel, near the galleries, but set back inside a small room, there is a kind of recapitulation picture of the principal figures, which control the composition of the sanctuary, accompanied by the punctuation of a set of signs.

In the same way at Rouffignac *, long trains of mammoths escorted by bisons, ibex, rhinoceri, painted and incised horses, reveal the aesthetic preoccupations in which myth takes a dominating place; for instance, the procession in which two files of mammoths face one another, led by two males.

## Superpositions and organic figures

However at Lascaux, as at Les Combarelles, the Paleolithic artist often shows his preference for more complex and ambitious means of portrayal. It is again in the Dordogne, at Les Eyzies, in the cave of Font-de-Gaume, at Niaux * in Ariège, and in the cave of the Trois-Frères *, that themes and multiple superpositions, the richest in the whole of the Magdalenian period, are discovered. To understand such works, those criteria which we have already shown to be without foundation must be avoided. In the word of Leroi-Gourhan, "they have been judged by civilised men, with the aesthetic criteria of Western men in the nineteenth century tradition; the absence of symmetry in the groups has been interpreted as absence of composition, the confusion

33

**Marsoulas,** Haute-Garonne
*Barbed Line (perhaps sign of masculinity)*
Middle Magdalenian

▼

**Marsoulas,** Haute-Garonne
*Bison in Lozenge design*      ▶
Middle Magdalenian

**El Castillo**      ▼
Province of Santander, Spain      ▶
*Joined signs.* Middle Magdalenian

of the themes as the piling up of successive isolated images"[1]. We now know that most of these superpositions are not the result of an accumulation of figures over several epochs, that they played no part in the needs of the hunter. On the contrary they reveal the creative desire which obeys the particular demands of expression while partaking in a narrative, in the celebration of a myth. This is not only an aesthetic convention, an artifice of composition, but a principle of communication, a language reflecting the mythical or religious thought of a social group.

At Font-de-Gaume, among more than two hundred overlapping figures, is a herd of polychrome bison, whose red and brown masses are depicted by short and sharp incisions in the rock. A group of small mammoths, superficially engraved and coloured, full of life and crammed together, producing a kind of spacial counterpoint which is infinitely fluid and subtle, surround them. In spite of a different scale, changing the treatment of space, there is great unity of style in the two portraits, the result of a similar kind of drawing, Thus, the modulations of the dorsâl line, common to both the bisons and mammoths, is used with the sole aim of creating a similar rhythm between them, a graphic concordance. It goes without saying that such a concordance implies others, more intimate and decipherable only with difficulty, of which we still perceive only the symbolical association of two species evidently united in a mythical space. But there can be no doubt that this manner of composition by superpositions cannot be read continuously, logically, or in a detailed manner, because its aim is to give a global view of the expressed action.

This search for an organic way of depicting figures, presupposing a coherent

[1] André Leroi-Gourhan, *Histoire de l'Art*, Vol. I, Encyclopédie de la Pléiade, Gallimard 1961.

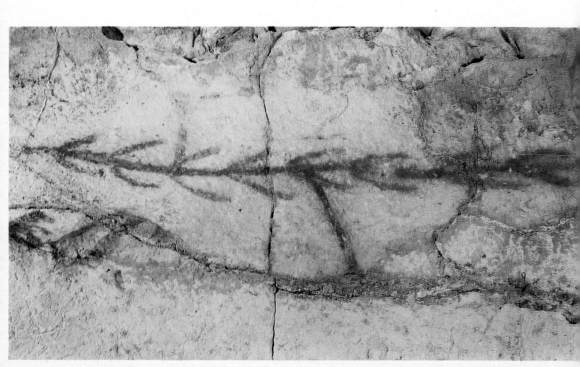

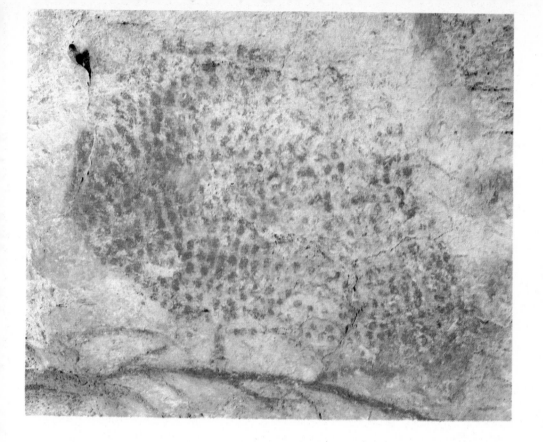

form of thought, is found again at Niaux, and at the Trois-Frères in a more elaborate form. At Niaux, where there is great similarity between the wall paintings and the engravings in the clay soil, the observer is struck by the highly effective manner in which this natural canvas is used. This creative work — and only true painters could have undertaken it — is well described by Annette Laming-Emperaire: "The rock has never been prepared, never planed; it must be used as it is, an almost living natural canvas in which all the asperities, humps, crevices, ridges, hollows, and the reliefs, far from embarrassing the artist have, as it were, guided and inspired him. For it is the rock, with its natural shapes, evoking sometimes a rump, sometimes a belly, some-

times a trunk, sometimes an almost complete animal, which often seems to have been responsible for the painting"[1]. Here at Niaux, as at Altamira, the rock seems to crave exploitation, inspiring the artist — at once material, shape and colour. No constraints are put upon him; the rock offers a large range of solutions of which he takes advantage, without however falling into any kind of mannerism.

It must have required extremely receptive painters to react to this so sincerely, in the definite manner which even today delights and fascinates us. No attempt is made to use polychromy, or coloured flat tints — an absence of colour which could not fail to blind the first commentators on the Niaux cave, so that they even described the principal hall by the term "black salon". It is true that black dominates, effective in its firm direct tracing, as incisive as an engraving, imprinting itself on the stone better than other colours; it appears to have been chosen essentially for these graphic qualities and the many possibilities of superposition. It is clear, simple, effective, and the scenes which it depicts can be immediately read. The lines are not concerned only with the figure which is drawn, but with the unity of the artist's inspiration as seen in the whole composition.

The "black salon" is not a thing apart; it belongs to the four groups which

[1] Annette Laming-Emperaire, *La Signification de l'Art rupestre paléolithique*, Editions Picard 1962.

compose the sanctuary, repeating the central theme of the whole cave. The principal role in this theme is played by powerful bison, sometimes wounded by black or red arrows; ibex, deer, a lion, and especially horses are associated with them, have a part in their movement, initiating it or terminating it, without ever complying with the same plan. In spite of the clumsiness of the line, and its multiplicity, all these associations are harmoniously accomplished, organically, in a space where the shapes become lighter, purer and more transparent. This takes nothing from the monumental character of the composition which relies on the principles of superposition — to be found spread over the entire Franco-Cantabrian domain; one animal between the paws of another, some of them doubled up, one on top of the other, confused one with the other, facing one another, alternating. There is, moreover, at Niaux a recapitulation panel at the end, where all the elements of the theme are repeated, as well as the actors who people the walls of the sanctuary, and the graphical situations in which they take part.

The cave of the Trois-Frères has equally varied superpositions, no less disciplined, although there is a certain lyrical quality in the groups. The animals are painted to different scales, yet related to one another. A troop of small bisons, for example, accompanied by ibex, deer, rhinoceri, is placed above an enormous bison associated with a horse between his paws. Elsewhere in the deepest part of the cave, the composition is divided into three groups, each an individual unity, in which bison, horses and reindeer are preponderant, all dominated by the strange and celebrated figure of the "magician".

## Synthetic figures

This "magician" has been interpreted in a number of ways, most of which betray an inadequate view of Paleolithic realism. Attempts have been made to justify this anthropo-zoomorphic person, whose sex is clearly marked, by identifying him with a masked and disguised hunter, dancing or celebrating some magic cult. He has been described as a magician, but also as a great spirit, the god of hunting or fecundity.

We must go beyond these ideas of voodooism, and not always look for illustrated stories of the daily life of the Ice Age in the rock paintings. If we do not know how they are connected, or cannot follow the thread which explains them, or the ideology which inspires them, we nevertheless possess enough proofs of the social and cultural activity of Paleolithic humanity not to regard it and its artistic works only as something "curious". We must attempt to read these designs, to decipher them in their natural context.

In this way, Leroi-Gourhan considers the "magician" of the Trois-Frères as a "synthetic" person, similar to the recapitulatory panels which end the groups of Niaux and of Portel, gathering together all the main characters of the principal theme. Combining painting and engraving, the human as well as the animal element, the "magician" takes on the various characteristics of the species which surround him: from the reindeer, he takes the antlers; from the bisons, the beard and the ears; from the horses, the tail and the movement of the bodies. He is therefore a composite figure, occupying a position which allows him to dominate the whole of the composition and the entire sanctuary, thereby displaying his holy quality. This is not the portrait of a masked dancer, whether a magician or not; but rather of a mythical creature, a supernatural being expressed by the means of a symbolism preceding from a general conception of the world, and whose effects are to be found again in the bearded person with the antlers and horse's tail, engraved on a small plaque at Lourdes.

## Tensions in painting

At the boundaries of the Franco-Cantrabrian expansion area in Spain, in the province of Santander, the Altamira cave contains remarkable paintings by a Magdalenian hunter, rivalling those of Lascaux. Covering the vault of a relatively low and narrow room, the paintings have long been considered as independent of one another, although Altamira has been described as the Sistine Chapel of pre-history. But we have no need to compare the work with that of Michelangelo, to recognise the greatness of this sanctuary. About a hundred horses, does, stags, ibex, wild boar, among other animals are distributed across the wall; while about twenty life-sized bisons project their brutal bulk into this swarming mass of shapes and colours, as if to petrify it.

The horns, the eyes, the nostrils and hoofs are often set in with a firmly incised line, and most of these animals possess a polychrome effect hitherto unknown in Paleolithic rock art, underlining the presence of highly contrasted flat tints of colour. The big figures particularly, while conceding nothing to naturalism, are powerfully modelled by the application in varied styles of red, yellow, brown and an extremely subtle and delicate rhythmical line. Moreover, to accentuate the modulation of the surfaces, the Altamira painters have exploited the uneven nature of the rock, combining their colour with that of the rock, which confers on their works a natural intensity. The animals are not simply attached to the wall, coloured pictures on stone, but seem to be born from the stone, to live in terms of the material.

It is clear that before undertaking these paintings, the artists must have studied the shapes of the caves most carefully, drawing up a plan for the distribution of the different groups of figures, a general order of composition. But this would mean that certain parts of the rock surface are best suited to certain animals, as we can judge by the frequence with which given associations reappear, in particular that of the bison and the wild boar. The whole animal group is connected by punctuation signs, feminine and

**Niaux,** Ariege
*Wounded bisons*
(detail of illustration on page 38)
Middle Magdalenian

**Niaux,** Ariège
*Wounded Bison*
(detail of illustration on page 38)
Middle Magdalenian

masculine, which were long thought to be clubs and ladders, manual imprints, incomplete paintings, and anthropomorphic figures engraved with a bird's head. The composition is most clearly ordered, with the great bison as the central element, full of light and chromatic variations.

Altamira has often been compared to Lascaux, particularly for the rare plastic quality of the wall paintings; it has even been said that the figurative conventions are the same in the two sanctuaries. This comparison appears doubtful, because if the conventions have a common source, and correspond to the designs of the same inspiration, they are expressed differently in each cave. At Lascaux, most of the compositions, in particular in the hall of the Bulls, give the impression of violent movement, tumultuous yet full of lyricism. The theatrical nature of the place endows the whole scene with a monumental quality; a painting of action and celebration. Altamira however reveals a more static form of pictorial expression. The composition of the vault in the principal hall has a maximum concentration of figures, ending with the formation of a compact coloured mass; taken individually these figures, and particularly the biggest ones, seldom appear to be in movement, they differ further from those of Lascaux. The bison of Altamira, and to a lesser degree the does and the wild boars, are part of a subtle arabesque design, an effect enhanced by close hachuring. It is a painting of tensions, pent up forces, oppositions, while at Lascaux the movement is simple and direct.

In the province of Santander, the caves of Castillo, and Pandal possess further interesting groups of paintings and engravings. Isolated from the Franco-Cantabrian cultural area, but displaying certain affinities with it, the caves of Levanzo, in the Egadi Isles, and of Addaura* near Palermo, possess engravings with deep incisions, but of considerable finesse.

# The disappearance of the sanctuaries

After 10,000 B.C. approximately, the great Magdalenian period entered its last phase preparatory to the sudden decay which Paleolithic art was about to experience. Severe climatic changes at the end of the last glaciation repulsed the great herds of reindeer towards the North, destroying its economy and culture, and giving its civilisation the death-blow. After this we find no more sanctuaries; the rock engraving becomes set in a sterile naturalism notable only for conventional painting and technical artifice. By 8,000 B.C. all was over. In the Dordogne, the sites of Teyjat*, Limeuil, la Madeleine, Villepin* and Isturitz in the Basses-Pyrénées contain some of the last examples of Franco-Cantabrian art.

The many engraved stones found at Limeuil, long considered the work of
students from some "studio of prehistoric art", are difficult to decipher, and have little
graphic interest. The superpositions of the bovids are still visible; a bull in an unusual
position is well adapted to the surface of a small plaque; there is a mysterious scene
which may be a parturition, or a funeral lamentation. The bone engravings of Teyjat
reveal a sure sense of ornament; one depicts in a confusion of antlers a line of reindeer
in movement. But these are the last liberties which the Paleolithic allowed itself.
Henceforth, painting in the caves is precious and mannered, while the decoration
remains geometric and schematic, little altered since the earliest Aurignacian period.

Contrary to the general belief, it appears that the principal cultures of the Upper
Paleolithic possess a certain unity over the whole period, that is between 30,000 B.C. and
8,000 B.C., just before agriculture makes its first tentative steps in the Franco-Cantabrian area. The inspiration appears always the same, dominated by a meaning, and a
traditional order of great severity, which we still today do not entirely understand, but
intimately connected with the expression of the main theme. As Annette Laming-
Empéraire writes "They may be mythical, and recall the origin and history of a certain
human group in its relations with the animal species; they may embody a very ancient
metaphysical idea and express a terrestial system in which each species, animal or
human, plays its part, and where the sexual division is of the first importance; they may

[1] Annette Laming-Empéraire, *La Signification de l'Art rupestre paléolithique*, Editions Picard
1962.

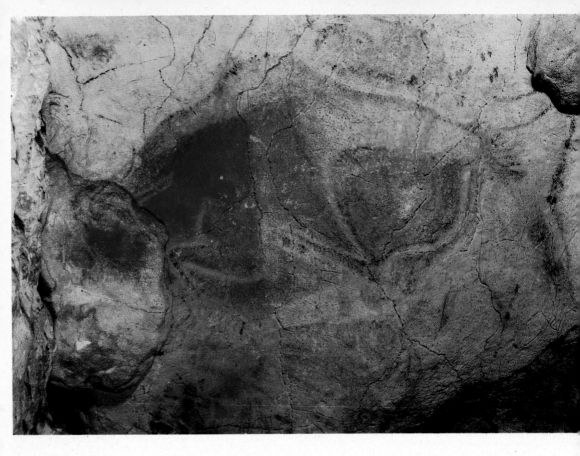

be religious and depict supernatural beings"[1]. They may also be mythical, meta-physical and religious, reflecting the spiritual and social experience of Paleolithic humanity, revealing that they are conscious of future continuity.

The art of the hunters of Altamira, Lascaux, Pèch-Merle, and Niaux are the result of a creative process which appears to be much closer than we think to historical periods which we know better, or even to those which we live in. This art which we thought was magical, to satisfy some obscure need of the intellect to escape from the present, is now, thanks to patient research, revealed to us in all its original fullness; and these first attempts at expression, face to face with nature seem to us contemporary and neighbourly.

## The mesolithic transition

Coming after the Pleistocene * which followed the Ice Age, whose huge troops of reindeer had perished or emigrated northwards, the Mesolithic * is a relatively short period between Upper Paleolithic and Neolithic; it marks the transition between an economy based on hunting, berry gathering, fishing and an agricultural economy, in which man at last cultivated and produced from the earth. After about 8,000 B.C. Mesolithic man hunts with the bow and arrow; he invented the sledge and small boat, improved his snares and tools, in particular the harpoon, the scraper and the weapons with flint points. One side of his production, in the Mediterranean regions and in northern Africa, is distinguished by the use of microliths which differ little from those at Capsa * and Mas-d'Azil while passing through the Spanish Levant *. Elsewhere, in the Baltic and Scandinavian zone, the age is notable for flint hatchets, hammers, picks, heavy tools inherited from the Paleolithic, to which were added the bait, the net, and many other devices for sea fishing, the principal activity of Maglemosian culture *.

Figures now tend to be confined to essentials; but the art of Maglemose goes to the extreme with the many geometrical motifs found throughout the entire Upper Paleolithic period. Incised, spotted, or punched, this form of decoration has a complex symbolism, closely related to the schematic graphism of human or synthetic portraits, the product of triangles, lozenges and angular lines.

The painted pebbles of Mas-d'Azil, which are sometimes engraved, display this new symbolism with even greater originality. The crosses, circles and rectangles with cross pieces, the marks, crenellations, the short hachuring repeated along a curve, possess a sense of style and an abstraction which can hardly be explained as a simple

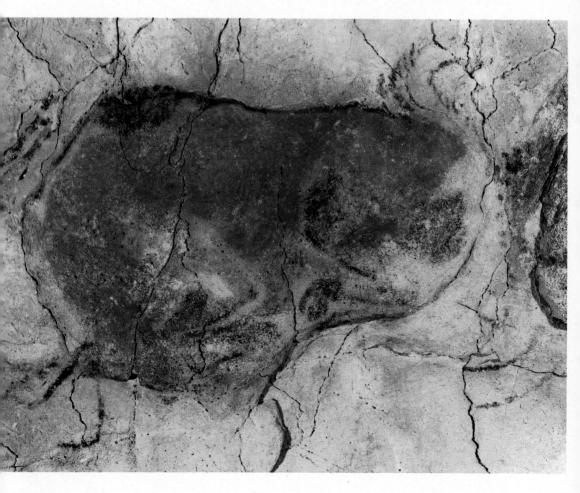

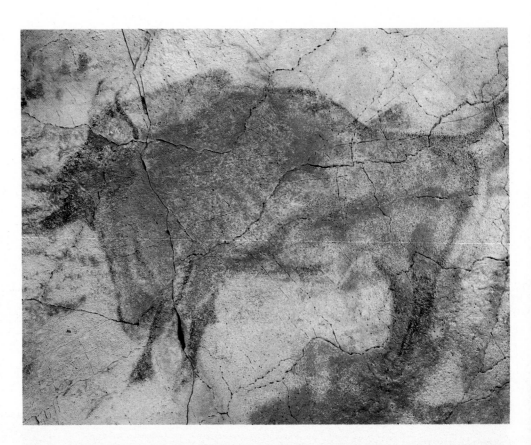

44

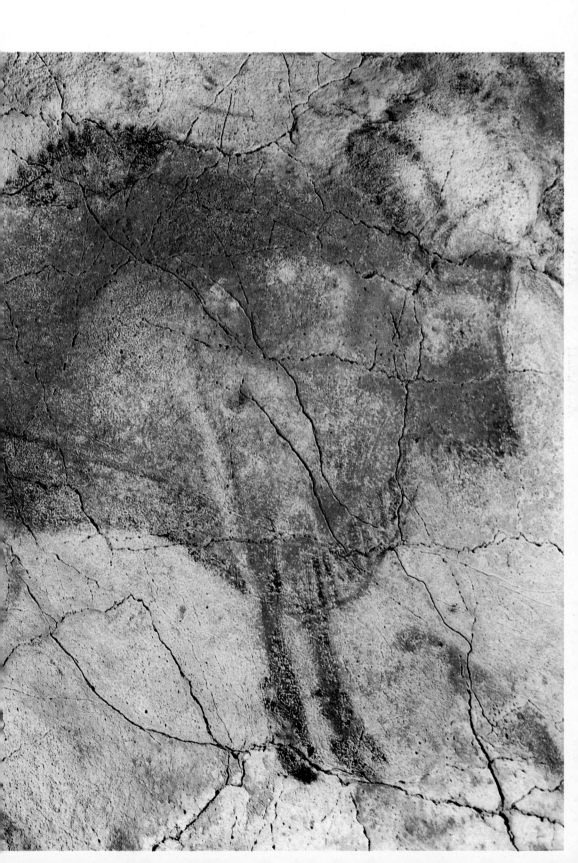

taste for ornament. Painted in red ochre and faithful to the shape of the pebble, these signs, which are derived according to Breuil from southern Italy, started a kind of pictographic * form of painting to be found in certain rock paintings of the Spanish Levant, precursors of schematic figures and anthropomorphous Iberian plaques of shale, related to the Neolithic "idols" of the Mediterranean basin.

Unlike Franco-Cantabrian art, the paintings of the Spanish Levant are not inside deep caves, but on the walls of shelters beneath rocks, in natural anfractuosities exposed to the daylight. The difference is not confined to this, but is repeated in both aesthetic and social terms. In the first place, although the art of the Levant displays, in its paintings and engravings, a type of life based on hunting and berry-gathering, it seems to possess from the Paleolithic tradition only survivals which have been re-generated by other cultures, dominated by other types of signs, perhaps by other myths. Without placing it as late as the Neolithic, as do certain Spanish authors, it appears improbable that it reached its zenith before the Mesolithic period, approximately between 8,000 and 5,000 B.C. If it flourished as a result of certain foreign contributions (all incidentally assimilated), there is little point in looking for animal and human figures of Franco-Cantabrian origin for the first, and of African origin for the second. It is a unified, original art, reflecting certain cultural affinities, rather than real relations with Africa.

With the exception of groups such as those of Alpera *, and Minateda *, the paintings of the Spanish Levant never reached the dimensions of those in the Magda-lenian sanctuaries. On the other hand they are full of human and animal pictures, in equal proportions, which have no effect of modelling, for all movements and living figures are shown in two dimensions. Their creators had no practical knowledge of polychromy, adopting a linear outline and flat tints of red brown and sometimes black, more rarely white, which are sometimes replaced by scratches. There are a few bichromes and engravings. Whatever the technique employed, this is essentially a graphic manner of portrayal; the paintings are spread out upon a surface of the stone, they do not "work" it, or exploit the material. Supple, free, rapid, the artists want them to be immediately intelligible, schematic, even calligraphic, without any lyrical flourishes.

Different ways of treating the human form are sometimes found in the same region, in the same site; it appears that they do not signify any stylistic evolution. They possess, however, a common manner, a shadow theatre type of portrayal, which places the figures and their attributes in profile, neglecting no detail of their clothes, coiffure, ornaments or armament. In the gorge of Gasulla * are animal forms, ibex, wild boar or ox, freer and less systematically stylised. But there is a fundamental opposition between the art of the Franco-Cantabrian domain and that of the Spanish Levant — seen in the profusion of hunting scenes, those of war or social life, and their many animated figures.

**Santolea,** Teruel. *Shelter of the Bowman*     **La Cenia,** Tarragona. *Shelter of la Poudrière*

The "dance of the women" of Cogul *, the procession of warriors, the battle, or the "execution" of Gasulla, deal without any theatrical or dramatic flourish, with the anecdotic side of the incident in a most succinct manner. A mythological story appears most improbable; if most of the pictures have a votive quality, the narrative element refers to historic events. Their position may, however, indicate that certain paintings were the object of a cult, or some religious ceremony.

## Syntax and signs

This schematical simplification of the contents, the interchangeability of figures and their excessive repetition, finished by impoverishing creative expression. The painters of Lascaux discovered the mythical power of the bull and allowed themselves to be carried away enthusiastically by its movement; but the painters of Cogul and of Alpera took possession of this movement, caught it in an instantaneous photograph, neutralized its expressive liveliness, and turned the figures into signs or symbols. They are transformed from live creatures into a kind of syntax or set of rules, relating one to the other according to their position. Collective scenes like the great frieze of Alpera, or the warlike hordes of Charco del heua Amarga *, or the wild boar hunt in the gorge of Gasulla, appear animated; it is not because of the action repre-sented, but simply owing to the large number of animal and human figures.

These animals are a vocabulary of signs, a wall writing, of which the artist takes advantage for whatever he wishes to represent. It is as if these artists had foreseen the cinema, in which the pictures, each possessing individually no emotional content, becomes alive when put in series.

In this way, the groups of archers in the gorge of Valltorta * are the first sign of an anthropomorphic alphabet; while the art of the Spanish Levant is a decisive step forward, if not aesthetically, at least in the creation of a system of graphic conventions which will lead later to a written alphabet. But Breuil's question still remains un-answered. Is this an African influence in Europe, or a Spanish influence in Africa, or are they meeting on some vaguely common ground? Because "an undeniable relation-ship, in spite of the enormous distance which separates them, connects the paintings of the Saharan and the South African hunters with those of the Iberian. Between these two groups, so far apart, the Sahara appears as an intermediary region[1]".

With its many sites full of engravings and paintings, the Sahara * is evidence of the last phases of the great change accomplished by humanity at the dawn of the

[1] Henri Breuil and Raymond Lantier, *Les Hommes de la Pierre ancienne*, Payot, Paris 1959.

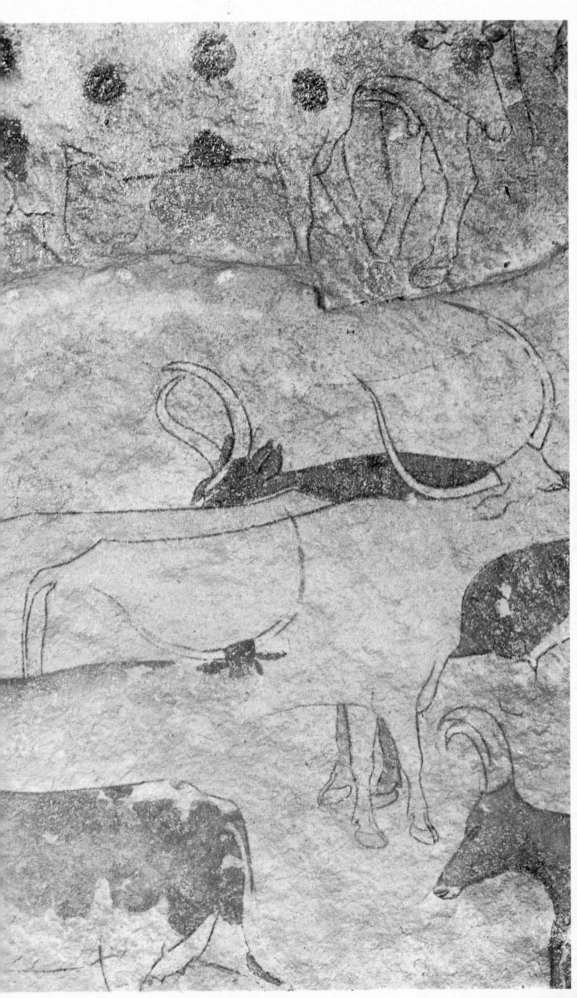

**Tassili n'Ajjer,** Sahara
*Composition with women, archer and
various figures (ritual scene),* Séfar

Neolithic age, the change to agriculture, to ceramics and metallurgy. These last stages, before an economic revolution as important as was our own industrial one, are the products of a pastoral civilization which, in successive migrations, was to spread out from the Mediterranean across Egypt and the Sahara, then green and watered with river courses, as far as the most remote regions of South Africa *, bearing with them material progress, an increase of productive forces conducive to the evolution of the human spirit, and the development of its thought and knowledge. Rock art of the Sahara is therefore the creation of cattle breeders, the direct ancestors of the Nilotics, of the Puels *, of the present Bantu * linguistic groups.

## Paintings to be deciphered

This at least appears to be the task after the recent researches of Henri Lhote *, and Jean-Dominique Lajoux * on the plateau of Tassili n'Ajjer *, an immense natural reserve of paintings and engravings. Compared with pictures in other Saharan sites, these are in a state of exceptional preservation. They reveal a remarkably homogeneous evolution both in inspiration and subject, so that Tassilian art appears to be the expression of a powerful socio-cultural complex. Its roots are in ancient Neolithic times, and its heyday was reached between 3,000 and 2,500 B.C., when the Sahara first showed signs of dessication.

The most archaic paintings are of gigantic animals, huge masked men with painted or tattooed bodies and, at Sefar, anthropomorphic figures, giants and phantoms. Their white figures are bounded by a purplish blue line, and dominated by a strange symbolism of geometrical signs and superpositions. At Tin Tazarift, a garland of masked dancers is rhythmically depicted on all the lower part of a painted wall — mythical creatures, whose meaning is still not clear. The era of the cattle-herders possesses painters which are easily comprehensible: antelopes, giraffes, ostriches, rhinoceri, elephants, and oxen, all generally associated with man. The coloured mass of the animals, profiting from the subtleties of the ochre colouring, are contrasted with the soft, supple lines of the human figures, endowed with a harmonious elegance and lack of tension. This plastic equilibrium between man and ox is less connected with the buccolic spirit which such a scene might suggest, than with the mysterious and organic bonds uniting them, a part of the culture and beliefs of these people. As at

Inaouanrhat, strange compositions are also found combining in the same space human and geometrical figures. The latter are very large but not schematic; they are used as emblems within the scene, having an allegorical meaning. Lastly, the archers of Sefar and Jabbaren show signs of natural movement, not still and frozen as are the warriors of the Spanish Levant. During the two last periods, those of the horse and the camel, a strong tendency towards sign pictures took place; then came the ideogram*, which weakened the importance of the ordinary symbol, without effecting the liveliness of the line.

Photographs taken at Lajoux[1] reveal Tassilian art in its monumental grandeur, and with all the force of its creative imagination. They contradict the tendentious and sometimes apocryphal surveys which are always given the "artistic" flourish to which we are accustomed. Thanks to infra-red photography, superpositions of figures which the eye cannot see have been revealed, throwing the existing chronology of paintings with superpositions into disarray. The object has been to discover the original qualities in Tassilian art; rather than the foreign influences and certain common grounds, on which the cultural and aesthetic effects of neighbouring civilizations, more Mediterranean or African, are seen. Systematic archaeological excavations alone can reveal the true origins of the man of Tassili. While waiting for these, it is fruitless to dream of Atlantide, and dogmatic to limit research to known references, Egyptian or otherwise, simply in order to draw definitive conclusions. Tassili N'Ajjer possesses no "great Martian god", or "judges", or "bather with naked breasts swimming on her back", no "Greek warrior" or "Antinea". It posseses a host of paintings yet to be decyphered, whose shapes, as powerful as the finest artistic expressions of humanity, are the precursors of those described today as Negro-African art.

[1] Jean-Dominique Lajoux, *Merveilles du Tassili n'Ajjer*, Editions du Chene 1962.

**Australia**
*Painting on bark*, Arnhem land
Geneva, Musée ethnographique

# Oceania

What is meant by the South Seas, and to what extent are we entitled to talk of a South Seas art? There is a geographical South Seas area, containing all the land in the Pacific Ocean, and an ethnological South Seas area extending to neighbouring continents, and beyond Indonesia and the Indian Ocean, as far as Madagascar. For our purposes here, it is understood as four geographical classical regions, corresponding to four great human groups: the Australians, the Melanesians, the Micronesians and the Polynesians.

In spite of slight differences, a cultural and ethnical unity is shared by the peoples of Polynesia *, Micronesia * and Melanesia *. Australia alone has special characteristics, although in a distant past the continent had close relations with New Guinea *. Moreover, if only from the linguistic point of view, it appears that the South Seas populations almost all had a common origin, somewhere to the south-east of China. For many centuries, they moved across the Indonesian archipelago as far as New Guinea, then to Australia, perhaps even to the Bismarck Isles. They knew nothing of agriculture, and they lived by fishing, hunting, berry picking, just as Australian aborigines live today. They can be divided into three main physical types: the first related to the Ainu, the second to the Vedda, the last a Negroid type going back to approximately the same epoch. In this way various extremely diverse peoples, the issue of successive cross breedings, spread across the Pacific; after further new maritime infiltrations, agricultural techniques appeared.

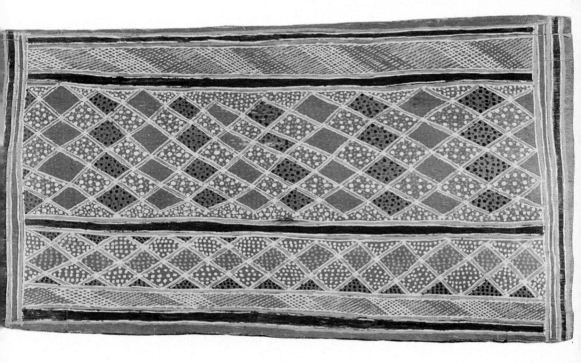

**Australia**
*Painting on bark*, Arnhem land
Geneva, Musée ethnographique

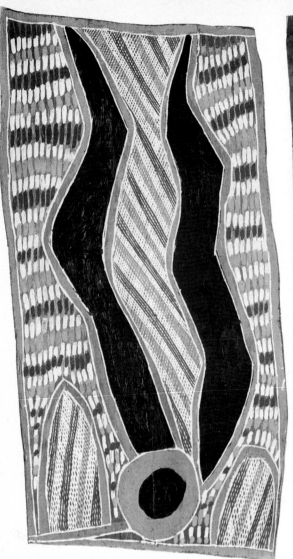
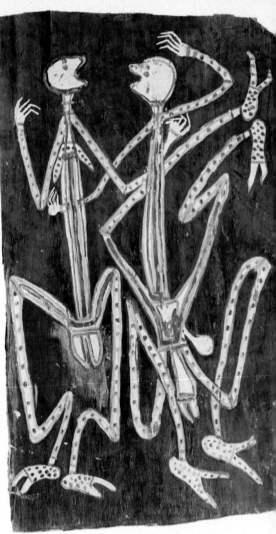

The South Seas therefore appear geographically as a place of human re-grouping, in continuous transformation, most of which have never been completely explained. Particularly in New Guinea do the migrations appear mysterious. On the other hand, it is becoming increasingly clear that South Seas humanity has, in the last four or five hundred years, had much more contact with other peoples than is generally supposed. Well before the explorations of Captain Cook, the coastal regions must have been visited by the Indonesian, Chinese or Spanish sailors, sailing across the Pacific. In New Guinea, for example, as a result of enquiries on the Papua * coast, it is clear that great cataclysms shook these societies, massacres from which their members were forced to flee. Entire populations were decimated or dispersed, cultures annihilated or impoverished.

The result of migrations and forced alliances required for survival, of innumerable exchanges, this socio-cultural complex produced a whole group of artistic activities, all characterised by a certain unity of expression. An attempt was made to associate the objective world with a mythical universe, in a visual art form, using the shapes in which the curve, the spiral and the tracery predominate.

**Australia.** *Paintings on bark*
Paris, Musée des arts africains et
océaniens

None of these populations, with the possible exception of the Australian, was entirely isolated. In Melonesia, new human groups were constantly appearing, so that an area like the valley of Sepik* is still today the permanent theatre for a continuous exchange of decoration motifs. The art of the South Seas may be interpreted in many ways, although aesthetically it possesses a unity; its compositions have not changed greatly in the course of the centuries, just as they are the same over the entire South Seas area.

## A mythical potential

Comparatively, Australian art may appear austere; its elaborate social and religious setting is now recognised, but certain specialists still contest or underestimate its aesthetic richness. Unlike other South Sea civilizations, whose economy depends upon agriculture, stock-breeding and fishing, the Australian has remained in the Stone Age, dependent upon hunting and berry-picking, his existence reduced to a form of permanent nomadism. Their pictorial tradition is best illustrated where nomadism exists only intermittently, even rarely. Nevertheless, if the material culture of these peoples is dependent upon their nomadic life in the great deserted spaces of the continent's interior (conditions of life which are so limiting that they are even responsible for the bareness and sparseness of their creations) we should not regard them as some prehistoric residue, but as one of the rare "primitive" contemporary cultures.

There must have been a regular renewal of their institutions, because they were maintained with such vitality down to our own time; as well as a system of rites, corresponding to the various stages of initiation for the male adult. This initiation, combined with religious rites was bound up with human reproduction, as well as with that of the vegetable and animal kingdom. The totemic myths were celebrated either in a graphic or pictorial manner, or by a choreographic display, in which the initiates were the principal actors. In the latter, in the land of Arnhem, the participants imprint their body with a close network of black and ochre geometrical motifs copied from the local paintings on bark. Elsewhere in central Australia, they apply vertical bands of the down of birds to the flesh, whitened or reddened by the blood which is used as a fixative for these ceremonial ornaments. In both cases, the corporal decoration makes man the mobile sign of a visual language.

In north central Australia, paintings on the ground depict mythical events conventionally. Most are treated collectively, on a flat emplacement previously watered, either with human blood or water, hardened in the sun, and marked out with lines of white down on the earth. Some of these depict the journeys of the giant serpent

Wollungua, who deposits in water-holes the seed which fecundates the women; the sinuous motif of this painting, a black or red double volute on a yellow ochre background twists its way through blobs of white and concentric circles. Other paintings, using the same colours, recall the animal totems of prosperity, but are more votive than magic. In eastern Australia, engravings deeply hollowed in the hard earth add a series of lozenges and squares to the figurative theme. Here too, the collective character of these designs presupposes, in the case of each individual, a relatively strict observance of a set of rules, an operational lithurgy expressive less of symbolism than of the rhythmical movement of the human bodies in communal celebration.

However, the Australian has not confined his art to insubstantial backgrounds; he has also painted and engraved on the walls of the shelters beneath rocks, or in the shallow caves lit by daylight, following an ancient tradition which goes back to the beginning of our Bronze Age *. These are in general ritual propitiatory paintings whose outlines were periodically renewed, some quite recently. The best known and most finely worked are in the north, in the land of Arnhem, in the district of Kimberley, in the area of bark painting. In black, white or red, the "wondjina" of the region of Kimberley are great phantom-like anthropomorphous figures, the faces clearly delineated, surrounded with a halo, mouthless. Mythical beings connected with the origins of each clan, they possess the power of fecundating women and causing rain-fall. They are accompanied by human and animal pictures, in particular the rainbow serpent, with its broad supple movement. Once again this is not simply a piece of magic; it is a ritual act, invoking and celebrating a holy presence.

Apart from their many schematic and lively effigies of tenuous and slender figures, or squatting creatures decorated with parallel stripes, generally in monochrome, it is in the land of Arnhem that the most daringly stylised wall paintings are found. Known by the naive description "X-ray paintings" their graphical structure has been interpreted as the exact transposition of animal or human organism. This pseudo-realist "explanation" does not correspond with the reality which it attempts to explain, but in fact deforms. These figures, often more than two metres high, reveal another system, which does not depend only on an architectonic portrayal, but on a complete collection of precise signs. Fishes, kangaroos, human-beings coupled sexually, appear in excited movement on the rocks and the eculyptus bark plaques which serve as weather boards to the Australian huts. These, publicly exposed, are the coats of arms of the tribes, the badge or index of a tradition. They have no religious function as such, although the execution of most of them is based on a pedagogic exercise connected with the cycles of initiation *. On the other hand, each describes some episode in a myth, using elements borrowed from the animal or vegetable world.

Painting on bark, an experimental field for corporal painting, employs many themes, in which drawing of a geometrical kind soon loses all pictorial or figurative quality. They become polychrome networks of black lozenges, rectangles made of parallel bands, with concentric circles, vertical diagonal and horizontal lines, red, yellow, white, black, light brown, all crossing one another rhythmically, the striking design emphasised occasionally by pointilist effects.

## Engraving and tattooing

A graphical invention of this kind was unlikely to be used only on painted bark; its curves, hachuring, and spirals, are found incised on the boomerangs, shields, clubs, propellants and assegais; attempts at rock engraving by hammering, incision, or point marks are also found. It also appeared, clear and precise in the engraved writing of the "tjurunga" *

These tjurunga are thin plaques of wood or shale, elongated and ovoidal in shape, sometimes circular and of varying dimensions, found principally in the interior. Both faces are generally engraved firmly and closely. Being holy objects, they may not be viewed by women or non-initiated persons. According to Claude Levi Strauss[1] they were "piled up in the natural shelters, far from the beaten track, inspected, polished, greased and coloured periodically to the accompaniment of prayers and incantations; they are the tangible evidence of a mythical period, of the bond which unites living man to an ancestor who had undertaken this type of modelling at the dawn of human history".

All the engraved motifs are therefore precise and permanent, constantly related to a general symbolism. In the graphical compositions, with their complicated system of parallel lines, straight, sinuous, or broken, the groups of spirals or concentric circles are the fundamental element in a language which is not only visual. In fact when, accompanied by a chorus of initiates, the high priest reads one of these "tjurunga" following the engraved phrase with his finger, he is reading an incantation full of sonorous images, pronouncing myths contained in Australian engraving. No other example exists in the South. Seas in which the message is concentrated with such rigidity and power.

In graphic terms, Polynesian tattooing alone can equal this, if not in intensity at least in complexity; although religious content is denied it, it is impossible to con-

---

[1] Claude Levi-Strauss, *La Pensée sauvage*, Plon 1962.

sider it as simple corporal decoration. By repeating the incisions of New Zealand*, or the perforations of the Marquess Isles*, tattooing technique could produce bands, flat tints, a linear network to cover the entire body; but the operation would then be so long and painful, that a lifetime would be needed for it. Whatever skill may be required, these incised motifs on the surface of the skin share an aesthetical quality common to reliefs and engravings. They do not simply belong to a body of ornamental signs; they have a definite meaning.

Thus the facial tatooing of the New Zealand Maori*, with their spiral arabesques, are repeated on their big sculptures, which bear traces of their migrations from the Society Isles*, the Australs*, and the Cook Isles*. Supple, wavy, continuous, proliferating, they are chiselled and dug into the flesh of the human face, in the same way that they perforate the lintels and beams of the houses, the prows of the canoes. Tattooing in the Marquess Isles is somewhat different; it is not localized, but applied to the whole body, undulating, and curvilinear. The figure of a divine ancestor, the "diki", is frequently seen in this tattooing. Although this is the only human figure in the art of the Marquess Isles, it is not thought that its existence, particularly in tattooing, has any religious significance. In the South Sea art, one particular design may represent several different symbols.

## The engraved and the pictorial

Engraving plays an important part in Polynesian decor. The potteries of the Fiji Isles*, the wooden vessels from the Marquess's and the Australs, the perforated handles of ritual howels of the Cook Isles, the New Zealand, Fiji, and Tonga clubs, are covered with geometric signs. But engraving is found further afield than tattooing; beyond Polynesia, and through the entire Melanesian archipelegos, where it gave birth to a form of writing in colour, before directly influencing the polychromy of the masks, statues and shields.

In the Bay of Astrolabe*, bamboo containers, and scale armbands, are freely engraved with a geometrical decoration. Shields bear strongly incised symbolical figures, adapted to their shape. On the other hand, the engraved decoration of the drums, plates, and wooden cups in the Tami Isle* and in the Huon Gulf*, consists of the same theme repeated many times on a flat surface, with the intention of emphasizing the shape of the object. Scenes with human figures depicting traditional life and colonization in New Caledonia * are finely engraved on bamboo, contrasting with the heavy door jambs, in which lozenge-shaped chevrons are scooped out, surmounted by a human face of exaggerated breadth.

This engraving, although possessing a certain formal monumentality, is free and unconstrained. A wooden comb from the Soloman Isles, for example, depicts a bird with outstretched wings emerging from an irregular network of broken and sinuous lines; the bird is not a passive ornament, it clearly has a goal of its own. In the same way, the designs in the sand at Ambrym *, in the New Hebrides *, are not drawn to any scale. Here the finger traces in the black sand a continuous, complex and symmetrical figure full of volutes and rosettes crossed by straight lines in the form of lozenges, which then coil back on themselves. The line must be continuous, never passing the same point in the same direction more than once. These designs were not simple exercises in technique, but were used by the elders of the tribe to instruct the adolescents in the essential principles of group life.

So pure and melodic is the line of Melanesian engraving, that a pictorial effect is achieved without the use of colour, as we see in the sooty incisions in the Caledonian bamboos, the brown highlights of the bamboos in the Bay of Astrolabe, or those in chalk on the drums in the Gulf of Huon. In the chalk spatulars of the Trobriand Islands *, the white colour reveals animal or human figures, difficult to identify in the curvilinear decor. In the interior of this cultural zone known as Massim *, the prows of canoes seldom bear painted spiral reliefs, and we cannot determine their exact meaning.

# The emancipation of colour

The aim of colour is not simply to make engraved decor more comprehensible; it is a part of the composition, as seen in the animal figures on the exterior of the oval wooden plates of Lake Sentani *. In another part of New Guinea, in the valley of the river Ramu, and as far as Potsdamhafan, shields, drums with slots, and wooden panels, bare shallow incisions, destined simply to receive a white coating. The spirals, ellipses and concentric triangles neutralize any figurative element.

Two New Guinea peoples, the Papuans and the Asmats *, have ingeniously

combined the expressive possibilities of relief and polychromy. In the Gulf of Papua, the bark belts unroll in an ornamental fashion a long engraved phrase with motifs painted in red and white, derived from the anthropomorphic themes which, with their chevrons, arabesques, indentations, are also found in the elliptical shape of their shields and votive plaques.

In the south-west of New Guinea, the great ceremonial shields of the Asmats are decorated with champleve * heraldic figures, the general effect being varied according to the colour used. The motif itself is hollowed and coloured with red ochre, or yellow; the relief, painted in brown or black appearing as a whitened circle. Extremely elaborate themes are often attempted. Some of the shields are decorated with a double line in an indented framework, or associate the line with a mass of curves and countercurves.

These signs are taken from man, fish, and birds, and occupy an important place in New Guinea symbolism; with the passage of time they have become simpler, freed of all extraneous matter. The geometrical decor of South Sea art is based upon the shape of the human body. Maurice Leenhardt[1] writes, "The tendency of South

60      [1] Maurice Leenhardt, *Arts de l'Océanie*, Editions du Chene 1947.

**Australia.** *Tjurunga*, engraved pebble
Geneva, Musée ethnographique

Sea art to slip from realism into geometrical style should be studied. It would be fruitless to regard the two styles as in opposition, and to see in the geometric style a retrograde step." Jean Guiart * has asked if the motifs of the Asmat shields "are not connected in some way with the changes of fortune which the tribe has experienced in the past?"[2]

On these shields colour is no longer merely an accessory; it bites into the wood as acid does into copper, perforating the prows of the canoes and the sharpened part of the lances of Asmat, or the great plaques of the middle-Sepik, where shapes recall certain works of Massim.

Colour belongs to a social language part of a symbolism; the facial painting of man, his corporal ornaments are not intended simply to "impress" the public at the time of a fete, nor are they simply aesthetic. In New Guinea, a face painted white is a sign of mourning; it can also be painted with schematic motifs associated with rites while they are being celebrated. The colour also controls the choice of certain vegetable dye ornaments which accompany masks and polychrome wickerwork in the Sepik region. In Melanesia, the painting of masks and statues is very seldom

---

[2] Jean Guiart, *Océanie*, collection «L'Univers des Formes», Gallimard 1963.

61

**Australia.** *Tjurunga*, engraved pebble
Geneva, Musée ethnographique

decorative or illustrative, as is often the case in Micronesia, in the gable ends with figures in the Carolines *, in the posts of the meeting-houses of the Isle of Yap *, or in the illustrated engravings which decorate those in the Palau Isles *. On the contrary, Melanesian colour has such a sense of movement that it is almost sculptural in effect. The wooden or bark masks of the Witu Isles * in New Brittany * are symmetrical and linear, a labyrinth of red and blue bands on a white background. The statuary of Tami Isle in the Gulf of Huon has more varied geometrical designs in brown and red or green and ochre on a white background.

## Polychromy and material

In New Guinea, in the region of Maprik, the ridge-boards of the great ceremonial dwellings of Abelam * are surmounted with a small plaque, whose polychrome composition alone reveals that it is based on the human face or two human profiles facing one another — yellow and black surfaces overlapping, outlined by a double red and black circle like a rosette, drawn in a double scallop with the same tone. This lively colour reappears in the heads in the gable fronts of the middle-Sepik, where eyes and stars are the reference points for concentric circles with sinuous and continuous rhythm. In certain Papuan masks, morphological details of the face disappear in favour of a coloured flat tint, spread evenly across them.

But it is in the New Hebrides, in an often monumental sculpture, which always retains its plastic liberty, that Melanesian polychromy reached its height. The material on which it is placed is carefully chosen — a trunk of bracken, the texture full of hard serried needles. Particularly at Ambrym, the statues of rank *, greying and ochre-coloured, spring from the soil, as if erupted by the force of nature. At Malekula *, violent blues and reds are used on the masks, with heavy coiffures. Sometimes a light blue tint reappears on the lengthened body of an effigy, like a water colour.

Elsewhere it was on account of this violent colour that many coloured feathers

 **New Guinea**
*Shield*
Polychrome relief decorated with vegetable
fibres
Geneva, Musée ethnographique

**Marquesas Islands**
*Model of tattooing drawn on Bamboo*
Geneva, Musée ethnographique
▼

**New Ireland**
*Fragment of a Malanggan Pole*
Geneva, Musée ethnographique

**New Hebrides,** Ambrym
*Monumental drum* (detail of the head)
Paris, Musée des arts africains et océaniens

were chosen and fixed on basket work, representing the terrifying head of the god of war, which the priests of the Hawaian Isles* took with them to battle. With these feathers were mixed mother of pearl shells to represent the eyes, and sometimes even human hair. With the expressive use of such materials, these people contrived an original form of plastic composition.

## Polychrome architecture

The Malanggan* masks, bas-reliefs, and statues, an amalgam of the techniques of sculpture, engraving and painting, must not, if we are to appreciate theis aesthetic quality, be regarded simply as the product of an ingenious technique. They were inspired by an extremely rich mythology. Jean Guiart, describing one of these sculptures, gives a precise idea of their complexity, and the constructive imagination which they display. "The person, or a number of persons and animals sculptured in the round, is surrounded with different objects, human or animal figurines, and decorative motifs which sometimes conceal the essential theme. In some of the more complex examples, we see clearly the principles which inspired the local artist; a contrast between the massive internal sculpture, and the slenderness of the lateral network; between the flat colours of the exterior network, and the subtle touches and hachuring of the decoration painted on the principal parts; between the cohesion of the internal theme, and the multiplicity with which it is surrounded"[1].

Light, slender, proliferating, these spacial constructions are developed symmetrically on either side of an axis, and in spite of the elaborate geometrical constructions, it is always possible to make out the mythical being represented. In the bas-reliefs, for instance, the bird is clearly visible: his wings are outspread, while the serpent which he holds in his beak is rounded in a circle. In profile, they show a number of beaks, and the wings coil back on the bird, absorbing the serpent in their plumage. Painted according to the same principles, the masks have as many perforated surfaces, incorporating in their structure the bird, the serpent, the fish and other

64      [1] Jean Guiart, *Océanie*, collection « L'Univers des Formes », Gallimard 1963.

creatures connected with the original myth. There are others which are even more expressionist, formed by a combination of painted bark tissues, mounted in pieces of cane. The art of New Ireland reveals a vision of the world unique in South Seas art. According to Guiart, an aesthetic relation exists between certain paintings on Australian bark, and the complicated graphical designs of the Malanggam — the latter being the development in three dimensions of the former.

## The Tapa

South Seas painting is free from all sculptural support and can be expressed freely in two dimensions. The South Seas produced a vegetable tissue generally known under the name "tapa" *, made exclusively by women, which became a remarkable means of pictorial expression. (Certain South Sea areas did not produce this: Micronesia in which, as on the island of Yap, and on the Santa Cruz * and Marshal * islands, different materials plaited in yellow, black and red fibre were found; in New Zealand, where

65

◀ **New Guinea**
*Decorative Shield*
Polychrome relief decorated with
vegetable fibres
Geneva, Musée ethnographique

**New Ireland.** *Polychrome Statuette*
Geneva, Musée ethnographique
▼

**New Zealand,** Maori
*Headman's Cloak* (woven linen)
Geneva, Musée ethnographique

the Maoris with similar plaiting technique produced pieces of linen with a geometrical motif; or the Hawaian ceremonial capes formed from yellow feathers and red knots in the meshes of a net).

In Polynesia, the decoration of tapa is essentially geometrical, but it reveals a remarkable sense of invention in the choice of the figures depicted, as in its use of colour. The motifs of the Futuna Islands* are of a web-like finesse, sometimes very widely spaced. Those of the Wallace Isles* are superimposed in horizontal lines of unequal breadth, while those of the Tonga Isles* are composed in a kind of red and black checkboard, broken up by sharp triangles. The various squares of Samoa* and the Fiji Islands demand a relatively symmetrical treatment of the surface; while those in the Cook Isles are very varied and covered with tresses, chevrons, triangles facing one another, and diagonally placed heads of grain. Hawaian tapa is subtly coloured, an effect which is heightened by hand painting. The same can be said for certain Fijian pieces, which exploit all the resources of the texture.

New Guinea tapa does not display the same invention, nor skill in application. The decor in the Bay of Astrolabe is defaced, and cannot be compared with engraving of shell or wood. The tapa at the mouth of the Sepik is not deeply enough incised. Only the neighbourhood of Sentani Lake and the Bay of Humbolt have left us good calligraphic compositions of animal figures, often interconnected and punctuated with stars.

**New Guinea**
*Panels painted with Polychrome vegetable
pigment*
Paris, Musée des arts africains
et oceaniens

# A field of monumental expression

It is however in the region of the river Sepik, on the pediment or the inside of the great ceremonial dwellings* of the men, that the South Seas genius for colour is best displayed. It is seen painted with extraordinary plastic liberty on bark, and on the open leaves of palm trees; the human form, and particularly the human face, are combined closely in allegorical compositions connected with the architecture and the houses in which the cults are celebrated.

The curvilinear style of Bas-Sepik reveals male and female figures alternately separated by decorations of an animal or vegetable design. The Kanigaras* of the middle-Sepik, in the neighbourhood of Tambanum, depict the human face by a system of interweaving curves, with large, closely pressed bands of colour. On certain shields, the colours are sometimes so close that they seem to run into one another. Sometimes too, on other panels, the colour is so thick that it appears to overrun the line which contains it; we find dark spots of colour, violent harmonies (blue, green, mauve) from which emerge fantastic creatures. The Upper-Sepik saw the birth of a system of designs which was less fluent, made up of rough rather brutal markings but making use, however, of a whole range of earth pigments. With equally rudimentary means the Washkuk* drew with a free flowing line expansive figures which seem to grow out of a complex of white spirals.

In the region of Maprik, the Avelams erected imposing polychrome compositions inside as well as on the exterior of their buildings for cults. Using reds, browns, and yellows, they painted giant ikons, in human form but expressing the all powerful myth.

69

**New Guinea**
*Panels painted with Polychrome vegetable pigment*
Paris, Musée des arts africains
et oceaniens

**Ivory Coast,** Baoulé
*Door carved in Monochrome relief*
Paris, Musée des arts africains et
océaniens

# Africa

Comparing the ceiling of the Sistine chapel with a Negro-African sculpture, Elie Faure* wrote in 1935, "The latter strictly obeys the rules of rhythm which are at the basis of every work of art, whatever its form or intention. These rhythms belong to the dance, music, and architecture. By their shape, colour, symmetrical decor, arbitrary grouping of natural elements, obstinate refusal to imitate, limitless ability to evoke reality, combined with the elements of a dream, they produce an entirely new creation of which the only real subject is rhythm. . . . They reflect cosmic order without discussing it"[1].

It is the plastic quality in Negro-African art which impresses us today, the product of socio-cultural conditions which are extremely varied, brutally interrupted by colonisation while they were evolving. Only now are we beginning to distinguish one from the other, without being able to reconstruct what has been irreparably destroyed; for in the words of Aimé Césaire "Wherever colonisation has existed, entire peoples have been emptied of their culture". However we may regard it in future, this art is in no way different in principle from that of civilizations which are better known and more familiar to us. In all its manifestations, it expresses the relationship between man and the universe, and reveals a mythical knowledge of nature.

In Africa, all is sign and symbol. To dance, sing, sculpt, paint are not isolated acts, but imply communication and communion between men, an interrogation of the obscure forces which rule the world, an affirmation of humanity in the world. One of the first to note this was Marcel Griaule*: "These people, who are thought to possess no archives, are precisely those who have left to posterity — and continue to outline, sculpt, dance or model — the greatest number of comprehensible signs, comprehensible at least by the initiated, which any people has ever offered for our research"[2]. In the same way, those people who were thought to have no painting, simply because they paint "otherwise" from us, are those who can best help us discover the sources of pictorial creation.

The technique of the relief depends upon the composition and exploitation of a theme in two dimensions; engraving, embroidery, corporal scarifications* provide rhythmical variations of pure graphism; finally, polychromy does not use exclusively walls, rocky surfaces or normal objects, but invests all objects on which it is applied with its own symbolical meaning — objects such as the mask, the statue or the human body.

We are therefore confronted with an art important both aesthetically and spiritually, which it would be absurd to consider as no more than a group of signs bearing social and metaphysical implications. To disassociate its "beauty" from its "function", or to approach it only from a utilitarian or religious point of view, would be no less erroneous than to judge it according to the norms and conventions which

71

[1] Elie Faure, in L'Encyclopédie française, Vol. XVI, 1935.
[2] Marcel Griaule, «Art et Symbole en Afrique noire», Zodiaque, October 1951.

are foreign to it. That system of signs, by which every society expresses itself, whatever may be its economic development, only proves that we are dealing with an art of a "functional beauty" (according to Senghor)*, not simply a delight for the eye or a mystification of the spirit.

There is no tradition, nor any Negro-African society, which considers artistic activity, even the most modest, as unproductive. The act of creation is an essentially social form of work; a language common to all, a manner of portrayal as much as a means of operating on nature. In most African languages, the terms beauty, goodness, well-wishing, happiness, action, movement, frequently have similar meanings, and are to be found in all their conceptions of work and efficacity. For Michel Leiris*, in "The Spirit of the Dogons" * work, whether it is technical or ritual, is never conceived other than as a function of the public weal, the common good . . . the efforts of the cultivator, or of the dancer during their respective ceremonies are not so different, because the correct accomplishment of these duties produces a similar good; namely, to take advantage of the "good man, whose activities have nourished others, just as the enthusiasm caused by the "beautiful dancer" awakens forces which help to assure the permanence of the community"[1].

In this way artistic creation, which is nothing more than a form of work by which man can develop his talents, becomes an integral part of social practices, a transformation of reality.


## Birth of a relief

At the end of the nineteenth century, when Europe discovered the art of Benin * thanks to some two thousand pieces of bronze which the European nations had just shared between themselves, nobody imagined their creators could be "bloody" people whom England had just "pacified" (during a "punitive expedition", 1897, terminated by the pillage of the capital and the massacre of its inhabitants). It was thought that these bronzes were the work of Egyptians, artisans who had come from Greece or India, or even of an unknown master of the Italian Renaissance. In another connection, the technique of the wax mould * having been perfectly employed, it was assumed that it had been introduced by the Portuguese, the first Europeans to enter the city of Benin in 1472. It appears today that these theories were erroneous.

The terra-cotta figurines discovered by Frobenius * in 1910 on the emplacement of the Holy city of Ife in the south-west of Nigeria, and the bronzes found by chance in 1939 near the palace of Oni, attest the great age of their technique and their repertory

[1] Michel Leiris, «L'expression de l'idée de travail dans une langue d'initiés soudanais», in *Présence africaine*, No. 13, 1952.

of shapes. These discoveries justify the tradition by which, in about 1280, the king of Benin, the Oba, asked the Oni of Ife to send him a man who knew how to smelt bronze, a process which could be taught to his subjects. In 1949, new excavations confirmed the greater age of, and the spiritual and formal influence exercised by, the art of Ife over that of Benin. They also confirmed the influence of Ife in the present art of Yoruba *, principally in the ornamental element of the statuary of these people numbering nearly five million, who live in the south-west of Nigeria, and of Dahomey as far as the delta of the Niger. This statuary evidently belonged to a civilization whose originality and unity we are only now becoming aware of, and whose source went back well beyond Ife.

According to their traditions, the Yorubas came from the East during the first centuries of our era. They lived on the banks of a great river, probably the upper Nile, and practised the wax mould method well before their migration, following a technique used in the Egypt of the Pharoahs, and the last Greco-Nubian civilization of Meroe *. It was in northern Nigeria that Bernard Fagg* excavated about fifteen years ago the oldest evidence of African art in the southern Sahara. Buried near the villages of Jabia, Jemaa, Wamba, and Makafo, these terra-cotta figurines were made between the fifth and the first century before our era; they belong to what is generally known as the "culture of the Nok", to an epoch of transition between the use of stone and that of iron in these regions. Somewhere between the Lakes of Chad and Benoue, where the Paleo-Mediterranean civilization could penetrate, the area dominated by the Nok culture was probably passed through by the Yorubas, who absorbed some of its influences.

Earlier than the thirteenth century, the art of Ife marked the high point of the Beninian relief which, in the form of bronze plaques, decorated the pillars of the covered walks inside the courts of the royal palace, from the end of the fifteenth century. In the terra-cotta head coiffures, graphic decoration was already very marked, to be found in its extreme form in the bronze portrayals of the royal couple, or of the Oni. In these, the necklaces and ornaments, the jewels and bracelets, the diadems, clothes, and other ornaments seem the pretext for decorative variations, which even the moving humanism of the faces cannot contradict. The grouping of these incised motifs, their quantity and stylization, are forerunners of the exuberance of Beninian decoration, with its similar hierarchical order. We can understand this better when we see the ritual bronze cup, in the form of the sacred monolithic seats of Ife. The royal figure who twists around this cup, resting one hand on the handle, and flourishing in the other a sceptre, is not sculpture, but engraving and relief. It is a part of the cup, while the simple chevrons of the geometrical network of the clothes possess an emblematic character.

The reliefs of Benin are, in fact, the high point of this ornamental genius;

73

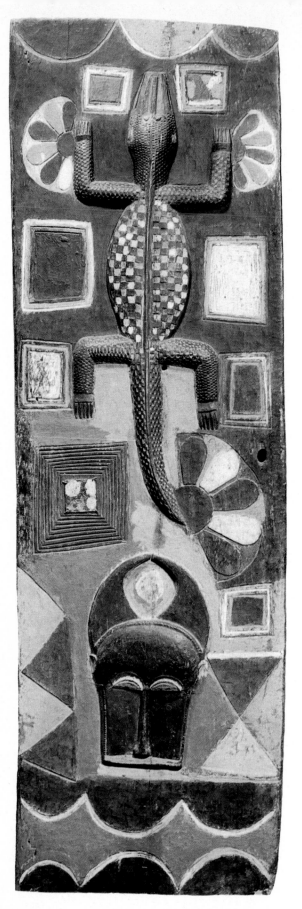

**Ivory Coast.** Baoulé
*Door carved in Polychrome relief*
Geneva, Musée ethnographique

**Dahomey.** Fon
*Tapestry with overlaid motif*
Paris, Musée des arts africains et océaniens

**Dahomey.** Fon
*Tapestry with overlaid motif*
Paris, Musée des arts africains et océaniens

although they are used in frankly allegorical compositions, no imagery can detract from their intrinsic beauty. On a background of floral or abstract embossment, man appears in all the glory of his arms, his attributes, his splendid apparel, becoming a part of the tracery of a vegetable decoration.

## Incised coats of arms

This aesthetic conception is not peculiar to the bronzes of Ife or Benin; we find them equally in Chad, in the ancient art of the Sao *, in the firm decor on the breastplates, the bracelets, the pendants or the libation cups, in the confusion of the lines, the broad and deep incisions, the regular chevrons, the light and twisted reliefs, the curves, the pattern of checks, none of which fulfill only an ornamental function. Whether they are in ceramics or in bronze smelted by the wax mould method, their function is symbolical, and their graphical meaning is connected with the Sao civilization in all its aspects.

The country of Lake Chad possessed one of the most ancient peoples of Africa. From the end of the upper Paleolithic, it conserved the rock engravings of Tibesti *, the wall paintings of Ennedi *, and, from the ninth century, was the meeting point for hunting and fishing peoples. These last celebrated an ancestor cult, characterized by ceramic effigies and a manner of burial in jars. They knew about the techniques of arts concerned with fire, and on the emplacement of their villages they left a large and varied production in clay and bronze. This grouping of peoples, who maintained their religious and cultural independence until the sixteenth century — when they were decimated, forced to flee, or to embrace Islam — are described by the generic term of "Sao" meaning "men". They carried the art of the ceramic very far, in both utilitarian objects and those required for their cults, and particularly in strange human and animal figures, whose essential features are borrowed from Negro-African art.

Small scale masks and schematic figurines depend either on the modelling or the engraving, or both, and are accentuated either in volume, or in a faint morphological relief on a flattened face, with a coarse outline. Their shape is of little importance; they are merely the background upon which short incisions can be made. According to Lebeuf * "the portrayal of scarifications (or tattooing) on certain images are so clear that they are the main feature of the object, which is itself merely a background for these kind of native coats of arms"[1]. The function of these masks is

[1] Jean-Paul Lebeuf, *Art ancien du Tchad*, Ministère d'Etat des affaires culturelles, exposition du Grand-Palais, Paris 1962.

essentially religious; they protect against illness, appease the spirits, and are to be found *ex-voto* in public sanctuaries, and on family altars for the cult of the dead. The animal figures recall the distant existence of the propitiary rites of hunting and fishing.

The effigies of ancestors and masked dancers, intended for the public sanctuaries, are of a contradictory nature. While the second are modelled in a violent manner, with a pronounced sculptural effect, the modelling of the first is most restrained, aimed merely at accentuating the incision of the chevrons and whorls, tattooings, ornaments, or signs of chefferie *, which cannot be justified by any decorative fantasy. Their graphical value appears to be the main thing about them, full of a symbolism which, according to Lebeuf "allows them to reach, through schematic designs, the domain of the metaphysical, bonds linking the terrestial world with certain celestial elements, recalling mythical facts, relations with other fundamental elements of the universe, portrayals of a system of the world which can be equally clearly seen on the cauldrons, plates, drinking vases, bowls of pipes, and on objects used for rites"[1].

This form of expression, as in that of Ife or of Benin, has its own life, and its intrusion on any object whatever it may be is accompanied by its own independent movement. In the extreme case, it gives a wall-like dimension to the reliefs which in the Cameroons, decorate the jambs of doorways, and the pillars of the Bamileke * architecture since the beginning of this century; it is this which produces the repetition of the figures, their rigid stylisation, even the order of their composition. It is to be found again in the graphic rhythms of Mali, perforating and cutting up geometrically the crest of the antelope mask of Bambar *, and in the hierarchical position of certain figures with uplifted arms to be seen on the shutters of the Gogon granges.

However this form of portrayal, using successively engraving and relief, or sometimes both together, this form of portrayal, only reaches its full plastic effect in two peoples of the Ivory Coast, the Baoule * and the Senoufo *, whose sculptured doorways are clearly a "pictorial" conception, confirmed moreover by the frequent traces of their original polychromy, which are still visible. But colour, or whatever remains of it, appears to be less important than the treatment of space, the positioning of shapes and forms.

## Two figure systems of the world

Most of the Baoule doorways have figurations of the world far more elaborate than any allegory with a proverbial meaning. Borrowed from statuary or the goldsmith, the

---

[1] Jean-Paul Lebeuf, *Art ancien du Tchad*, Ministère d'Etat des affaires culturelles, exposition du Grand-Palais, Paris 1962.

masks and animals are always depicted in a graphic language, which means that the artist always has to think of the surface on which he is working. Wearing anthropomorphic masks, the buffalo and the ram recall the mystical bond which unites them with Niamye, a celestial god in the Baoule pantheon. The horns of the first, which point upward, almost meet and are sometimes surmounted by another animal; those of the second, which point downward, can become a part of the traditional tresses of the Baoule women. Both cases recall the design of a crescent moon. Buffaloes and rams are often found inside engraved geometrical figures, in which triangles and lozenges, the symbols of femininity, are predominant. A shutter at Dimbokro is a more complex example of insertion, in which a ram is associated with a linear incision effect, semi-lunar or quadrangular in shape (the curve of the horns corresponds well with the former) dominating a hollowed out checkboard and a broken triple line, a symbol of the fecundity effect of water. Some form of symbolism must be implied here, in which the buffalo and ram, closely related to the cults of fecundity, are fundamental signs. The incisions accompanying them are certainly not ornamental. Graphically, they appear to derive from the geometric relief of certain weights used for weighing gold powder before the seventeenth century, smelted by the wax mould method of the Baoules, whose numeral writing reveals mathematical motifs. But their doors, evokes another kind of relief, the no less elaborate or symbolical result of corporal scarification.

Although there are more animal portrayals, displaying more daring in their stylization, most of them occupy the greater part of the surface of the doorway or the shutter; they fit into a background of geometrical engravings, or are surrounded by signs such as the square, the crescent, the lozenge and the triangle. The species in the greatest number are those which inspire the most rich formal inventions; the crocodile and the voranian lizard, which are combined frequently on the doorways and in the oral tradition, then the fish, creatures belonging to the same element, the same mythical cycle, the result of a sacrifice made by the Queen Pokou to the spirit of Comoe.

However, portrayals of animals are not limited to this fable. Crocodiles alternate symmetrically biting their tails, whose firm engraving and energy possess an emblematic rhythm; there are crocodiles with two heads, their bodies covered with rows of scale triangles, laid out on a background of a chessboard; there are fish covered with broken lines and surmounted with the crescent of the moon. A doorway of Toumodi has four squares unequally cut; a big fish with its fins spread out holds a small fish in its mouth; the same decor brings them to life, while a "water line" ties them together, and an aquatic bird, by touching another, establishes a supplementary contact between them. This organic group, water — fish — bird, is accompanied at the side by a narrow band of engraved triangles and, at the top, a light circular relief divided into four segments cut in broken lines. We are here confronted by one of the strangest expressions of Baoulean aquatic mythology.

The Senoufo doorways have many origins, but they are derived essentially, as we have seen among the Baouleans, from statuary and articles of adornment. However, they can be distinguished from one another by depicting on a same panel, and sometimes in great quantities, masks and human and animal figures. If the technique seems much the same, as in the plastic effect attained, the sense of the image is different.

The Senoufo artist set up his work in a different way from that of the Baoulean artist; it is always there, active but never demonstrative, and where we find it more confused, it is simply more complex than elsewhere. In this way if often does not correspond to the horizontal or vertical nature of the material on which the portrayal is made. It makes this material appear bigger by the intrusion of a composition with concentric themes. The point of view, the angle of vision one might say, is turned upside down.

On a doorway in the region of Korhogo, masks and human figures, among them horsemen, animals, and in particular a crocodile, a tortoise, a serpent and a bird gravitate around an umbilicus, the hub of the universe. Placed at the two extremeties, pulsating force, their emblematic character as pronounced as in the engraving on the other persons and other animals do not appear to frame the central figures but to accentuate its circular movement. This is the doorway to the place of a cult; it was the boundary between the sacred and the profane worlds, bestowing the form of the esoteric symbols of the "lo", the initiating institution of the Senoufos, whose function was to create by stages men who were socially perfect. On another door in the neighbourhood of Korhogo, in the middle part, between two horsemen armed with a lance and three tortoises with engraved discoidal shells, the traditional motif of umbilical scarifications can be recognized, the solar image of four deeply incised branches, which run out from a square surface, interrupted by a double broken line.

Another manner of composition, based largely on symmetry, can be interpreted in many ways. Such a door, for example, possesses two serpents which limit it on two consecutive sides, a large crocodile which divides them and, on one side and another of this second, successively, two tortoises, two varanian lizards, and two non-identified quadrupeds. There is nothing static about this, for each of these figures emerges in a living space, peopled with many delicate geometrical engravings, in particular rectangles with crosses, and aligned or more or less overlapping triangles.

From what remains on the Baoulean and Senoufen doorways we surmise that not much colour was used for the shapes, with the exception of scenes dealing with colonization, treated summarily but frankly. Colour, on the contrary, appears to have been part of the relief, of the engraving, to obtain its effect in the interior of the

field of expression. It helps the effect of relief in the Baoulean by using wide black flat tints in lozenges and twin triangles; it also employs a strange mixture of natural red ochre, porcelain clay and laundry blue; with rhythmical red incisions it animates the work of the Senofo artist. Lastly it appears sometimes to have attempted to neutralize or unify by its monochromy the polymorphous creations — Baoulean doorways entirely painted in brick red, Senoufen doorways in black (apart from the case when they have been blackened by fire).

## From relief to colour

On the other hand, the polychrome reliefs of the ancient royal palaces of Abomey or Dahomey are often coloured. However, the modelling of the clay is so defaced in a number of these that it would be illegible without the help of colour. By using the same vegetable colourings as those employed for the decoration of the leathers — particularly in the sacks, dagger sheaths and machets — this polychromy is very revealing, accentuating the modelling of the surfaces, distinguishing the masses among themselves, the gestures, the attitudes and costume. From the beginning of the eighteenth century until the "French pacification", the reliefs of Abomey depicted in the clay

Ivory Coast. Sénoufo
*Ceremonial bird used by the Lo tribe*
Paris, Musée des arts africains et océaniens

Ivory Coast. Baoulé. *Mask in painted wood*
Paris, Musée des arts africains et océaniens

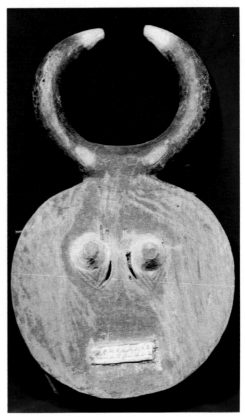

the great deeds of the Fon * people, whose first kingdoms go back to the sixteenth century. This is not historical painting of a theatrical nature; the historical event, like the myth, undergoes an allegorical metamorphosis which is hard to decipher if one does not know all its implications. In Fon art, all figures are based essentially on animal symbols. A confirmation of the proverbial origin of these different portrayals is often shown by the influence of certain myths. According to tradition, the kings liked to speak by means of proverbs or sentences, to express changes or alterations in the national life. The animals referred to were used without the intervention of rigid composition principles.

It seems, however, that the mythical figures, in spite of a smaller plastic variety, are inspired by a more elaborate language. Every element is symbolic and belongs to a given rite. Heviosso, the god of thunder, appears as a ram spitting fire. He is violent, virile, retributive; he strikes bad men with a flame shaped like his horns, and gives his shape to the axe of thunder which the priests of his cult flourish. Other spirits, other "Vodoun" accompany him, such as Lissa the chameleon, who illustrates the sentence of King Akaba, "chameleons move slowly, however they get to the top of the cheese basket"; or as Dan, the rainbow serpent who bites his tail, the incarnation of continuous movement, of the generating force, at once made by the red colour signifying male sex, and female from the blue colour, the auxiliary of Heviosso when the latter wished to leave earth and return to heaven. Dan also protects the "tohossou", supernatural beings who inhabit the marigots, and likes to reveal himself in the body of abnormally born children.

The Tohossous are the object of huge mural paintings in their own temple. Their first leader, Zomadonou, has the face of a large bird which eats fish, and whose spotted body has the sinuosity of a meandering river. Another painting in his temple associates a decorated leather sack, a double bell and Dan the serpent, all encircled with the particular marks of the tohossou, with So Bragada, the nocturnal guardian who whirls about himself with the appearance of a haystack. So Bragada and the decorated leather sack are to be met again in a painting in the temple of Adomou, accompanied by a throne and a guinea-fowl. Occupying the centre of the composition, the sack is dominated by two buffaloes clad, recalling the challenge delivered by the king Tegbessou, "A dressed buffalo is difficult to undress". These paintings do not only possess the motifs suitable to reliefs, they integrate them into a plastic order reflecting a system of communication among men, as well as perpetuating tradition.

This more or less mythical formulation of the history of a civilization also constitutes aesthetically the pictorial translation of a polychrome relief, and never an incomplete sculpture. If we compare the modelled buffaloes with the painted buffaloes, the proof is clear; the second, as well as other figures, are the result of a flat relief, levelled, completely transposed in two dimensions — hence the puffed-up shape. But it is in the case of the tinting of the materials that the relation is clearer. The motifs are a part not only of a space common to the reliefs and to the paintings; but by the daring of their stylization and the freeness of their colouring they enrich the whole composition.

## Visual parables

In technique these wall hangings which decorated the interiors of the Abomey palaces go back to the middle of the nineteenth century. Mythical themes are hardly dealt with, but popular proverbs are, and royal mottoes abound, frequently referring to historical events. All the animals play an important part, in particular the lion, the crocodile, the python, the toucan, the buffalo and the panther, who, according to tradition, fecundated the daughter of the king of Tado and became the holy symbol of the dynasty. These animals are depicted in relation with the tree, the pineapple, the dwelling, the snare, the Indian club mortar, the sabre, the flintgun and the boat of the victors. . . . It is also possible that the wall hangings describe episodes of every day life, hunting and fishing scenes, but this cannot be stated with certainty owing to the extremely metaphorical nature of Fon art. One wall-hanging depicts a large vertical crocodile seizing a man surrounded by fish, while two hunters armed with lances stand on either side of his hind legs. This composition in successive stages, with no effect of continuity, presupposes an understanding of the demands of mural painting.

The material background on to which the motifs are sewn is not passive. Often black or yellow, it is not used only to make the patches of colour stand out; the red, blue, green, violet, white, stand out in blazing clearness on the golden background which they illuminate. These figures, in turn emblems, ideograms and signs, produce mural "images", visual parables, whose spirit has survived the kings and flourishes in the life of the people. Thus when a young man wished to declare his love for a young girl, it was customary to design on the sand a dwelling and a broom, a graphical message which meant "If you do not come and sweep in front of my door, grass will grow there".

## Engraving and symbolism

Most of the proverbial motifs, which children learn to decipher very young, are engraved "in reserve" on the gourds used in domestic life. Birds, palm trees, serpents, moons, suns, varanian lizards, crocodiles are clearly depicted on the brown surface, often linked with the geometric decor which surrounds them. This technique, which goes back to the fifteenth century, was applied in a strange way in the last century. At Dahomey, the Fons were not the only peoples to use it; more to the north, the Baribas * adopted it to depict the complexity of a graphic rhythm, based upon the circular repetition of a linear motif, or the continuity of a wave undulation occasionally interrupted by a reverse rhythm. The Bariba composition appears to be developed from the centre of the gourd; it generally remains hemispherical, taking advantage of the background on which it is placed. This graphical mastery of the Baribas is to be found also in the engraving of their knives and the decoration of their leatherwork, which is full of traceries, small flowers, rosettes painted black and dotted.

Engraving on gourds is not confined to the Dahomey. The Peuls sometimes practised it, as well as the Songhais of the Niger, who produce a poker-work, lines drawn from one end to the other of the surface of the container, preserving the parts which are hachured, or simply blackened. The Dogons and the Bambaras use it for deepening the stylization of certain themes; the Falis* in the Cameroons use it to cover their utensils with triangular incisions grouped in concentric circles. As for the gourds engraved or poker-worked of the Konkombas of northern Togo, they possess a large variety of animal, human and esoteric figures, distributed inside in a geometrical manner in compartments.

But there is an even more absolute form of graphism in symbolic themes, produced by wood engraving for the decoration of household objects. Thus the clogs of the Bambaras offered to the young married woman have engraved on them the double image of the couple and of the world, twin lines which, issuing from the heel, cross with one another and multiply. Clearly sexed, the Fali furnishing can be regarded as the depository of the myth inside the house. Portrayals of the Ark, which God sent from Heaven to organize life on the earth, their stools are loaded with compositions reflecting the religious and philosophical thought of the Falis. Some of them intended to recall the continuity of the movement of the world and of humanity, are organized symmetrically in associations of feminine and masculine signs, to the right and to the left of central mats on which four primaeval couples are united. Others show the search for order through an anthropomorphic structure. There are others in which the interior system becomes complicated, on the basis of an organic principle, so that the signs of the primaeval tortoise of the first human ancestor and fruit of solar energy are interpenetrated. In a language which is exclusively graphic, by the use of continuous lines, repetitions of parallel shapes enclosing quadrangles, unequal triangles assembled in indentations, twin lozenges, Fali engraving reveals a conception of the world stripped entirely of anecdotic overtones.

Tent pickets which the Touaregs * cut geometrically out of small planks of wood, and cover with a fine linear decor, possess a symbolism which is no less imperative. Their angular stylizations, possessing the plastic force of the sign, reappear in the poker-work decor of their soup ladles, and the handles of their cups, as in the decoration of certain travelling sacks. They too endow the art of metalwork with forms and motifs of astonishing energy, particularly in the diversity and the preciosity of the famous "crosses" of Agades, and in the heavy pectoral pendants shaped in multiple triangles, "moveables" covered with short and light incisions. The source of this Saharian symbolism is probably to be found in the old copper pendants which the women of Agades still carry in pairs at their throat. They represent a highly schematized anthropomorphic figure, and are engraved in solid lines crossed and heightened by a transversal touch of red copper. They are implicitly given a sexual quality, in two parts: one is the curve, broad generous; the other is short brittle and jutting out. Together they compose an emblematic image of the couple, a sign of fecundity which is to be found again in the keys of the chains for trunks and sacks whose locks are more symbolic than real.

# The art of leather

Apart from their daggers, their ankle bangles, their locks for boxes, their richly chiselled key chains, it seems that the Moors* had an unusually rich leather art, not only by developing a precise and delicate technique, but in using great plastic liberty in the treatment of themes. Thus the "tassoufra", a fairly large travelling bag, is an example of several processes, principally painted or incised decorations, applied ornaments and leather embroidery in different colours. Thanks to its formal invention, the vigour and dazzle of its polychromy, its expressive effect, it symbolises the pictorial genius of the Moors.

The Haoussa of the Niger were masters in leatherwork, elaborating simple sandals. By the use of various black and red tints, cut across by green, yellow and silver lines, they developed a group of motifs for use in various harmonious combinations with the support of the "samara". It is probable however that certain of them were not interested only in decoration, as doubtless in the case of the "Boubou" embroidery, that broad tunic in which the skill and elegance of Haoussa work is so well seen. With small local variations it is worn in all the Moslem regions, particularly in the Cameroons, Nigeria, Dahomey, Mali, and on the Niger.

# The importance of weaving

Weaving, at least in its traditional forms, also implies a certain method comprehensible to all members of a society. Cotton is generally woven on long narrow bands on a Sudan-type loom; the bands are then sewn laterally in blankets, which almost always causes a slight shifting of the alignment of the motifs. In the Niger these are principally geometrical: black and chestnut squares, or blue and white, embroidered with yellow and red; triangles or lozenges in blue and red, distributed between blue transversal stripes. On the Ivory Coast, the Baoules and the Gouros* use colours for schematic figures, all of which belong to a strictly codified repertory.

But the Dogons have given weaving its greatest importance. According to Marcel Griaule, "weaving is the symbol of culture;" so typical of the Dogons is no more than the reflection of the square shape of fields, an image of the mask of the Stage House; in the other black rectangles in the centre, a filigree motif of two drums is to be seen, the symbol of the Word revealed to men. Of this Griaule says "Weaving, the interplay of straight lines, is the most authentic and profound expression; weaving is in fact the ideal spokesman, because it encloses the Word in each of the interstices of the thread"[1].

[1] Marcel Griaule, *L'Art et Homme*, Vol. I, Larousse 1957.

## Pottery

If weaving is the work of the men, pottery is an exclusively feminine activity. Only the wives of blacksmiths have the right to remodel what comes from the entrails of the earth. This implies that the vases, jars, cauldrons of all sizes and shapes, which they make by hand and by turning, which they decorate or leave plain, cannot be regarded as simple recipients, whatever their use in the house, or for the cults. The pots of the Songhis in the Niger have a painted triangular motif passing beyond the neck of the vessel. Using white and various shades of ochre on the natural colour of the clay, they produce a motif which covers the entire bulge of the bottle, superimposed and returning on itself, inserting itself between the lines or horizontal bands, accompanied by a slight pointillist effect, before ceasing suddenly in front of the parallel and vertical lines. Sometimes they frame an anthropomorphic figure which is vaguely given a sexual connotation, but this never possesses the energy of the decor. In the Cameroons, the decoration of the Fali pottery is obtained by incisions or impressions with the finger, or by a linear tracing in ochre, continuous and supple. Some of them carry beneath the handle, groups of cavities in which the marks of the potters can be recognized.

All these arts which are wrongly considered minor — embroidery, weaving, decoration of leather, pottery or metal — all the techniques and materials used for engraving, cannot be disassociated from the most elaborate Negro-African art. We have seen that in most cases their aim is not decorative fantasy, but that they constitute, or partake in, forms of expression, decipherable languages, based on the ideogram, the symbol or a conventional sign, and that they proceed from a style, from a conception of the world, from a civilization. Doubtless until quite recently we found it more convenient to ignore this graphic potential, blinded as we were by our thirst for exoticism and savageness, tempered by the reassuring dream of finding the antique ideal in the bronzes of Benin. We must now admit that such a graphic power is at the basis of all Negro-African creation, that it has changed the form of the materials, that it works inventively, and finds in the human body its most extreme means of expression.

## Corporeal scarifications

Technically limited, corporeal scarifications can have great variety through the repetition and arrangement of the scars which, when regarded individually, have little interest. Their principal purpose is as distinctive marks among members of the same tribe, or the same clan, or the same degree of initiation, the same religion, and they almost always possess an aesthetic quality. The process itself is painful, demands courage, and may be repeated on several occasions during one lifetime. It takes place in a ritual ceremony, and is applied only to certain parts of the body. With the exception of some aesthetic or even religious scarifications, most are concentrated on the face; the part of the body looked at first, it makes a person easily identifiable.

In Togo, where the custom is very common, in Gourma, Konkomba, Bassari, Kotokoli, and Kabre tribal, clan, or initiatory scarifications are distributed on the forehead and cheeks: parallel lines, diagonal lines, which sometimes bend back on themselves, straddle one another, accompanied by stippling. In Dahomey, the Yowabous make incisions on their cheeks with parallel lines crossing at right angles; while the Sombas entirely cover their faces with a very thick system of fine lines running from the nose or the mouth, the nose itself being scarified. The Kabres carry their initiation scars over the whole body, in particular on the stomach and the breast, incised with large parallel chevrons meeting one another in an X; the Bassaris introduce squares, lozenges with triangular summits in the interior of their clan motifs, harmoniously spread on the neck, and the cheeks.

The body, it appears, is reserved for religious scarification. The votaries* of Datin, at Porto-Novo have their breasts and backs covered with a multitude of small incisions lined in intersecting diagonals, or grouped in triangles, lozenges, and chevrons. At Abomey, the votaries of Heviosso, the Thunder, and of sakpapa the Smallpox, carry on their arms and body scars in three rows, indicating a cult.

Scarifications called "aesthetic", perhaps because they are better composed and less readable than the others, appear in general on the body and are to be found more among women than men. Although they play a purely decorative role, it must not be forgotten that they all derive from a very powerful symbolism broadly spread across Africa. Generally speaking, they are the ramification of complex umbilical scarifications, the centre for parallel lines intersecting in concentric curves, setting out their

bundles of lines across the breast, punctuated on the star studded breasts with regular marks, and invading the back with several bands of chevrons and stippled triangles. This structure of rays emitted from a centre is an image of the sun, the source of life through the body, the entire being with its fertilizing power; and the women of Chad bear the mark on the belly.

Comparison must be inevitably made between these scarifications and other objects of aesthetic value. Their incisions whether deep or light, lively, multiple and sometimes rubbed with dark blue powder, the sensuality of their reliefs, recall the rhythms and spacings of engraving, the relief on the Baoule, Senoufo or Dogon doors. There are bronzes of Benin marked in the same way with these linear and projecting modulations, which can be compared with those flush with the skin of human beings.

## Colour takes possession of man

Less rigid, but no less elaborate than the scarifications, corporal paintings possess an essentially ceremonial design. They perhaps add to the pleasure human beings have in being looked at, and betray sometimes a legitimate desire for elegance; this does not prevent their serving man as they serve the mask or the statue, not in order to decorate or embellish a background, but to give form and movement to a language. We have already emphasised several times that in Negro-African art the intervention of colour is unusual, sudden, and always for a very good reason. It does not aim at refinement, giving pleasure, even elegance; but is defaced, direct, "natural". When human beings are painted, colour has its most elementary aspect, it reveals its vegetable, animal or mineral origin.

When the body is covered from head to foot with a mixture of palm oil and red powder, it is clearly taking part in some form of symbolism. Red is a sign of life. Often it indicates, during initiatory rites, the passage from childhood to adult life. For many African peoples every ascent to a superior stage of knowledge is emphasized in this way by a particular colour. It is worn publicly, and indicates the new man. In the Congo, the Basonges* of both sexes paint white and red flames on the torso, white circles around the eyes; the Mangbetu women draw crosses, stars, flowers, bees, black lines on their body; the Batekes trace a china clay motif on their arms, breasts and shoulders, encircling the neck and emphasizing the mouth, nose, eyes, and ears, thereby enhancing a geometrical facial painting, composed of different shades of ochre. Only the Bororo Peuls display a real interest in refinement, in the choice of their ornaments as in their care about corporal decor which is most suitable to their "gheraoul" fete. Young men tattooed with blue dots in a square or diagonal on each cheek, and a bifurcated line traced in black on the crest of their nose, also place a red coating on the oval part of the face in order to dance the "bamoul" before a jury of girls, who have to select the best looking.

On the Ivory Coast collective spraying of a whiteish liquid is used by the Atie *, in particular at the annual procession of the effigy of the leopard. In the interior, in the wooded zone, the Manons *, the Dans *, the Gueres *, the Wobes *, the Oubis *, and the Krous solemnly celebrate new dissections when they leave the initiation reserve. Corporal paintings with a base of china clay, yellow or red ochres, and imported washing blue mark the end of their period of seclusion. The Wobes enclose their breast and face with a network of white lines; which encircle the mouth, cover the nose and the forehead, and trace the outline of the expression in a peculiar way. The face of the Cubis is barred with a white line at the height of the eyes, which branches into diagonals on the cheeks, stretching up the forehead as far as the hair. The Gueres wear on their eyes two twin, subtly painted triangles, which frame the nose and give the forehead a fretwork appearance. The Manons, half of whose breast is coloured in blue and sprinkled with white marks, use a facial painting with blue, yellow and red curves and diagonals, traced "in reserve" on the white.

When these many colours are enlivened by the ritual dance, granting them a kind of organic rhythm, the whole assembled populace becomes part of the physical exaltation of a "living painting", its symbolic gestures revealing something fundamental about the society. Leroi-Gourhan is therefore right in saying that "the direct application of paints and colourings on the skin produces a figure design which is all the more dramatic when it is put in movement by the muscles of the face and the limbs of the actor. More than a mask, it is a transfiguration"[1]

## Polychromy frees itself of its support

Colour is not found on all the masks, but it takes advantage of the many forms of action. Violent and harsh, it adds blue, red or white to the dishevelled expressionism of the Guere masks. In its simplest form it emphasizes the white in the Dan masks, or divides its contemplative gravity symmetrically into four black and white zones. In the Upper-Volta a white layer covers the Bobo-Fing * mask irregularly with white, enlivened with two tribal masks. Dull red or white marks punctuate the "Waniougo" of the Senofos, a zoomorphic mask with large horns symbolizing the original state of the world, and bearing the chameleon and the hornbill, two of the primaeval creatures. In Gabon, the enigmatic smile of the mask of the Mpongwes * is given an oriental pallor. Multi-coloured pearls, cowries *, metal applications compose the iridescent polychromy of the Bakuba masks of the Congo. While in the Cameroons, the Bamilekes wear huge blue copes, embroidered with white and red motifs, decorated with pearls,

[1] André Leroi-Gourhan, *L'Art et l'Homme*, Vol. I, Larousse 1957.

which mask them from head to foot. Colour can equally affect the structure and emphasize the dynamism of the shapes. This is so in the "Banda" masks which are worn by the Nalous *, and the Bagas * in Guinea, in the antelope stylization of the Kouromba dancers, as in the effigy of the buffalo of the Bobos, in which a chromatic geometry distinguishes the main masses of colour. In the same way in the Congo, concentric bands of colour which the Balubas * develop around the protuberant eyes of their masks, or the variation of the rhythms which imposes a composition with delicate but deep veins on the masks of the Basonges and the Bamilekes, gives a new conformation to the masses of colour.

There are masks possessing no volumetric effect, which provide the barest background to the colour. Colour here acquires a liberty of application and invention which recalls the corporal arts or wood engraving. In the Congo the Bakweles * have a mask in the form of a heart which would be incomprehensible without the colour which surrounds it, hollows it, models it; and the Batekes would not be able to dispense with the third dimension, if their daring polychromy were not supported by a purified graphism, and an order as strict as that of the ikon. It seems, however, that it was the Bobo race who freed the mask from its sculptural tendencies. Above the facial part, a narrow panel geometrically cuts out curving and angular shapes of various kinds, capable of being used for innumerable graphic compositions. These combine principally motifs in a checkboard pattern and a triangle of broken lines, or chevrons, or diagonals, their expressive power residing in the forceful way in which the emblem, even the heraldic quality, is depicted. The liking for a repetition of figures and rhythms inside the surface, their constantly renewed association, prove that these are certainly signs of a visual language, spoken in the domain of social life. The checkboard structure, just as the superposition of the aligned triangles, is frequently repeated in lozenges, a black and white theme, an interaction of major and minor keys, within which the red can if necessary create supplementary tension.

Statuary by its very nature does not allow colour to be expressed with such liberty; contrary to painting, engraving or relief, the sense of space is around the material, not within it. For this reason the sculptured ornaments of the canoes of the Doualas, and the royal thrones decorated with pearls of the Bambouns *, in the Cameroons, provide nothing more than a noisy and naive medley of colour. However discreet and exact may be the colour in the weatherboard posts of the Yorubas and the Nagos *, it in no way enriches the mythical figures worked into them. On the other hand, the stylized portrayal of the traditional tattooings of a Denguese chieftain interests us more than the statue itself, because it brings us back sharply to a specifically pictorial spacial conception, which we shall find even in the Congo. Stretched on elliptical wood frames tinted bark plaitings present architectural motifs which are perfectly integrated into their format, and are later used as ornaments for the young

Mangbetu girls. The Bankanous * and the Bayakas * use polychrome bark tablets when initiating their novices. Although they often contain a figurative element in relief, this, under the influence of a coloured graphism, tends to become a part of the background on which it is depicted, inserting itself into a geometrical symbolism. However it is Mali, on the prows of the canoes of the Bozo * fishermen of the Niger, that we discover pictorial themes which are more delicately elaborated, an ornamental method of expression modulated like a melodic phrase.

## Pictorial expression and mural space

It was again in Mali, at Songo, in the cliffs of Bandiagra, that the wall paintings were formally renewed periodically by the Gogons during their circumcision ceremony. According to the rite, they recall the descent of the Ark, which came to bring order on the earth; and they are the source or the ideographic transposition of the masks and their system, as well as the instruments for the cults required for the celebration of the "sigui", a quasi-national ceremony, which took place every sixty years to commemorate mythical ancestors. But we cannot be sure yet if these paintings preceded the mask society, known to have existed among the Dogons since the end of the eighteenth century. Different writings of the "kanaga", the Hand of God, are seen

*Detail of painted African textile*
Paris, Musée des arts africains et océaniens

among the masks, whose arms raised alternately to the top and to the bottom of the shaft symbolize the primaeval gesture of the pancreator who had just created the world. Various translations of the "sirigue", the House with Floors are to be seen, which with its high mast perforated with jewels and crosses, numerous figures with chevrons, was simultaneously an image of the Ark descended from heaven and of humanity.

During the circumcisions, these paintings were retraced by children, as well as those of the mobile stones on which the blood of the operation flowed. By its use of black and white surrounding a sign in red ochre, this initiatory form of writing reveals the extent and the complexity of a language expressing all its knowledge in graphic images as varied as those of the palm tree, a cosmic tree uniting heaven and earth, or of the child in the womb, or of the entire man leaving the hands of the circumcizer. In the same way, the totemic coats of arms painted in red, black and white inside and

93

on the facades of the sanctuaries at the time of the fete of sowing, bear figurative and geometrical signs, which can be interpreted in a number of symbolic ways.

As a means of specific expression, painting was to display itself frequently throughout Africa in the interior and exterior décor of the houses. There are examples in Gabon and in the Cameroons which go back to the middle of the nineteenth century; but many of them have been degraded, and in certain countries this art has completely disappeared, or it has been replaced by anecdotic illustrations, borrowed from laborious copying in school books, completely without interest.

In the lands of Upper Cavally, in Guinea, the Konos* until quite recently used to decorate the interior and exterior of the circular walls of their dwellings, previously whitewashed with china clay. Engraved or painted, this decoration unrolled across the whole length of the dwelling, above an ochre band following more or less regularly the plan of the foundations. In this way, large motifs covered almost the entire surface of the wall geometrically, animating it with their grey and ochre masses which succeed or overlap one another. But the portrayals of the masks are many and generally sealed in their function, so that the smallest anecdote cannot be introduced. On the contrary, all the figures are the object of a transcription which is a proof of the greatest daring or invention in engraving as in painting. Most of the incisions are painted in red, yellowish grey or black, and some of them, engraved "in reserve", allow the clay colour of the wall to appear.

Engravings and paintings are found on the dwellings of the Oubi and the Grabo, on the frontier of Cavally, on the Ivory Coast, in the regions under the influence of the Dans, the Gueres and the Wobes (who once had an extremely powerful mural tradition). The engravings are executed by knife, the paintings generally by finger. The latter are often polychrome, using all the chromatic sources of the natural ochres and their red tints, vegetable cinders for black, washing blue, and more recently industrial colours which have been imported. According to Holas, both men and women do this; but the women tend to paint the geometric motifs more, as well as the animal and vegetable stylizations, household objects, while the men "dip with greater advantage into the inexhaustible spring of legends and myths"[1].

In this way, the division of work depends on the sex of the painter, and on the profane or religious nature of the figurations. Besides the portrayals of dances and hunts, superpositions and the associations of ceremonial figures, such as the masks with mythical or symbolic figures, appear on the double basis of the meaning and the organic structure of a composition. The paintings inspired by that aquatic spirit known under the name of "Mami Wata", for example, display a rich plastic continuity spread across a varied wall space.

94       [1] B. Holas, *Cultures materielles de la Cote-d'Ivoire*, P.U.F. 1960.

# A total figuration

Revealing another kind of spiritual quality, the paintings which decorate the interior courtyards of the houses of the Oualata * are inspired by an Islamic tradition, by the infinite multiplications of the curve, the spiral, the arabesque, the filigree, the inexhaustible energy and suppleness of their logical sequence, their conception of absolute space. No other Moorish village possesses décor of such importance, nor is anything of this nature known elsewhere in the whole of black Africa. Discreetly portrayed on the exterior walls of the dwelling, confining itself to frame a doorway with a continuation of black designs, to emphasize an opening hollowed in the reddish facade, this décor is visible as soon as the threshold of the courtyard is passed, covering entire panels, stretching out along the walls, vividly encircling the attic windows, niches, doorways, in the form of small flowers and of rosettes, and continuing in each of the bedrooms.

After the rainy season, these paintings are renewed according to an old custom, principally by the wives of the smiths; without the least hesitation they retrace it with their finger, using a dark red ochre for the whitened surfaces, as for the colouring of the relief. The work is in monochrome — few attempts at polychromy having been made — rigorously coherent in its style and technique, demanding the complete submission of personality; one might suppose that such a pictorial expression would be an integral part of its real decorative function and could not escape it. In fact this is not so; this lively graphism is based on no unfounded suppositions; it embodies the contraction of the world, thereby formulating Moorish thought. As Odette du Pugiaudeau[1] has shown, all these compositions, from the simplest to the most elaborate, are developed from basic motifs derived mostly from masculine and feminine ideograms, whose influence is repeated in certain pendants, the decoration of pottery, the incised metal appliques of wooden trunks, corporal designs, and above all in the polychrome décor of Tassoufra, and of the circular cushion-pillow, accessories reserved almost exclusively for the use of women.

It is also significant that the door of the conjugal bedroom possesses the greatest amount of decoration in the courtyard, as much for the richness of the motifs as for their organic elaboration. All the elements of this sexual symbolism, which are already highly stylized, are less combined with one another than actually married, thereby finding their internal unity. It is here as in these synthetic panels, that the pictorial composition of the Oulatas achieves a certain hieratical gravity, fully achieving its mural ambition, by the creation of a continuous space, born from the white

[1] O. du Puigaudeau, «Contribution à l'étude du symbolisme dans le décor mural et l'artisanat de Oualata», *Bulletin de l'IFAN*, No. 1-2, 1957.

wall and acting as a golden background, on which ideographic signs in reddish brown are placed or stretched.

As the other extremity of Africa, in the mountains of the north Cameroons, the Falis have a conception of mural space which corresponds more with what we know of Negro-African art. It is primarily fitted into an architectural space, corresponding to a geometrical cosmological portrayal. In the words of Jean-Paul Lebeuf, who studied it in all its material and spiritual implications, "The house represents the successive faces of an original myth, of which it is the total symbol, the way in which the plan is traced, the choice of materials, the order adopted for the construction, the manner in which the buildings are erected and disposed; in the architectural details, the placing of the furniture and utensils; in the painted and incised motifs which cover the walls; in the form of the opening as in certain privileged spaces"[1].

Whether painted or engraved, the mural décor of the Falis derives from a geometric symbolization which is often an extreme form of abstraction. Small marks imprinted with fingers give life to the rectilinear engravings, whose broken lines reflect back the vibrations of the sunlight. These elementary signs return frequently, as much in the mosaics of black and white stones surrounding the fragments of pottery on the soil in the courts of Toro, as in the paintings which decorate the dwellings and granges of the Kangous. These paintings which cover an entire wall are composed of red and black alternating flat tints, dotted with white points and cut up unequally in rectangles by white bands. These flat tints represent the essential element in the skin of a toad, and the bigger ones, sometimes surrounded and barred by a large black line, the shell of a tortoise, both mythical animals which presided at the organisation of the world.

The elements, species, events and mythical animals, the cosmic system, weave these motifs of graphic symbolism, by means of disseminating small cavities on a whole surface, or as a result of rows of parallel lines, oblique, intersecting, divided into lozenges, in red cross rulings on a white background — the red being the generator of force and life, the white a sign of impotence and death. The exterior decor of certain granges, sanctuaries, is related to the three principal masks. Superposed ranks of broken lines, marking the successive generations in white or in black on an ochre background, form triangles facing the bottom, representing the loincloth of the primaeval ancestor. Finally, the facade of certain shrine chapels contain real compositions, in which the simplicity of the elements which constitute them contrast with the quantities of meanings.

96     [1] Jean-Paul Lebeuf, *L'Habitation des Fali*, Hachette 1961.

# Evidence and documents

## Marks and pictograms

It is probable that in the course of the evolution which produced language, means appeared for supplementing it materially, and conserving it fairly well. We refer to the great period of "marks" (understood in the largest sense) which preceded writing, and existed beside it for certain purposes. Art on the other hand, or at least some graphic skill which took its place, is at the origin of all systems attempting to present visually what cannot be expressed by word. First, we find pictography everywhere from the Latin root "to paint", and the Greek root "to trace, to write"), in different forms of proto-writing, presenting to the viewer a fragment of figured speech which is not decomposed into separate words, with the result that there is no effective link with any known language.

Generally speaking, we are dealing with those "stories without words", with image-situations or thing-signs. Of various types, these correspond with the shapes and different usages in societies which are themselves different, but all having remained at materially inferior stages, societies of hunters, fishermen, modest farmers, in Africa, northern Asia, America, the South Seas.

The pictograms must be considered separately; these are signals which have no descriptive details, but whose function is to launch the recitations, by acting as a memorandum for the narrators. Real writing, corresponding to an analysis of phrases formed by successively figured words, new evidence of observation and abstraction, only appears in societies which were evolved to the point of possessing towns; this presupposes complex and regular exchanges, particularly to ensure the food supply to the citizens from the rural areas, and first of all, the development of architecture, by artisans and artists.

Marcel Cohen

«L'Art de l'Ecriture»
Courrier de l'Unesco, March 1964

## Colour

Every system of figurative signs depends upon the direct sensibility of the eye to colour — and equally of the mind. Colour does not imply simply a process of more or less faithful imitation, which is bound up with a design or the discursive thought about the Universe's fugitive appearance. For generations, colour has been combined with *trompe-l'oeil*. One of the principal aesthetic events of the last half century is certainly the rediscovery, however clumsy its execution, by artists of the specific qualities of a means of perception, as important as that expressed by lines and arabesques. Colour is one of the fundamental categories of vision, and the employment of colours allows the direct depicting of perceptible values as significant in themselves as those supported by a line or a plan. Fundamentally, colour gives the depths of space, that is to say movement, just as a line gives the divisions of space. All civilizations which have not used exclusively a written language — an exceptional state of affairs for the last five hundred years — have attached great importance to colour. However, the ability to distinguish colours was much more limited than it is today. This is doubtless why the language of colours has been subordinated in highly developed societies to that of lines or abstract symbols.

Pierre Francastel

in «Emblèmes, Totems, Blasons»
Cat. de l'exposition du Musée Guimet
Paris, March-June, 1964

# Franco-cantabrian wall paintings

Paintings are more expressive and eloquent than engravings; they give a better portrait of the tastes and talents of the hunters in the last stages of the glacial epoch.

When our eye passes from the natural tint of the engraved walls to the brilliance of the painted surfaces it is held, whether it wishes to be or not, by the magic of colour. We then realise to our amazement that these remote artists not only used colour as a powerful element in figurative art, but that, to master the material more absolutely, they had to recognise the various possibilities of expression which unknowingly they possessed.

In brown, redi black and allied tints, monochrome, in two colours or polychrome, the paintings stand out on the walls, occasionally on the vault, defined sometimes only by their contours, silhouetted, covered sometimes by an entirely flat colour, sometimes by polychrome compositions achieved by a combination of colours.

As far as contents are concerned, paintings and engravings are similar, both representing contemporary animals, sometimes also human or anthropomorphic figures, or a large number of "symbolic" signs; and lastly, which is new, enigmatic coloured prints of hands and, outlined in red or black, hands "in reserve".

The artist of the upper Paleolithic period did not possess a very extensive palette. His colours were prepared with the help of wood charcoal, furnished in abundance by his hearths, and some widely found and easily accessible minerals, ochre, ferrous and manganese oxide, allowing him to obtain a scale of gradations from light yellow to black by way of red and brown. It is doubtful if he used pure white; blue and green were also lacking. Obermaier has proved that the occasional use of violet is due to the effects of weathering.

Mineral colourings have often been found, in particular red ochre, sometimes shaped in small triangular blocks, or even cut in a pointed manner like a pencil or a stick of chalk. Did the Magdalenians use these colours for painting their bodies? We do not know. However it is probable that they used them in some way for painting "in pastel". Normally the artist of the glacial epoch reduced his colouring matter to powder, and introduced some greasy element, forming a kind of paste. In some of the geological layers stone recipients have been found which may have been used as mortars for crushing the colours; a tall vase found at Anval contains remains of red colouration.

According to Breuil and Obermaier, the binding substances were grease, blood serum, the white of eggs, less often vegetable juices, perhaps resin. Chemical analysis has not yet succeeded in confirming these suppositions, for the colours of the samples taken from the caves have long been decomposed. Some years ago a German specialist in colours, Kurt Herberts, basing his theory on practical tests of reconstitution of colours, said that the binding element was only water; the Franco-Cantabrian paintings had been applied dry onto the surface of a rock which had been previously moistened, and whose own humidity, after having absorbed the colour, was the principal element in the remarkable state of conservation during the painting's long sleep of several millenia. The semi-liquid pastes were applied with the finger or with a brush of some kind. These brushes, with or without handles, probably consisted of tufts of hairs, or feathers, or in wads of fur, or unravelled reed-heads, in small champed branches, or pieces of wood dipped in grease. There are paintings at Lascaux in which the colour is so thinly spread, that it must have been blown through a reed in the form of a fine powder on the prepared surface of the rock.

In this way these frescoes were born which, in spite of their almost immemorial age, have retained their brilliant colouring. This must be attributed to a thin and transparent film of limestone covering it all like a varnish. Elsewhere, it would appear that this film was already laid down, acting as a background which, aided by the passage of time, slowly impregnated the coloured layer and rendered it permanent. . . .

Johannes Maringer

«L'Art préhistorique»
Editions Massin 1955

# Techniques of rock art

About twenty thousand years ago, a pictorial art stretched over a large part of Western Europe, from the centre of France to the South of Spain. It evolved in the course of millenia, since it did not die until the end of the last glaciation, and at the beginning of the post-glacial epoch, about ten to twelve thousand years ago. It is extraordinary that over this extensive area, in the course of so many generations, this art has shown a cohesion and an extraordinary continuity. The technical processes may have varied, the styles, as in all domains of art, evolved from one epoch to another. But this variation does not conceal a fundamental unity. Paleolithic art possesses a coherent and continuous artistic tradition, revealing a definite social organisation, firm beliefs, and a true culture. Paintings drawn, or in flat tints, are found, sometimes stencilled, sometimes shaded off as if by a spray-gun, in monochrome or polychrome; also clumsy finger tracings on the clay: superficial or deep engravings, sculptures which range from the simple use of natural relief to real bas-reliefs; and clay modelling. The Paleolithic artists knew and used all these processes, and they could extend their skill from the delicate engravings a few centimetres in size, such as those in the cave of Teyjat, to monumental paintings such as the bulls of Lascaux.

These sculptures and engravings were made with the help of flint picks and gravers, whose incisions can be clearly distinguished from those made with metal tools. The techniques of application appear varied, using fingers, brush, wad, stencil, and primitive vaporizers; but we can hardly classify them in all their detail. The raw materials are better known to us. The colour which has survived always has a mineral nature, with an ochre base for the reds, the yellows and the browns; a base of manganese oxide for the blacks, and the very dark brown. Colourings of an organic nature may also have been sometimes used. These have decayed with the passage of time, and none have survived today.

Annette Laming-Emperaire

«Lascaux, peintures et gravures»
«Voici», Science-Information, Paris 1964

# The two great groups of paleolithic rock art and their themes of inspiration

Paleolithic rock art can be divided into two groups: works in the open air, and those in subterranean sanctuaries. This distinction is based upon an important element, the location, and it is repeated in other domains. Technically, the works in the open air are nearly all sculptures, while those in the subterranean sanctuaries are mostly paintings and engravings. Geographically, the sculptured shelters are to be found towards the west and the north, while the general area of the subterranean sanctuaries is much more to the south. There are overlappings, and classification cannot always be accurate, but these reveal the relations between the two groups, without however detracting from their clear identity.

It appears that the periods in which these two groups developed were contemporary, for the most part, with the exception of the beginnings and ends of the period. Paleolithic rock art started with rough, unpolished work on stone blocks, of which the best known are those found in the Aurignacian levels at La Ferrassie. These deeply engraved rocks are the first gropings of an art which was to flourish with hardly any change in its geographic location in the magnificent rock bas-reliefs of the south-west of France. The idea of painting human hands, animals, various signs on the walls of the caves, and in their depths, seems to have started with the first attempts at engraving on blocks of stone, perhaps in the same regions, and at a very early date. Then in the course of the evolution of subterranean art, these hands become less frequent or disappear altogether, replaced by animals in increasing quantities, surrounded by signs which are also increasingly varied.

Thus, and we can regard this only as a hypothesis, cave art must have been born somewhere in the region of Périgord at an early period in the upper Paeolithic, with engravings on large blocks of stone. The first gropings lasted probably a long time, but only traces are left today. It was only towards the end of the Périgordian epoch that this art suddenly flourished, spreading over a much greater zone, covering simultaneously the south-west of France and a part of Spain. However, the first traditions of art on blocks of stone are very seldom found away from their birthplace. They attain their aesthetic height in a quadrilateral contained within the places known today as Isturitz, Penne, Angles-sur-l'Anglin and Le Roc. They may of course also have been collected further afield earlier in their history, indicated by the very rare vestiges of their art to be found at Hornos de la Pena, Vento de la Perra, Altamira, in the south, and the caves of the Gard and perhaps of Italy towards the south-east. In any case, the Spanish group was ephemeral, soon submerged by the great artistic wave of the subterranean caves. As for the group in the east and the south-east, we known very little about it; and its associations with a centre at Périgord are uncertain.

While in the north sculpture was being developed, the artists of the more southern Paleolithic groups penetrated into the limestone caves. Without any definite aim, they began painting and engraving animals on the walls, sometimes hundreds of metres beneath the earth, in the most secret, mysterious recesses. For a certain time, the two groups developed in a parallel manner around the region of the Eyzies; but while the sculptures disappeared in the Middle Magdalenian period, the art of the caves reached its heyday.

Annette Laming-Emperaire

« La Signification de l'Art rupestre paléolithique »
Editions Picard, Paris, 1962

# Lascaux

At Lascaux it is clear that certain groups, for instance that of the black bulls or of the galloping horses, are thought of in terms of compositions; one animal is not to be isolated from another. But it is harder to determine what sort of relations existed between the different groups. Were they simply painted at different periods chronologically, and with different intentions? Or do the superpositions have a special meaning? It is hardly possible to decide from a simple examination of the wall-paintings.

It is certain however that the disorder is only apparent. Even when the artists superposed paintings from different epochs on top of one another they attempted to retain a certain harmony in the whole; the best example of this is doubtless a horse in bichrome framed between the horns of two immense bulls.

The composition was clearly planned aesthetically, and now it is also believed that it was planned to have a definite meaning. Generally, wall art is considered not to have been planned, and this for various reasons. The old discoveries of Paleolithic works often consisted of a jumble of paintings all running into one another. This would appear to dispel any notion that the composition was planned; the observers were particularly struck by this, and háve always insisted upon it. On the other hand, unlike all other artistic schools we know, the Paleolithic artists had as the surface on which their works were painted a coarse irregular uneven face of rock, very seldom possessing a flat surface. To take copies of these works on paper, with designs or photographs, is extremely difficult. Everything is twisted, elongated, stretched in every direction. Frequently, the portrayal of a figure in a group to which it belongs has to be isolated, because it is on a concave, convex, or very irregular surface. Sometimes even a photograph can portray only a fragment of a figure. For this reason, Paleolithic art has been generally regarded in terms of its fragments, and not its ensembles. These ensembles are to be found in almost all the caves, particularly well placed in Lascaux; and we must attempt to give them the exact meaning they were given by the artists who painted them. The simple enumeration of individual designs should not make us forget the importance of the whole.

The Lascaux artists knew and used a process which was rarely employed in the other decorated caves. As well as clear and precise brush strokes, they had mastered the ability to depict the hazy outline of a contour or a space. This process was used particularly for the manes of horses; but it seems that certain details of the animals which are modelled in black bands were not carried out by simple brush strokes. We know nothing about the process itself based, we are told, on a vaporisation technique of painting achieved with a very primitive airbrush, a reindeer bone cut longitudinally, or the hollow bone of a bird etc. It is important to note that this technique for the manes of horses is to be found only at Lascaux. The modelled black on the other hand is found in several caves. Most of the painted horses at Lascaux were executed in this way; but it is possible that they do not all date from the same epoch, some executed in one sudden painting operation, the others the result of retouching older figures.

The other processes, linear tracings, use of punctuation to mark the contours of the body, dappling of the spaces, portrayal of animals in large bands, modelled or not, or filling of the silhouettes in flat tints, are very varied and indicate great changes of technique from one period to another. At certain periods, one particular colour was preferred. This was probably due to economic factors and the difficulty of obtaining a rare raw material, or for religious reasons — the belief for example in the greater effect of a certain red or a certain black — or simply due to a variation of aesthetic taste. The variations of style are perhaps more revealing than those of technique, because they are basically unconscious and unintentional. The style corresponds with a tradition which is not easily broken. Among the stylistic qualities which are most typical, and the most difficult to isolate, the way of depicting the hooves is important, the horns or antlers of the bovids, and the ears of the stags. The spaces or white lines to mark the joints of an animal, or outline a limb, are also typical in many of the figures of Lascaux.

The hooves of most of the bovids in Lascaux are shown in a special way, the division being shown full face, while the fore-limbs and thighs are shown in profile. Sometimes, the two ergots are also shown, one placed above the other. This view of perspective, or "twisted perspective" in the phrase of the Abbé Breuil, is typical of the middle phase of Paleolithic art.

It has been customary to study in isolation and individually the figures represented on the walls of the caves, not only those which, being superposed, are considered as belonging to successive periods, but those which, in the same style, must have been executed at about the same period. However the Paleolithic peoples — their works reveal it — had approximately the same view of the world as we have, and they undoubtedly regarded their works in the halls and galleries as ensembles. At Lascaux, these ensembles are more striking than elsewhere, and it is clear that the Paleolithic peoples "composed" groups of animals, or one or more species, on the panels of their subterranean sanctuaries, and that this composition had a sense which was quite different from that of a simple juxtaposition.

In our art, depicted on a background of canvas, paper etc., there are geometric limits, and it is generally the décor (the landscape for example) which gives the picture its unity. In Paleolithic art, from which all drawn décor is absent, the proof of composition of a group is furnished either by the arrangement of subjects among themselves, or by the repetition of groups of identical subjects in a cave, or on the wall of a cave.

These compositions and successions of paintings take us far from the too simple idea of magic art, which does not incidentally mean that we know how to interpret them. How should we interpret the dominant idea in the decoration of a sanctuary? Is it the unfolding of a story with sacred overtones, like the stations of the Cross in Christian sanctuaries, whose panels, in spite of the variety of personal interpretations, always reproduce the same stories? Or is it an attempt to depict what was believed to be the structure and organisation of the world and human societies? According to this hypothesis, the Paleolithic sanctuaries should be regarded as a first Treatise of the Universe or of living beings, even before the invention of writing.

The first hypothesis does not exclude the second, and it is probable that what we attempt to decipher on the walls of the subterranean sanctuaries has something of the myth attached to it, and — why avoid the word? — of metaphysics. These subterranean compositions reveal a story of both man and animals, where we are in the domain of the myth; they attempt to state what man was among the animals, to draw up a classification, to put a little order in this great animal and human world, where chaos exists, ever new and ever inexplicable. . . .

Annette Laming-Emperaire

« Lascaux, peintures et gravures »
« Voici », Science-Information, Paris 1964

# The sense of paleolithic compositions

It is understandable that these facts of composition have not been satisfactorily studied, first for topographical reasons, and secondly because the compositions often overlap. A general theme, marked at the beginning and end by signs, may include several repetitions of the same subject, panel by panel, with proportional differences which often cannot be interpreted; only a statistical analysis can bring out the composition itself. When we consider it, the situation would hardly be different in a cathedral, if we did not understand the meaning of the images found there. We would see the Stations of the Cross depicting the Passion around the monument, when a certain reredos grouped its episodes in one panel, when such-and-such a chapel, by its pictures or its sculptures, showed isolated a descent from the Cross, a Crucifixion, or Saint Veronica's veil. Then the altar would repeat the theme of Christ on the Cross three times, and it would be found again opposite the Throne. We may imagine an archeologist ignorant of Christianity, who would suppose each time that an attempt was being made to put a spell on an enemy, each time by showing his image crucified, his sides wounded, in the sanctuary.

What the Paleolithic peoples wished to represent will probably never be known to us. But it seems that their repeated compositions deal with the illustration of a mythological story, in the large sense of that word, the play of events and persons operating in a time and space which are mythical, simultaneously both original and day-to-day events. Such a system centres round the great animals of the hunt, the horse, the bison, the ox, to which can be added the mammoth, sometimes the reindeer; it implies the association in pairs of species for the central theme. And also the participation of secondary elements, framed in the picture, generally the stag and the ibex, and the presence in a further or isolated place, of dangerous animals, the feline species and the rhinoceros. Signs are used to depict the opening and closing of the ensemble. Other signs depicting symbolically the male and female organs accompany the animals. The wounded animals, with spears in their bodies, are relatively rare. There is apparently a relationship between a spear and a male sign, between a wound and a female sign, so that wounded animals sometimes replace animals accompanied by signs. . . .

More compact in time than has been sometimes thought, more stable in space, Paleolithic art appears closer to what history of art has learned about superior forms of aesthetic development. It doubtless becomes less miraculous, losing its character of challenge to historical equilibrium, although it may be six times further away from us than the oldest arts of history; but it gains by plunging us directly into the thinking processes of those mammoth hunters, of being in our eyes more immediately human.

André Leroi-Gourhan

In « Histoire de l'Art », Encylopédie de la Pléiade, t, I, NRF, Paris 1961.
© Gallimard, Paris.

# Rock art in the Iberian peninsula

When we first studied the wall-paintings in the valley of the Batuaças, we noted a striking similarity between the points or strokes aligned in series and the paintings on pebbles at Mas-d'Azil. In fact, Obermaier has incontestably established by twelve series of figures that it is possible to interpret the symbols of Mas-d'Azil in the light of the less stylized figures on the Spanish rocks, generally representing human diagrams: the double or triple chevron connected with the design of a seated man. The simple cross or with a double bar, as well as the sign in the form of a ladder vertically cutting a large number of rungs stands for the upright man. There are too many similarities between the two series for their respective origins to be distinct from one another.

In the present state of knowledge, Iberian prehistoric art can be regarded as follows: in Upper Paleolithic times the Peninsula possessed an Atlantic province, primarily Cantabrian, which stretched to Castille and even as far as southern Andalusia, to La Pileta and the neighbourhood of Malaga and Cadiz; its naturalist art is the geographic prolongation of our Aurignacian-Magdalenian art of the reindeer age in the south-west of France. The best example of this is at Altamira. Nevertheless, quite early a flowering of schematic signs appeared, but rarely and later in the Pyrenees and Dordogne, less frequently in the latter. La Pileta is particularly rich in a variety of old signs.

The second Paleolithic province of art in Iberia is almost exclusively Mediterranean, stretching from Catalonia to the province of Almeria. Although in its fine animal art this Levantine art is a special evolution of the Périgordian-Franco-Cantabrian, it is notable, as we have already said, for the abundance and the movement of its human figures which are equally realist, but treated summarily, the production of complex figured scenes of hunting and war. Schematic elements which in certain cases, for example at Minateda (Albacete), preceded other realist figures, are found increasingly towards the end of this art period, and appear to derive from a mixture of elements in the Mediterranean littoral, increasing in numbers relatively to the original element, which was more northern. There is an undeniable similarity between the Saharan painting and even with that of South Africa, but it can be interpreted in the reverse sense, as an influence from the Mediterranean coast of Iberia in Africa.

Henri Breuil

in « L'Art et l'Homme »
Larousse, Paris 1957

# Photography in the service of prehistoric art

I have been concerned largely with photographic problems in connection with the beauty of the walls of Tassili, and the accompanying technical questions. The first of these is the simple fact that the wall space is ten, twenty, thirty square metres in extent, sometimes more. To take photographs with negatives measuring six by six centimetres or twenty-four by thirty-six millimetres, followed by the problem of enlarging them to twenty-four by thirty centimetres creates difficulties over lenses, emulsions and laboratory methods.

The human eye can go from one detail to another, and then take a general view of the painting. But the general view will never bring out the detail, just as the detail without its context cannot give a satisfactory reproduction. This means that the photographer must regard the problem from two points of view, photographing the whole, and then the detail, without being able to isolate any object, gesture or expression which particularly interests him.

Furthermore and no less important, the potentialities of sensitized film allow one to reproduce wall paintings that are so defaced that they cannot be photographed by the so-called traditional methods. Starting with negatives on slow film I make the prints on a paper that is normally used for half tones, which has the effect of considerably increasing the contrast.

Colours also presented a number of difficulties connected with light and its reflection. The frescoes are for the most part situated in the shade, lit by the reflections of daylight on the sand of the ground, and the gritty and coloured walls surrounding them. This gives an orange-yellow lighting of tints and intensities which vary so as to be particularly unfavourable to a colour film, which, incidentally, in these surroundings is insensitive to greys, blues and greens, colours which the eye sees perfectly clearly.

Filters cannot be used, because each painting creates a special problem which can be solved only by artificial light. Here I encountered another difficulty — carrying batteries for flash-lights into inaccessible passages by hand, far from the electrical sources necessary for recharging the batteries. In spite of these difficulties and limitations, photography proved again what an admirable instrument for study, research and investigation it is, even when submitted to the most stringent scientific disciplines.

I was therefore able to contribute by photography more objective and precise information on the remains of prehistoric art, which had hitherto been known only from manual surveys. I carried out my work as honestly as possible, my aim being to reproduce the true structure of the works of art and (a mere personal intention) to reveal that the other methods of reproduction were not as perfect as had been supposed.

Jean-Dominique Lajoux

## Aesthetics, the element of cohesion in south sea society

Long before myths became a part of literature, and were conserved in it, they had been depicted plastically in art. The art of the South Seas is an excellent example of this. It is this aesthetic element which gives a coherence to the South Sea society. By aesthetics we understand not the normal interpretation of the science of the beautiful, but aesthetics in the original sense, retaining all the sensations and feelings caused by observation of forms and shapes (understood in their most general sense).

Lines, motifs, feathers, colours, with which primitive peoples decorated all their objects, are not ornaments in the sense in which we understand them, but forms or signs. The Australian reads the colours placed in juxtaposition on a post, the Guinean saw mythical beings in engravings; in the sculptures perforated with arabesques, combining birds, fishes, and humans, which mean little to us, the Guinean reads the history of these beings. He therefore placed in juxtaposition signs corresponding to the forms perceived by his eye, and placed side by side in his mind, as objects are in nature. This ensemble took on a new form, in which he found everything he that wished to perpetuate. If he had to express it by words, his comment took the form of a myth. This method demands great comprehension of the objects seen and felt; the hand takes hold of the shapes of this world that are near it more quickly, and they are then depicted through the aesthetic sense. Decoration is an artificial language. There are many religious and psychic complexes which the spoken language cannot depict, because it cannot express abstractions; but decoration, thanks to its aesthetic language, can give plastic expression. It produces a symbolism which we can decipher, in which the crocodile is the eternal ancestor, the bird has a mythical or a religious sense, the colour white stands for the pallor of a dead person, the red colour for life, etc. We are so accustomed to irrational thought, that we relegate aesthetics into a department in which it is isolated, where it remains comprehensible only to experts. The people of the South Seas on the other hand, in their ignorance of scientific thought, have recourse to aesthetics to express any general idea, or portrayal which they cannot formulate in speech (social, magical, or clan prestige, shown in their tattooing, the portrayal of the myth in sculpture, etc.). They seize the shape of objects before they analyze them, a knowledge which is all they require. They communicate through the emotions these shapes provoke, before communicating by speech. Their thought is ordered by aesthetics, long before it displays any logical process.

Maurice Leenhardt

«Arts de l'Océanie»
Les Editions du Chêne, Paris 1947

# The Australian palette

By judiciously using materials possessing several tonal values, together with poly-chrome coatings, or the brilliant and multi-coloured magic of feathers, the Australian became highly skilled in the art of tonal painting.

For instance, he was so pleased with the effect of contrast caused by a light coloured motif on a dark background that he used his household objects for decoration: bark baskets, and water gourds from coconuts. His favourite technique was of champlévé wood. The lines of his design being, whether incised or hollowed, the sombre colour in the bark, were in contrast with the sap-wood, of lighter tone. Often the parts in the hollow were brightened by painting. The same technique was applied to the fresh skin of opossum, in which the linear composition was incised and coloured. The dry skin gave the impression of tattooing. But it should not be supposed that this success suggested tattooing motifs for the Australian; he decorated the human body with points and lines made by swollen scars.

There were only four colours in the Australian palette; red ochre, yellow ochre, china clay, charcoal. His palette was much used in the north, diminishing as he went further south; it was apparently unknown in the south-west. It is uncertain if this absence was due to lack of ochre. Colouring earths were unequally divided across the continent; but the Australian, who travelled very little, made excursions to obtain the most valuable of them all, red ochre.

The colouring earths were watered down; with his finger or a morsel of frayed wood used as a brush, the artist spread the background tint, generally yellow ochre. After drying it, he traced on this background a broad red line, or some other motif, the paw of an emu etc. In this way he decorated the handle of a tool, a wooden basin, or similar utensils. On the post which indicated a tomb, he would trace several lines connected with the totem of the dead person. Or he would carefully form a delicate network of lines to decorate a religiously conserved skull. This art of organising red, black or white lines on a yellow background demanded a technique of its own; for it was a form of language.

Maurice Leenhardt

«Arts de l'Océanie»
Les Editions du Chêne, Paris 1947

# Technique of painting on bark in Australia

After it is sufficiently dry, the bark is ready for painting. If a sacred drawing is intended, the bark is taken to the ceremonial ground or to some specially prepared place. In the meantime the artist has prepared brushes, similar to those used in body-painting.

He mixes his paints of yellow and red ochres on a stone pallet. The ochre is in the form of blocks, the red coming from rich deposits at Elcho Island, while the yellow is found locally in great abundance. Ochre has great trading value, and may be bartered over a wide area for other goods. Natives discuss the relative merits of different ochres in regard to texture and colour; some varieties are preferred to others while in one painting at least two colours of red ochre may be used, or two distinctive shades of the yellow. The lump of ochre is strenuously rubbed on a flat rock and moistened gradually with water to form a liquid paint. If the artist is particularly anxious that his painting should not flake or powder unduly, he will add oil from a swamp root, similar to a miniature bamboo shoot. He does this by rubbing the flat stone with the shoot, and then mixing the ochre and water; the same shoot may also be used as a brush. Only a small amount of yellow or red ochre liquid is mixed at one time, so that throughout his drawing the artist is continually rubbing his lump of ochre and mixing his paints.

White paint is also obtained locally. The clay is collected in lumps, crushed to powder, and mixed in water to a liquid paste. This is held in a shell or, to-day, in an old tin, and applied in the same way as the other paints. Black paint is obtained from charcoal mixed with water. For both of these, as for the others, the oily bamboo shoot may be used to ensure the durability of the drawing.

Having his bark board prepared, his paints mixed and brushes ready, the artist sits cross-legged before his bark and begins to outline the main design, usually, but not always, in yellow. The lines when dry stand out clearly from the red-ochred background. The next steps depend on the individual artist. He may sketch out the whole design, completely covering his board; or he may build it up gradually in sections, finishing each section before going on to the next. The way in which he sits before his board, or holds it, depends too on his personal predilection. He can choose from a variety of positions.

Elkin and Berndt

«Art in Arnhem Land», Melbourne 1950
quoted by A. Laming-Emperaire

# The expressive force of Australian engraving

To understand how the artist himself becomes a part of a figurative design, let us imagine a group of Australians seated in a circle on the sand taking part in an incantation. The reciter starts his rhythmical words with movements of the head, to the accompaniment of his assistants' interjections. As his recitative proceeds, he traces on the sand with the end of his finger a spiral design whose centre corresponds with the end of a period. He later adds a second spiral, a third, then more; each is rhythmically integrated with the periods of the recitatif.

Then whilst still talking, he associates all these spirals by lines, and finishes the design at the same time as the end of his recitation, fully master of a situation. The figurative drama is complete; its aim is not simply to produce these spiral designs, with what we would term a symbolic or a decorative value, which we can judge by our values. It is actually *lived* by the actors; and the plastic décor, which can incidentally represent the most different subjects is only a projection of the figurative rhythm.

A second proof is furnished by the same Australians. Among their works are small plaques of soft stone engraved with the same groups of spirals or concentric circles, plaques called "churinga". Considered in isolation, the image which they bear has no real meaning of its own, it is only a powerful expression. Placed on the ground in the centre of the same circle of men, it produces the same figurative drama; the finger of the reciter follows the circles, turning rather like the needle on a gramophone record, the recitative unrolls, the assistants give their replies in a rhythmical group which is identical with the first one.

André Leroi-Gourhan

in « L'Art et l'Homme »
Larousse, Paris 1957

# Melanesian painting

Whether we are examining self-contained works or merely ornamental colourings, we have in the first case an impression of a work which is spread over the surface, and in the second, on the contrary, of a varied colouring and lively contrast emphasizing the feeling of life peculiar to all this art. This confusion, force and feverish feeling of life is typical of the perforated neo-Irish statuary, which is complicated, heavily baroque, and whose surfaces are covered for every square centimetre with polychrome motifs. Very rarely does a line of demarcation between painting and the plastic element disappear, as is the case for instance of the commemorative plaques in the Gulf of Papua, on which the sculptured subject is only very roughly sketched, in the middle of a flamboyant red, white, brown and black polychromy. This lack of reality is one of the essential characteristics of Melanesian art, found not only in the pronounced taste for fantastic shapes, but in highly developed stylization. What is true for the plastic arts is also for ornamental art. In the plastic arts, this tendency towards stylization leaves the artist to sketch the bodies and the faces in a symbolical manner. In ornamental art, this tendency often ends with the employment of simplified geometrical motifs which hardly recall the models taken from nature. The combination of these two processes, for instance in the masks of Baining, where the face is almost entirely covered with concentric circles and ovals to indicate the eyes, gives these works of art a most striking effect. All the details reveal a deep feeling for aesthetics; one might even speak of a conscious desire for effect, of a highly evolved vision.

Tibor Bodrogi

« L'Art de l'Océanie »
Editions Corvina, Budapest 1961
Editions Grund, Paris 1961

# The painting of the Abelams (Mapriks)

These are always painted on the same bark of the palm tree, decorating also the interior surface of the roofs of the large dwellings where the men assemble for their own rites. The variation here is between flat colours, red ochre, yellow ochre, and parts which are finely hachured in white. The principal theme is the human body. Sometimes the face is barely sketched; it is then presented in a kind of halo of white lines, ochre lines, broken lines, and ordinary circular hachuring, also by large plaques hachured on either side. The face is broadly treated, beneath a conical coiffure embellished with a halo placed above the red line of the hair; the ochre forehead is separated in two parts by a triangle. A "T" motif frames the small eyes and indicates the nose; this is prolonged by a vertical line which limits two large surfaces beneath the eyes whose lower curves enclose a minute mouth, with quantities of pointed teeth arranged around its periphery. The trunk in lozenge form is limited by a double hachured band. On the ochre breast, a necklace and white pendant stand out. A lower red triangle might represent the pubis.

In the northern part of this region, the paintings are placed at the apex of the dwelling, protected by a protuberance of the roof. A row of sculptured heads attracts attention at the base. The manner of dealing with painted faces here is similar to that of the Washkuks, owing to a plaited motif, simple or triple on the forehead; the triangular surface beneath the eyes is carried on to the base by a sinuous red plaque surrounded by parallel white lines which rise up above the mouth. The southern part of the region provides a background which is less rich and coloured, and with less variety.

Jean Guiart

«Océanie»
NRF, Paris 1963  © Gallimard, Paris

## Massim

The décor is achieved by the means of broad engraved lines, which give way in certain places to gaps of variable size. The theme is still the bird, an almost abstract shape, whose body is a volute with a simple central motif opposed to an incised border of circles and the beginning of inter-penetrating spirals; here and there references to the motif of the human face or a bird's beak can be seen. The beak of the principal bird is placed on a transverse band, whose decoration suggests a head of a fish or a serpent. The incised lines are filled with chalk.

The prows of the canoes are made of two pieces; one is flat, transversal, and serves as a basis for a longitudinal piece turned towards the prow. The general shape of these pieces is asymmetrical; between two bands is a body from which sprout spirals of unequal size. The internal motifs resemble spirals which are completely flat, taking the form of elongated "S's", hooked on to one another. The construction itself of the décor implies the stylisation of the human body in the central part; a small reference to this is made at the top. The lateral motifs reveal quantities of birds' beaks. The longitudinal piece presents the development of the bird theme, in white or in the colour of the wood.

Jean Guiart

«Océanie»
NRF, Paris 1963. © Gallimard, Paris

114

# The ornament of Polynesian tapa

The ornamention of a piece of tapa can be achieved in three ways. The entire piece can be dyed in red or black; it can be painted by hand with general geometrical motifs; or a printing process can be employed. The two last techniques are of particular interest.

The pigments are of mineral or vegetable origin; oily soot obtained from an aleurite nut; a red pigment gathered around the seeds from the berry of a cultivated bush; saffron leaves, to obtain the yellow.

Its originality lies in the manner of printing the motifs. A vegetable plaque composed of large leaves of a species of pandanus palm is bordered with an edging made of plaited coconut fibres. On a small surface a motif is formed from a similar plait, or fragments of the ribs of coconut palms, held in place by a vegetable seam. The design generally is based on a group of geometrical motifs repeated according to the technique of subtle motifs in opposition to others, less numerous but on a larger scale. This matrix is generally placed beneath the prepared tapa, which is then rubbed with a wad of tapa impregnated with brown dye. Only those areas overlying the high reliefs of the pattern immediately below are coloured as a rather blurred design. Tapa can be left as it is, or certain motifs can be boldened with the brush in black; or again certain surfaces which have been left free can receive painted motifs; this gives a contrast in colours, somewhat effaced and dull in the first process, but brilliant in the second.

The matrix of leaves and plaits tended increasingly to be replaced by a wood matrix used in the same way. In the Cook Isles, this last was used for printing. In the Hawaiian Isles, slender sculpted plaques in wood carry geometrical motifs in relief which are printed dry in relief on the tapa, and repeated to cover the wide bands; the design of the motifs is carried out by hand.

In general, the motifs are geometric, sometimes with stylized representations of fishes or plants.

Jean Guiart

in « Histoire de l'Art »
Encylopédie de la Pléiade, NRF Paris 1961
© Gallimard, Paris

# The Marquesan tattooing

In his anxiety to assure the presence of the Tiki, the Marquisian decided to write it on himself. The custom of tattooing, general in the South Seas, became for the Polynesians a display of art; the Marquisian brought it to its highest pitch of perfection. The blue network does not follow the lines of the body, it clothes it. The technicians, in reality artists, boast that they never reproduce the same decoration twice. They do not possess many motifs, nor do they invent new ones; but they vary those they have. All these motifs and signs have been collected by enthnologists and classified. It appears that by the possession of such a large number of signs, to which he gave a name, the Marquisian found himself inventing, by means of tattooing, a form of writing. He would no doubt have developed it, if the invasion of the Pacific by the Europeans had not arrested the evolution of his race.

Maurice Leenhardt

«Arts de l'Océanie»
Les Editions du Chêne, Paris 1947

# The meaning of negro—african portraiture

The tendency towards design and painting goes back to a remote epoch, if we include the quantity of engravings and paintings which the deserts of the Sahara contain, under Egyptian and Mediterranean influence; as well as East Africa, the zone of transition, and above all, South Africa.

Few of these works have been explained, but some Sudanese celebrate rites in which the paintings and rock signs have a primary place. The porches of Songo in the cliffs of Bandiagara, reveal in sybiline figures the descent of the Ark bringing order on the earth, and in clear figures, the masks of human society; as well as the material of the sixty-years ceremonies for the renewing of the cosmos.

The Keitas of the Mandingue territory do the same, at the time of the seven-year restoration of the Kangabas, of "international" notoriety, because many peoples describe themselves as having derived from this "vestibule" of Mande. The sense of the exterior paintings had already been seen; the rudimentary characters, their limbs on a cross, the silhouettes of hands and gourds, the blobs and three coloured point decoration which surrounds them contained a static symbolism corresponding to each of the lines, and figures. But the profound human feeling is clearly depicted. The woman in charge of the work faced eastward and first painted a black circle; then facing north, a circle surmounting a vertical axis, followed by a similar figure, carrying a transversal bar as an arm. In a fourth, another bar was used for the leg. These four works were regarded as elementary human beings.

However, what mattered was to represent on the wall the beginnings of creation: the initial seed (the point) appears under the effect of the first vibration (the axis), followed by a second (the arms), giving the four cardinal directions, that is the scene of the Universe; a third furnishes the lower limbs of terrestial beings, and shows their sex. For a short moment these figures maintain this incomplete appearance which is quite forgotten when the edifice is completed; the sketches have then become human beings.

These paintings are reflected in the sign of the Universal-man, used some thousand kilometres away by the Dogons who, on the "international" basis, use the name of Keita when they live in the Mandingue country. This sign, an ancated cross, is described as "life of the world", a strange return to the hieroglyphic which bears a similar name. Like the Mandingue figures, denoting a common dwelling, the Dogon sign is linked with the great family house, but is here connected with the plan itself of the edifice, resembling a man lying on his right side, depositing on the altars of the entrance, then through the open door into the Universe, the seed symbolized by milk extracted from the barely ripe grains of the first harvest. The same images are found in the Cameroons, in the Fali granary in eight cells, recalling the bursting of the first grain; and in the Kotoko palace whose labyrinths denote the world.

Marcel Griaule

in « L'Art et l'Homme »
Larousse 1957

# Totemic coats of arms of the Dogons

The coat of arms is executed by the sacrificial man attached to the totem priest during the annual feast celebrated by each group. The instrument employed is generally a hen's feather, and the material boiled millet flower. They are painted on to the facade or an interior wall of the sanctuary, a mud surface rendered smooth by a recent restoration. In certain cases, when the sanctuary is formed by rocky walls, the designs overflow and extend onto the rock, which has previously been covered with mud. The coats of arms have two kinds of signs, some realist, clearly comprehensible; others geometrical, and conventional, and difficult to interpret. In the first category, certain paintings refer only to the object depicted, the sacrificial hen, a stick, the moon, the sun, etc. But sometimes the object reproduced is symbolic (a cross signifies a man; the sandals of a priest represent the priest himself). The second category includes principally check-boards, with alternate parts possessing either empty spaces or being full of ladders with many steps, whose bars are irregular and chaplets of lozenges which are either filled or empty. The check-boards and ladders are still an enigma, similar to that of the saw-tooth ornaments, and the zig-zag lines for decorating masks. It is no less true to say that the coat of arms gives to the member of the group the image of things and persons essential to the group. In many cases, it also provides an image of the system of the world, for the group is not an amorphous element of the Universe.

Marcel Griaule

in « Journal de la Société des Africanistes »
Paris 1937, t. VII, fasc. 1

# Totemic coats of arms of the Dogons

The totem possesses an important function for the ritual execution of the "signs" — the fundamental graphic expression of the creative "word" and the successive drawings which accompany them. All the "signs" and designs belonging to the category with which they are associated are executed on the interior or on the facades of the sanctuary during a collective ceremony called "bulu" (literally, "to make live again"), celebrated by each clan before the sowing season. For example, in the region of Sanga, signs of the "amma" category are executed in the sanctuary of the totem Yebene; of the category "person" in that of the Ogoine; of the category "twins", in that of the Tire; of the category "water", in that of the Goummoyane; of the category "red sun" (or warm season), in that of the Sangabilou, etc. These figures are the totemic "coats of arms", the objects of our examination.

The execution of the figures obeys the following rules:

1. The group of signs of the particular category must be carried out on the interior, or the facade, of each of the principal sanctuaries, over a period of sixty years (sixty being "the account of placenta"). The group is called "designs of all the years which come", or "designs of every sixty years".

2. There are eight signs or permanent designs on each totem and permutation of other figures. In practice, and bearing in mind the time taken for the execution, which often extends beyond that of the lifetime of a priest, the application of the rule is not necessarily rigid. However, the theory is regarded by those who follow it as fundamental.

3. The position of the drawings in the interior or on the facade are a function of the mythical portrayals. They depict:

(a) In the interior, all that belongs to the origins of creation, formed in the "womb" of God the Creator.

(b) On the exterior, all that has been achieved after the opening of the "womb". We see firstly, above the door what took place in Heaven; secondly, beneath the door what took place on earth; on each side of the door, what took place in the space "between Heaven and earth"; in general, if the form of the sanctuary allows it, on the walls "what has taken place in the four directions of space".

4. Chronologically, for the same object, the successive drawings were not executed in the same year, but during four successive years. Each totem is specially associated with a number of cereals, the seeds of this variety are drawn in the interior in the following manner: the "bummo" on the soil at the time of the building of the sanctuary; the "yala" on the rear wall the following year; the "tonu" on the wall to the right of the door on entering, the third year; the "toy" to the left, the fourth year.

5. The materials used for these paintings vary with the category represented, the type of design, and the moment when it is drawn. For example — mixtures of different cereals are used for figures, depending upon whether it is "bummo" "yala", "tonu", or "toy" of a given object.

6. The figures are to be "read" in general according to a polyvalent symbolism. For example, the check-boards which alternate in black and white, and are generally present on all the facades of the sanctuaries, signify: the Ark in which men came down from Heaven to earth; the members of a clan; the cultivated soil — or the principal fields, including that of the clan ("binu minne"); the blankets carried by the dignitaries, who are themselves images of the ritual field.

Germaine Dieterlen

in «Emblèmes, Totems, Blasons»
Cat. de l'exposition du Musée Guimet
Paris, March-June, 1964

# The social and symbolical meaning of fali painting

The motifs of the facades may, according to the talents of the priest in charge, cover a large surface with yellow ochre, red or black; they represent the most formidable wild animals, hippopotami, panthers, lions, who have been killed by the priest in charge, or by members of his family. Sometimes this is regarded as a hunting scene. The symbols are always complicated, requiring all the knowledge of the priests to interpret them.

At Pouri, one of the reliquary-chapels of the house of the Tondji Belgui bears on its facade, which gives on to a narrow court, a wide incised motif "wewicina", painted in white and ochre, surrounding and covering its opening. Rectangular and composed of an assembly of geometrical, square, rectangular, and triangular figures, and white lozenges, spread over a uniform ochre background, it is surrounded, apart from the top, by a band held laterally by a narrow ochre flat tint; the upper part is bounded by a white line, while the base of the motif carries three ranks of wolf teeth above an ochre band. In the centre, the rectangular opening is separated from the diagonals in four alternating zones, white and ochre. To the right and to the left of this orifice are two macaronic figures whose surface is entirely pitted with small cavities formed by finger, and covered with vertical bands in two colours.

The ensemble represents a collective hippopotamus hunt; the belly of the animal is a part of the construction itself. The ochre bands which surround the motif symbolize the road taken by the group of men in order to reach the hunting field;

they are supposed to go to the left and to the right of the edifice (seen full face) and stop the savage animals, represented by interior geometric figures, from coming out of the brush. This is indicated again in the two white bands traced vertically on the two sides of the opening; while the uninterrupted white line which surrounds the orifice symbolizes the grassy savana in which the hippopotamus lives. The two lateral macaronic figures, and the painted triangles on the door refer only to the antelope who, being considered at Pouri as the most powerful of the savage mammifers, of which she was the "head" in the anthropomorphic classification, represents them all. In the centre, the two white triangles are the image of the animals' belly, the two red ones of his back; the point of intersection of the diagonals determining these four figures corresponds to his navel, the diagonals themselves to his limbs. On the right is the palm of the hand, on the left the back of the hand, a meaning supported by the cavities of the macaronic writing, in which that of the right represents the head, that of the left the hairs of the extremity of the animal's tail. The bands of colour of these discs are similar to those painted on the hides; the entire right side and the corresponding horn are painted in ochre, the left side in white. In the right hand triangle the remains of the offerings of a millet-mash can be seen.

The order in which these motifs are carried out, and the direction in which the animal moves, vary according to the direction in which the construction is supposed to turn; it changes according to the "classic" identity of the hunters, the apparent course of the sun for the group with the tortoise, and a contrary movement for the group with the toad. But according to the conception of the Falis, the movement printed on the building is a double one because of the bi-sexual nature of the seed of the water-melon, "father and mother" of the edible grains.

Jean-Paul Lebeuf

«L'Habitation des Fali»
Bibliothèque des Guides Bleus
Hachette, Paris 1961

# Negro-african images and rhythms

We would not understand the essence of the literature and art of the Negro-Africans if we thought they were merely utilitarian, and that the Negro-African has no sense of "beauty". Certain ethnologists and art critics have claimed that the words "beauty" and "beautiful" were absent from the Negro-African languages. The contrary is the truth. It is that the Negro-African identifies beauty with goodness, above all with efficacity. Thus for the Wolofs of Senegal, the words "târ" and "rafet" — "beauty and "beautiful", are applied primarily to men. When they are talking about words of art, the Wolofs employ the qualifications "dyeka", "yem", "mat" which would be translated by, "what is seemly" "what is correct", "what is perfect". Again, this is a question of functional beauty. The fine mask or poem is the one which produces on the public the required emotion; happiness, joy, hilarity, terror. A significant Senecate word is "baxi", which means "goodness", used by the young dandies to describe a pretty young girl. In this, beauty is for them "the promise of goodness". On the other hand, a good action is often described as "beautiful".

In Greco-Latin aesthetics which survived in the European west, with the exception of the Middle Ages, until the end of the nineteenth century, art was an imitation of nature, or perhaps I should say a corrected imitation. In black Africa it is regarded as explanation and knowledge of the world, that is a participation in the reality which is an undertone to the Universe's "surreality", or more exactly to the vital forces which animate the Universe. The European prefers to recognize the world in the reproduction of an object, known by the word "subject"; the African Negro, prefers to understand its image and thythm.

The African Negro image is not an equation image, but an analogy image, a surrealist image. The African Negro abominates the straight line and the false "proper word". "Two and two do not make four, but five", said the poet Aimé Césaire. The object does not mean what it represents, but what it suggests, what it creates. The elephant is force, the spider prudence, horns the moon, the moon fecundity. All portrayal is image, and image, I repeat, is not an equation, but a symbol, an ideogram. Not only the image-figuration but the material — stone, earth, copper, ore, fibre — and also the line and colour. Any language which is not fable is boring; even more so to the African Negro who does not understand such language. The astonishment of the first white men on discovering that the "natives" did not understand their paintings, not even the logic of their speech . . . !

The two things — the strength of the image, the strength of the word. Thus in Dahomey among the Fons, the king at each important event in his reign pronounced a rhythmical sentence, in which the principal word gave him a new name, "the pineapple which laughs at the lightning". And the word, which was everywhere despotically written as pineapple, became an image; in wood, clay, gold, bronze, ivory; on the throne, the head coiffure, the soldier's baton, the walls of the palace.

However the image did not produce its effect on the African Negro if it was not rhythmical. Here rhythm was a part of image; rhythm was consubstantial with it, uniting in a whole sign and sense, flesh and spirit.

It is the architecture of being, the internal dynamism which gives shape, the system of waves which it emits for others, the pure expression of the vital force. Rhythm is the vibrating force which, through the senses, touches us at the roots of our being. It is expressed by the most material means and sensual means: lines, surfaces, colours, architectural volumes, sculpture and painting; poetry and music; movement in the dance.

For twenty-five years now, the mural paintings of black Africa have been discovered, reproduced and commented upon. The rhythm is not marked by divisional lines in shadows and lights; it is not an arabesque, as in the classical painting of Europe; for the African Negroes paint with flat colours, without shade effects. The rhythm is born here as elsewhere by repetition, often at regular intervals, of a line, a colour, a figure, a geometrical form; seldom by the contrast of colour. In general, on a dark background used as a space or a neutral area giving the painting its depth, the painter places his figures in clear colours: and inversely. The design and the colouring of the figures has less to do with the appearance of the real than with the profound rhythm of the object.

Leopold Fear Senghor

in «Présence africaine» Nos. 8, 9, 10
Ier Congrès international des écrivains
et artistes noirs, Paris 1956

# Calendar of the discovery of the principal sites of prehistoric rock art

1847   In South Oran (Algeria) officers notice engravings on rocks at Thyout, Moghar and Tahatani in the Djebel Ksour.

1848   In Karelia (USSR) engravings are noticed scattered on the East Bank of Lake Onega.

1850   At Fezzan (Libya) Henri Barth refers to the existence of engraved rocks at Tel Izharen.

1860   In the Sahara at Tassili and Fezzan, Henri Duverrier finds inscriptions and engravings.

1869   In Tibesti (Chad) Doctor Nachtigal notices engravings.

About 1870   In South Africa D. W. Stow surveys paintings and engravings known for two centuries.

1877   In Air (Nigeria) at Dokou, Erwin von Bary points out engraved rocks.

1878   Grotto of Chabot at Aigueze, discovered by L. Chiron the engravings were surveyed by Breuil in 1928 and later by Glory and Drouot.

1879   Cave of Altamira near Santander (Spain) discovered by Marcelino S. de Sautuola. Its authenticity is not admitted until 1901.

1880   In North Sweden paintings and engravings are studied by P. Olsen.

1890   The Grotto of Figuier at Saint-Martin-d'Ardêche (Ardeche) discovered by L. Chiron. Surveyed by Breuil in 1928.

1893/99   F. Foureau points out engravings in Tibesti (Chad) and Air (Nigeria).

1895   Grotto of La Mouthe aux Eyzies (Dordogne) discovered by Berthoumeyrou and Riviere. Surveyed by Breuil in 1900 and again in 1924 and 1930.

1896   Grotto of Pair-non-Pair at Marcamps (Gironde) discovered by F. Daleau. Surveyed by Breuil in 1934, 1935 and 1937.

1897   Grotto of Marsoulas near Salies du Salat (Haute-Garonne) discovered by Regnault and James, then studied by Carthailhac in 1902. Surveyed by Breuil in 1902 and 1903.

1901   Cave of Mas-d'Azil (Ariege) discovered and explored by Breuil who fixes its measurements.

Grotto of Combarelles at Eyzies (Dordogne).

Engravings were pointed out by Pomarel to Capitan, Breuil and Peyrony. Surveyed by Breuil from 1903 onwards.

Grotto of Font-da-Gaume at Eyzies (Dordogne) discovered by Peyrony. Surveyed by Breuil from 1902 onwards.

1902   Grotto of Bernifal at Mayraes (Dordogne) discovered by Peyrony. Surveyed by Breuil, Capitan and Peyrony.

1903   Grotto of Castillo, province of Santander (Spain) discovered by Alcade del Rio.

Paintings at Calapata near Cretas, province of Teruel (Spain) discovered by J. Cabre Aguilo.

Grotto of La Mairia at Teyjat (Dordogne) discovered by Peyrony and Bourrinet. Surveyed by Breuil in 1904 and 1905.

1904   Grotto of la Greze at Marquay (Dordogne) discovered by Ampoulange. Surveyed by Breuil.

1905   Grotto of Romanelli in Otranto (Italy).

1906   Cave of Gargas at Aventignan (Upr. Pyrenees) discovered by F. Regnault and Cartailhac. Surveyed by Breuil. Cave of Niaux at Tarascon-sur-Ariege (Ariege). Rediscovered by Mollard, these paintings had been known since the eighteenth century but their antiquity was not known. Surveyed by Breuil and Cartailhac in 1908 and 1909.

Cave of Bedeilhac (Ariege) discovered by Harle and Breuil. Surveyed by Breuil in 1925.

1907   Grotto of Croze-a-Gontran at Tayac (Dordogne) discovered by Vidal. Surveyed by Breuil in 1913.

1908   Paintings at Cogul, province of Lerida (Spain). Missionaries point out paintings near Boukoba on the west bank of Lake Victoria (Tanganyika) but the systematic exploration did not commence until 1923.

Cave of Portel at Varilhes (Ariege) discovered by Doctor Jeannel and Fauveau. Surveyed by Breuil and Vezian.

1909 Doctor Lalanne discovers the Laussel rock shelter relics at Marquay (Dordogne).

Strata at Limeuil (Dordogne) explored by l'abbe Bouyssonie. Captain Cortier (and in the following years Lanney, Kilian, Bernard) points out paintings at Tassillni'Ajjer (Algeria).

About this time and right up to the present day, numerous sites of paintings or engravings were discovered from one end of the Sahara to the other; by Frobenius at Fezzan; by Dalloni at Tibesti; by Zehrer in Adrar des Iforas; by Rodd and Nicolas in Air; by Odette du Puigaudeau in Adrar in Mauritania; by Gerard Bailloud in Ennedi . . .

1910 Blanchard rock shelter discovered at Sergeac (Dordogne) by Didon.

Madeleine rock shelter discovered at Marzac (Dordogne) by Peyrony. Cave of Pindal, province of Santander (Spain).

Paintings at Alpera and at La Cueva Vieja, province Albacete (Spain).

Adrianov points out engravings at the mouth of the Tibor in the region of Shalabolinsk in West Siberia (USSR). Near Vingen (Norway) along the North Fiord engravings are discovered by K. Bing.

1911 Rock shelter of Cap-Blanc at Marquay (Dordogne) discovered by Peyrille.

Grotto of la Pileta, province of Malaga (Spain) discovered by W. Verner, studied by Breuil and Obermaier.

1912 Rock shelter Labatut at Sergeac (Dordogne) discovered by Didon. Surveyed by Breuil.

1913 Grotto of Isturitz (Lower Pyrenees) discovered by E. Passemard.

Paintings at Charco del Agua valley Amarga near Alcanis, Province of Teruel (Spain).

1914 Paintings at Cantos de la Visera near Yecla, province of Murcia (Spain).

Paintings at Minateda province of Albacete (Spain).

1915 Grottos of Comarque and Nancy at Sireuil (Dordogne) discovered by Breuil and P. Paris. Surveyed by Breuil. Mount Ekeberg, near Oslo, discovery of the group known as "Eastern Norwegian".

1916 Cave of Trois-Freres at Montesquieu-Avantes (Ariege) discovered by H. Begouen and his three sons. Surveyed by Breuil in 1921, and then from 1930/40.

1917 Paintings at Morella la Vella and at the gorge of la Valltorta, province of Castile (Spain).

1919 Paintings at Els Secans, near Mazaleon, province of Teruel and of la Cueva de la Arana, near Bicorp, province of Valencia (Spain).

1920 Grottos of Marcenac and Cantal at Cabrerets (Lot) discovered by Lemozi. Surveyed by Lemozi.

Reverdit rock shelter at Sergeac (Dordogne) discovered by Castanet. Surveyed by Breuil.

1922 Pech-Merle cave at Cabrerets (Lot) discovered by David and Dutertre. Surveyed by Lemozi.

1923 Ganties-Montespan cave, at Montespan (Haute-Garonne) discovered by Norbert Casteret and H. Godin. Surveyed by Breuil and F. Trombe.

1924 Le Fourneau-du-Diable at Bourdeilles (Dordogne) discovered by Peyrony.

1925 Rock shelter of Laugerie-Haute at Eyzies (Dordogne) discovered by Peyrony.

1926 Paintings at Tormon in the valley of Olivonas, near Albarracin, province of Teruel (Spain) studied by Breuil and Obermaier.

Discovery by Linevskij, completed by Raudonikas, of engravings in the delta of Vyg, on the White Sea (USSR).

Grotto of Chaire-a-Calvin at Mouthiers (Charente) explored by P. David.

1927 Roc-de-Sera reliefs at Roc (Charente) discovered by Doctor H. Martin. New findings in 1950 by Germaine H. Martin and Raymond Lantier.

1928 In South Africa, A. L. Armstrong excavates the grotto of Bambata.

1929/31 Excavations by Pericot Garcia in the cave of Parpallo, province of Valencia (Spain).

1930 Paintings at Barranco de Gasulla, near Ares del Maestre, province of Castellon (Spain) studied and surveyed by Breuil and Obermaier.

1932 Cave of Labastide (Northern Pyrenees) discovered by Norbert Casteret.

1933 At Tassili n'Ajjer (Algeria) Captain Brenans discovers paintings at l'oued 'Djorat and l'oued Amazar.

1940 Grotto of Lascaux at Montignac (Dordogne) discovered by Ravidat and Marsal. Surveyed by Maurice Thaon and then by l'Abbott Glory from 1953 onwards.

Cave of La Baume-Latrone at Sainte-Anastasie (Gard) discovered by Sutter, Roque, Martin, Foiard and Morizot. Surveyed by Glory.

1941 Grotto of Gabillou at Sourzac (Dordogne) discovered by Charmarty and Truffier. Surveyed by Malvesin-Fabre.

1946 Grotto of The Horse (or the Mammoths) at Arcy-sur-Cure (Yonne) discovered by Bourreau, Papon, Meraville and Faren. Surveyed by Bailloud and Tendren in 1946 and 1947. Grotto of Ebbou at Vallon (Ardeche) discovered by Glory. Surveyed by Glory.

1947 Paintings at Cueva del Polvorin, province of Castellon (Spain).

1949 First discovery of Paleolithic paintings in a rock shelter in the forest of Fontainebleau by J. Baudet. Exploration undertaken during the following years.

Rock shelter of Roc-au-Sorcier at Angles-sur-l'Anglin (Vienna) discovered by D. Garrod at S. de Saint-Mathurin.

New explorations during the following years.

1950 Grotto of Levanzo, iles Egadi, on the west coast of Sicily.

1950/51 At Tassili n'Ajjer (Algeria) Yolande Tschudi studies and surveys paintings.

Since 1951 in Kenya, L. S. B. Keakey studies paintings at Kondoa.

1952 Grotto of Magdeleine at Penne (Tarn) discovered by Bessac, Verperini and Soulie.

Grotto of Cougnac at Payrignac (Lot) discovered by Borne, Couloumes, Maxet, Sauvant, M. and R. Boudet.

1956 Grotto of Rouffignac at Miremont (Dordogne) discovered by Nougier and Robert.

1957 At Tassili n'Ajjer (Algeria) Calude Guichard discovers the site of Sefar (Henri Lhote expedition 1956/57).

1960/61 At Tassili n'Ajjer (Algeria) during two successive journeys Jean-Dominique Lajoux discovers and photographs new sites amongst them Czaneare.

# List of Museums

## Pre-historic Art

### Principal Sites

France: Grotto of Lascaux, at Montignac (Dordogne)

Les Eyzies (Dordogne), grotto of Combarelles

Les Eyzies (Dordogne) grotto of Font-de-Gaume

Cave of Niaux, at Tarascon-sur-Ariege (Ariege)

Cave of Trois-Freres at Montesquieu-Avantes (Ariege)

Cave of Pech-Merle, at Cabrerets (Lot)

Grotto of Cougnac, at Payrignac (Lot)

Grotto of Rouffignac, at Miremont (Dordogne)

Grotto of Cheval, at Arey-sur-Cure (Yonne)

Cave of Gargas, at Aventignan (Northern Pyrenees)

Spain: Grotto of Altamira near Santillana del Mar (Province of Santander)

Cave of El Castillo, near Peunte Viesgo (Province of Santander).

Grotto of Pasiega, near Puente Viesgo (Province of Santander)

Grotto of Pindal near Pimiango (Province of Asturias)

### Principal Museums

Museum of National Antiques, Saint-Germain-en-Laye (Seine-et-Oise)

Musee de l'Homme, Paris

Museum of Prehistoric Art, Santander

Museum of the Transvaal, Pretoria

University Museum of Pretoria

Museum of Prehistory, Les Eyzies (Dordogne)

## Oceanic Art

### Principal Museums

Musée de l'Homme, Paris
Musée des arts africains et oceaniens, Paris
Museum fur Volkerkunde, Basle
Museum & Institute of Ethnography, Geneva
Museum of Primitive Art, New York
Natural History Museum, Chicago
Museum of Ethnography, Budapest
Museum of Anthropology and Ethnology, Leningrad
British Museum, London
Roninklijk Instituut voor de Tropen, Amsterdam
Musées royaux d'art et d'histoire, Brussels
Bernice Pauahi Bishop Museum, Honolulu
National Museum of Victoria, Melbourne
University Museum, Philadelphia
American Museum of Natural History, New York.

## African Art

### Principal Museums

Musée de l'homme, Paris
Musée des arts africains et oceaniens, Paris
Rietberg Museum, Zurich
Ethnography Museum, Neuchâtel
British Museum, London
Musée de Tervuren (Belgian Congo)
Musées Royaux d'art et d'histoire, Brussels
Museum of Ethnography, Antwerp
Etnografiska Museet, Göteborg
Statens Etnografiska Museum, Stockholm
University Museum, Philadelphia
Natural History Museum, Chicago
Museum of Primitive Art, New York
Centre of Human Studies, Abidjan
Federal Department of Antiquities, Nigeria
Museum für Völkerkunde, Berlin
Städtisches Museum für Völkerkunde, Frankfurt-on-Main
Linden-Museum, Stuttgart
Hamburgisches Museum für Völkerkunde und Vorgeschichte, Hamburg
Museum für Völkerkunde, Vienna

# Chronology of prehistoric art

The following tables were established following studies in chronology by Andre Leroi-Gourhan, Annette Laming-Emperaire, Jean Guiart and the works of Theodore Monod, Hans-Georg Bandi, Johannes Maringer, Alfred Buhler, Georges Balandier.

| Approximate Datings BC | Cultural Periods | Movable Art | Mural Art |
|---|---|---|---|
| — 35,000 | **Paleolithic Superior** Chatelperronian (Upper Perigordian) | First decorative objects Incisions on bone and stone | |
| — 30,000 | Aurignacian | First engraved or painted figures on stone: Belcayre, La Ferrassie, Isturitz, Les Bernous. | |
| — 25,000 | Gravetian (Lower Perigordian) Inter - Gravetto - Solutrian | Engraved or painted slabs: Rock shelter Labatut, Isturitz. Laugerie-Haute Female statues called "Aurignacian Venuses" | First Sanctuaries with wall paintings: Pair-n Pair, Gargas la Greze. |
| — 18,000 — 15,000 | Solutrian Upper Magdalenian (Magdalenian I - II) | Painted and engraved slabs: Bourdeilles, El Parpallo, Isturitz. | Reliefs at Roc-de-Sers and Bourdeilles. Shallow or medium depth sanctuaries; Lasc; le Gabillou, Pech-Merle, Cougnac, la Pasi Ebbou. |
| — 12,000 | Middle Magdalenian (Magdalenian III - IV) | Pierced batons, Catapaults Spatulas; la Madeleine, Laugerie-Basse, Arudy Bruniquel, le Portel, Isturitz | Open Sanctuaries, Angles-sur-l'Anglin, ( Blanc la Magdeleine. Sanctuaries of medium depth: Arcy-sur-C Font-de-Gaume, les Combarelles, Bernifal, N soulas, le Portel, Altamira, Pindal. Very c Sanctuaries: Rouffignac, Labastide, Niaux, Trois-Frerès, Montespan. |
| — 10,000 | Lower Magdalenian (V - VI) | Decorated objects: La Madeleine, Villepin, Isturitz. Engraved slabs notably at Limeuil. | Decline of wall painted sanctuaries: Te; Limeuil. |
| — 8000 | **Mesolithic** Maglemosian | Geometric decorations and incisions at Maglemose. Small engraved or painted stones at Mas-d'Azil. | Between — 8000 and — 5000 the paintings of Spanish Levant appear to reach their fu expansion. Possible beginnings of South Afr art as practised until recent times. |
| — 4000 (Western Europe) | **Neolithic** | | Certain paintings and engravings from N Africa and the Sahara date back probably to period although the date of a large number been brought forward to the period of recor history and some are fairly recent. The peak of art of Tassili is found between approxima — 3000 and — 2500. |

| 19th century | Beginning of 20th Century (Breuil) | Chronology of Breuil and Peyrony (1934) | | | Approximate datings by Radiocarbon | Chronology of Leroi-Gourhan (1958) | |
|---|---|---|---|---|---|---|---|
| | | | Upper Perigordian or Chatelperronian | Perigordian I Perigordian II | — 33,000 | Chatelperronian | |
| | Aurigna-cian | Aurignaco-perigordian Cycle | Aurignacian | Aurignacian I Aurignacian II Aurignacian III Aurignacian IV | — 29,000 | Aurignacian | Pre-figurative period / Style I |
| | | | Lower Perigordian or Gravetian | Perigordian III (Lascaux) Perigordian IV Perigordian V | — 24,000 | Gravetian | Style II |
| | | | | Aurignacian V Proto-magdalenian (Peyrony) | — 1900 | Inter-gravetto solutrian | |
| utrian | Solutrian | Solutrio Magdalenian Cycle | Solutrian | Proto-Solutrian Solutrian I Solutrian II Solutrian III | — 17,000 | Solutrian | Style III |
| gdalenian | Magdalen-ian | | Magdalenian | Proto-magda-lenian (Chrynier) Magdalenian I Magdalenian II. | — 14,000 | Upr. Magdalenian (Lascaux) | |
| | | | | Magdalenian III Magdalenian IV | — 12,000 | Middle Magdalenian | Style IV |
| | | | | Magdalenian V Magdalenian VL | — 10,000 | Lower Magdalenian | |

# Chronology of oceanic art

| Australia | New Guinea and the Melanesian Archipelagoes | New Zealand and the Polynesian Archipelagoes | Micronesia |
|---|---|---|---|
| Driven away from Indonesia, the large population found refuge in Oceania. | | | |
| Nomadism. The economy is founded on food gathering and hunting. Arms of stone, boomerangs of wood. | | | |
| | Interrelations between the Melanesians and the Polynesians. | | |
| Migrations of Australoids | First migrations of negroid peoples, Pygmies in Papua in New Guinea. | Settlement of Polynesians in successive waves. First settlement by unknown people in New Zealand. | |
| | Migration of the Melanesians to other islands. | Migrations to the Islands of of Tonga, Samoa and Cook. | Progressive settlement tribes related to the Melanesians and to the Malayans. |
| | | Migrations from the Islands of Cook to Eastern Polynesia and down to the Easter Islands. | |
| | Culture, Fishing and Hunting. Axes and Adzes in polished stone. Use of the bow. Various types of boat building. | | Caste society principall in the Marshall Islands Culture relating to that of Polynesia. |
| | First use of technique of painted pandana leaves. | | |
| | Melanesian pottery technique using pidgeon dung, use of slip (Ochre) engraved motifs. Figurative motifs in New Caledonia and New Guinea; Geometric motifs in the New Hebrides. | Polynesian technique of painting on mulberry bark (Tapa). Archeological presence of Pottery. Progressive modernisation of the techniques of painting and printing on Tapa. | |
| Wood Sculptures in Arnhenland. | | After the 12th Century summit of Polynesian migration from island to island. Pottery in the Fiji Isles: Varnished slip, geometric decoration in relief or engraved. In the Marquesas: ritual art of tattooing and the representation of the Tiki. | |
| | Trade in mineral pigments for dyeing and painting. | | |
| | | The sculpture reflects a caste system and a hierarchy of Gods. | |
| Ritual paintings on the ground; representations of clans totem animals. | Polychrome sculptures on fern trunks in the New Hebrides. Totem poles in Ambrym. | Anthropomorhic art of Eastern Polynesia: the lesser Gods are represented in human form. | |

| stralia | New Guinea and the Melanesian Archipelagoes | New Zealand and the Polynesian Archipelagoes | Micronesia |
|---|---|---|---|
| | Sculptured drums and in the sand on the New Hebrides Poker-work bamboo in New Caledonia. | Around 1330, settlement of New Zealand by the Maori of Hawaii, culture, hunting and fishing. Extinction of the primitive population. | |
| ntings on rock in the nberley district: nal and vegetation tifs, representations he human figure or ndjina". | | | |
| arunga" rituals in atral Australia: slabs wood or schist raved with symbolic ems and representations myths. | Death doll effigies at Malekula (New Hebrides). | Stone statues of the Marquesas. Monumental statues of Tufa and Basalt in the Easter Isles. Representation of the god Oro in the Hawaii Isles: scrolls of Tapa decorated with feathers. | Religious statuettes ("tino") |
| emonial dress of atral Australia. | Magic engraved stones in the New Hebrides. "Pig Stones" from Ambrym | Sculptured forks in New Zealand. | |
| | Reliefs on huts in New Caledonia. | Commemorative Maori art: statues and cabin reliefs. | |
| | Sacred objects from the communal huts of Papua. Funerary masks and initiation masks from New Guinea. Ritual masks from the New Hebrides. | | 1521 Magellan at Guam and then in the Phillippines. |

——————— Beginning of the discovery of Oceania by Europeans. ———————

| | New Guinea and the Melanesian Archipelagoes | New Zealand and the Polynesian Archipelagoes | Micronesia |
|---|---|---|---|
| | 1526-1528 The Portuguese from the Molakas reached the northern coast of New Guinea. | | |
| | 1567-1568 Alvarez de Mendana discovers the Ellis and subsequently the Solomon Islands. | | |
| | | 1595 Discovery of the Marquesas by Mendana and Quiros. | |

5-1607 Explorations of Torres between Australia and New Guinea.

| Australia | New Guinea and the Melanesian Archipelagoes | New Zealand and the Polynesian Archipelagoes | Micronesia |
|---|---|---|---|
| | 1606 Quiros in the New Hebrides. | | |
| 1616 Dirk Hartogszoom explores the west coast. | 1616 Exploration of Tonga by the Dutchmen Lemaire and Schouten. | | |
| 1642 The Dutch in Tasmania. | | 1642 Tasman lands on the west coast of New Zealand. | |
| 1644 Second voyage of Tasman. | | | |
| 1699-1711 Voyages of Dampier. | | | |
| | New techniques for wooden masks in the north of New Caledonia. | | |
| | | 1722 Discovery of Easter Island by Roggeveen. First European hypothesis concerning the "mysterious" statues. | |
| | | 1767 Discovery of Tahiti by Wallis. Voyage of Bougainville. | |
| 1769-1770 First voyage of Cook. | | 1769-1770 First voyage of Cook. | |
| | | 1769 Cook introduces the pig and potato into New Zealand. | |
| 1770 First landings at Botany Bay by Cook. | | | |
| | 1772-1775 Second voyage of Cook: Tonga, New Hebrides, New Caledonia. | | |
| 1776-1779 Third voyage of Cook. | | 1779 Death of Cook on the Hawaii Islands. | |
| European influence: Introduction of western colours, iron gradually takes the place of st◄ | | | |
| | The poker work bamboos of New Caledonia show the influence of the first contact with Europeans. | | |
| 1788 Sydney founded by the English | 1788 Death of La Perouse at Vanikoro. | | |
| 1797-1870 Differences between the missions. Conflict between missions and traders. | | | |
| Between 1802 and 1877, extinction of the Tasmanian people. | | | |

| stralia | New Guinea and the Melanesian Archipelagoes | New Zealand and the Polynesian Archipelagoes | Micronesia |
|---|---|---|---|
| 29 Extension of lement to Central stralia; Melbourne. | After 1817 the resumption of exploration by the French. | | |
| | 1834-1844 Extension of French Catholic Missions. | | |
| | | 1840 Settlement of the English in New Zealand. | |
| | | 1843 French Protectorate on Wallis and the Fortune Islands. | |
| | | 1849 American influence preponderant in Hawaii. | |
| | 1853 France annexes New Caledonia. | | |

From 1856 onward, French missionary schools. Local language and customs written down by the missionaries.

| | Disappearance of the technique of pottery in New Caledonia and the New Hebrides. | | |
|---|---|---|---|
| | | 1861-1871 Maori War of resistance against England. Recession of their traditional life. | Germans preponderant in the Marshall Isles. |
| | | 1874 England annexes the Fiji Islands. | |
| | | 1880 French Protectorate on Tahiti. | |
| | 1884 Annexation of Papua by England. | | |
| | 1886 Anglo-German Convention and the sharing of zones of influence. | | |

ter 1870, end of the isolation of Oceania; regular sea links with America, Europe and the Far East.

| | | 1893-1901 Gaugin at Tahiti. | |
|---|---|---|---|
| | 1894 First Protestant mission in New Caledonia. | | |
| | | | 1898 United States annexes Guam and Wake. |
| | 1899 Agreement between England, Germany and the United States: new division of Polynesia. | | |

| Australia | New Guinea and the Melanesian Archipelagoes | New Zealand and the Polynesian Archipelagoes | Micronesia |
|---|---|---|---|
| 1901　The Australian Commonwealth controls British New Guinea. | | | |
| | 1903　Beginning of the Mission of Maurice Leenhardt in New Caledonia. | 1903　Death of Gauguin in the Marquesas. | |
| | 1906-14　Anglo-French Agreements for Condominium of the New Hebrides. | 1907　New Zealand and English Dominions. | |
| 1919　Transfer of German possessions to the Allies. | | | |
| | Studies by Leenhardt on Melanesian Art. | Samoa, the Tuamotu Islands and New Zealand keep their traditional costumes. Extinction of Hawaiian Art. | |
| | Art and ancient traditions survive in the centre of New Guinea, in Malekula and Solomon. | | |
| 1941-1942　Japanese advance into European Oceanic possessions. | | | |
| | In New Caledonia Sculpture and mural paintings are renewed. | Centre of popular art of Tahiti: restoration of the technique of Tapa. | 1945　Apart from the Gilbert Isles Micronesi comes under U.S.A. "trusteeship". |
| | Drawings collected by the missionaries in the Solomon Isles. | 1955　West Samoa becomes autonomous. | |
| | Melanesian drawings collected by R. P. O'Reilly. | Authentic tupa technique continues in the Islands of Fortune, Tonga and Samoa. | |
| | Survival of the art of mask making in the New Hebrides. | | |
| | Pottery in New Guinea. | | |

# Chronology of African art

| | |
|---|---|
| 5th-1st c. B.C. | Nok culture (Nigeria): Baked earth. |
| 4th c. B.C.-350 c. A.D. | Kingdom of Meroe (Nubia): castings in bronze by the lost wax process. |
| approx. | Indirect contact with Mediterranean civilization. |
| 4th c.-8th c. | First dynasty of Ghana (West Sudan). |
| 7th c. | First Songhai dynasty in Sudan (Mali). |
| 8th-11th c. | High point of Ghana culture. |
| 9th-13th c. | Civilization of Zimbabwe: monumental architecture in granite. Elliptical temples particularly in hundreds of cities situated between Zambesi and the Limpopo (East Africa). |
| 9th c. | Spread of Islam in the Sudan, then in East Africa. The Arabs introduce cowry which reached interior of Africa. |
| | Importation of various techniques to the Sudan: weaving, dyeing, tanning. Possible introduction of the lost wax process. |
| 11th c. | King of Songhai is converted to Islam and sets up his capital at Goa: beginning of commerce between the Maghreb and the Sudan. Beginning of the migration of the Bantu from central to southern Africa. |
| 11th-12th c. | First civilization of Benin (Nigeria): bronze cast by lost wax and the ceramics of Ife. |
| 1076 | Ghana is forced to adopt Islam by the Almoravides. |
| 1235 | Kingdom of Mali. |
| 13th c. | Foundation of the kingdom of the Congo. Settlement of the Bambara in the upper valley of the Niger. Beginning of the urban civilization of the Yoruba: the artists of Benin are influenced by the bronze workers of Ife. |
| 1307-1332 | High point of Mali culture. The gold market at Goa serves the Berbers and the Egyptians. |
| 14th-16th c. | Baluba Kingdom (ex Belgian Congo) |
| | In West Africa: manufacture of masks, jewels and ornaments of gold. Baluba wood sculptures. |
| 1325 | Capture of Goa by Mali. |
| 1352-1387 | Decline of Mali. |
| End of 14th c. | Commercial activity in copper from the Maghreb. |
| Beginning of 15th c. | First waves of migration by the Ashanti in the Gold Coast (Ghana). |
| 15th c. | The Hottentots settle on the Zambesi. Spread of the technique of engraving on calebashes and basket-work. |
| 1446 | Cao da Mosta rounds the Cap Vert. |
| About 1450 | Cowry shells become the courtesy of Senegal (until the 17th c.). |
| 1463-1493 | Hegemoniy of Songhai over Mali. |
| 1472 | Discovery of Benin by the Portuguese: statues and reliefs in bronze cast by lost wax process. Contact between the Portuguese and the Yoruba. |
| 1482 | Diego Cao finds the mouth of the river Congo. |
| 1487 | Bartolomeo Diaz rounds the Cape of Good Hope. The Baoules create hanging ritual masks in gold cast by lost wax process. |
| | In the Cameroons, bronzes cast by lost wax process and ivory work by the Bamouns and Bamilekes |
| 1491 | Portuguese found San Salvador. |
| 16th c. | First kingdoms in Dan-homey, Capital Abomey. Beginning of the conversion of the Bakongos by the Portuguese to Catholicism. Decline of the kingdom of the Congo. |
| | Beginning of commerce and exportations to Europe by the Portuguese of "Objects d'art" in gold and ivory. |
| 1546 | The Construction of the capital of Mali by the Songhai. |
| 1575-1648 | High point of Benin bronze art. |
| 1591-1612 | Morocco rules Songhai. |
| 17th c. | High point of Yoruba art. Apparition of the decorative art of the Bakuba. Choreographic rituals and costume art in the country of the Watutsi (Ruanda). |
| 1625 | Dutch in South Africa. |
| 1625-1708 | Extension of the Kingdom of Abomey. |
| | In the north of Dahomey, the Somba built fortress villages with towers, walls, interior courtyards, such as may be seen today. |
| 1630 | Independence of the Bambara. |
| | Struggles of Abomey against negro slave traders. |

| | |
|---|---|
| 1645 | The Bambara and the kingdom of Mali. |
| 1699 | Formation of the confederation of the Ashanti. Development of the Ashanti art; bronzes, thrones, drums, jewels and ornaments in gold. |
| 1725 to the end of the 19th c. | The Baoule related to the Ashanti found a kingdom on the Ivory Coast: development of statues carved in wood. |
| 1738 | Victory of Yoruba over the Dahomey. |
| | Gold funerary mask of the Ashanti King. Ritual dance masks in wood of the Yoruba and the Fon (Dahomey). In the Congo, survival of Bakuba art until the Belgian colonisation. In Gabon, tattoo masks and encrusted helmets of the Ogoue. In the Sudan (Mali) the appearance of mask societies among the Dogon and Sanga. |
| 18th c. | The Yoruba people are decimated by slave traffic: disappearance of Yoruba art. Important engravings on colour bashings of Dahomey. Huts decorated with shells of the Mousgoun and Cameroon. Bantu stop their migration to South Africa. |
| 1818-1858 | Ghezo re-establishes the power of Dahomey. |
| 1835 | The Boers in South Africa: The Great Trek. |
| | In the Congo, vases in baked earth of the Mangbetu. |
| | Wood statuary of the Batshick of Angola and the Belgian Congo. In Gabon, the funerary art of the Bakota. |
| About 1850 | Gold work at Grand-Bassam (Ivory Coast) and sculpture in baked earth of the Bamoun. |
| 1850 | Conquest of the Yoruba by the Dahomey. |
| 1851 | First trade treaty between France and Dahomey. |
| 1857 | Founding of Dakar. |
| | Found in the south Cameroon: painted huts. |
| 1860 | Beginning of the systematic exploration of Africa and of European colonial rivalry. First polychrome bas reliefs of the Abomey. |
| | Funerary art of the Kissi in Guinea and Sierre Leone: sculpture in stone. |
| 1869 | The Ashanti resist European invasion. |
| | Development of the arts of weaving, dyeing and embroidery of Dahomey, velvet of the Kassai. Baluba statuary. |
| After 1872 | In north Angola, destruction of "fetihes". |
| 1874 | Raid by the English against the Ashanti. Ivory work in Dahomey. Decadence of the bronze and ivory art of the Benin. In the middle Congo, appearances of wood engravings blackened in fire. |
| 1883 | The Germans in Cameroon. |
| 1884 | The Germans in Togoland. |
| End of 19th c. | Migration of the Fang from the plateau of Adamaoua to the estuary of the Gabon river. Custom of the societies of masks continues among the Dogon. Stylised head crests in the form of the antelope among the Bambara. |
| | From the Congo to South Africa, the Africans return to their traditional cultures but use in their rituals christian emblems. |
| 1894 | Dodds dethrones Behanzin: Dahomey becomes a French Protectorate. |
| | Hieratic statuary of Fang: ancestral figures. |
| 1897 | Conquest of the Benin by the English: destruction and pillage of the capital, massacre of the inhabitants. |
| 1899-1902 | The Boer War. |
| 1900 | The last Ashanti uprising. |
| 1908 | Colonisation of the Congo by the Belgians. |
| 1910 | Creation of the Union of South Africa. |
| 1914 | Boer Uprising. |
| 1914-18 | German colonies are shared by the Allies. |
| 1919 | Treaty of Versailles. |
| 1930 | Preservation of the art of Bamileke in the Cameroons, notably in architecture and wood sculpture. |
| | As colonisation progresses, negro art degenerates and then expires. |
| 1944 | Conference of Brazzaville. |
| 1956 | First international congress of black writers and artists in Paris. |
| From the beginning of 1958. | Various people in Africa free themselves of the colonial system and achieve independence. |
| 1965 | World Fair of negro-african art at Dakar. |

# Franco-cantabrian domain

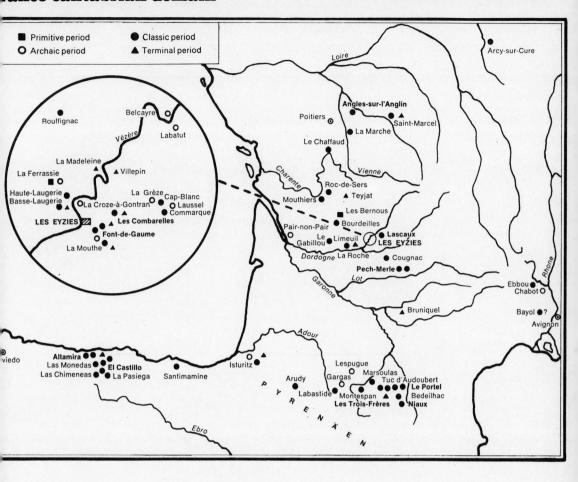

**Legend:**
- ■ Primitive period
- ○ Archaic period
- ● Classic period
- ▲ Terminal period

Rouffignac, Belcayre, Labatut, Vézère, La Madeleine, La Ferrassie, Villepin, Haute-Laugerie, Basse-Laugerie, La Grèze, Cap-Blanc, Laussel, Commarque, La Croze-à-Gontran, LES EYZIES, Les Combarelles, Font-de-Gaume, La Mouthe

Arcy-sur-Cure, Loire, Angles-sur-l'Anglin, Poitiers, Saint-Marcel, La Marche, Le Chaffaud, Vienne, Roc-de-Sers, Teyjat, Mouthiers, Charente, Les Bernous, Pair-non-Pair, Bourdeilles, Le Gabillou, Limeuil, LES EYZIES, Lascaux, Dordogne, La Roche, Cougnac, Garonne, Pech-Merle, Lot, Bruniquel, Ebbou, Chabot, Bayol, Avignon, Rhone

viedo, Altamira, Las Monedas, El Castillo, Las Chimeneas, La Pasiega, Santimamine, Isturitz, Adour, Lespugue, Gargas, Marsoulas, Tuc d'Audoubert, Le Portel, Arudy, Labastide, Montespan, Bedeilhac, Les Trois-Frères, Niaux, PYRENÄEN, Ebro

# Saharan rock art

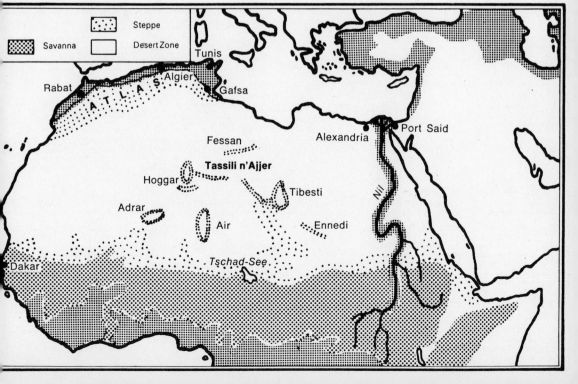

**Legend:**
- ▨ Savanna
- ⦙ Steppe
- ☐ Desert Zone

Tunis, Rabat, Algier, Gafsa, ATLAS, Alexandria, Port Said, Fessan, Tassili n'Ajjer, Hoggar, Tibesti, Adrar, Nil, Air, Ennedi, Dakar, Tschad-See

# Principal prehistoric sites

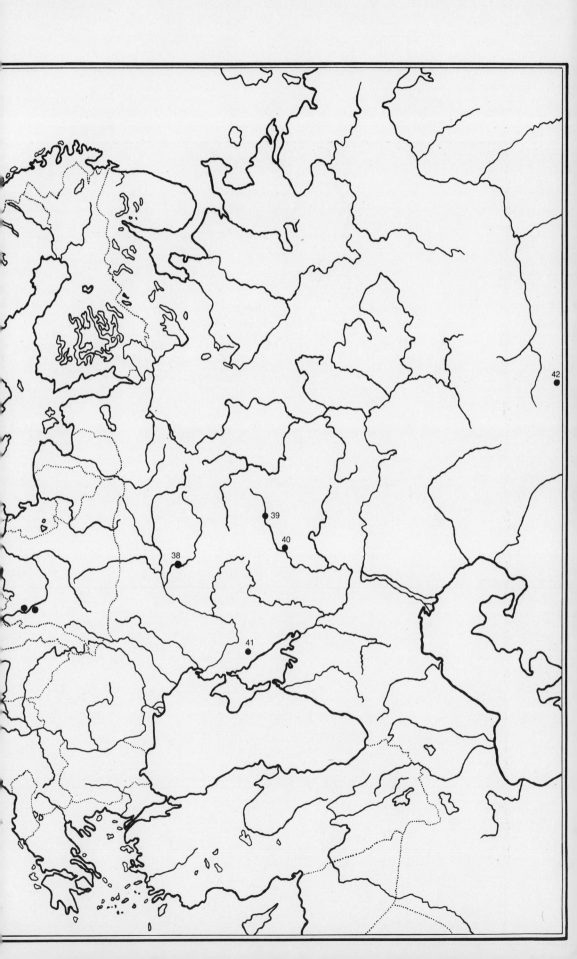

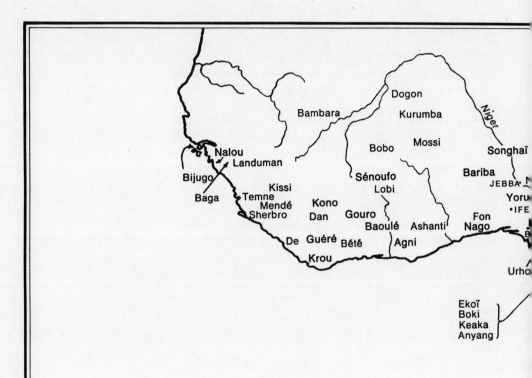

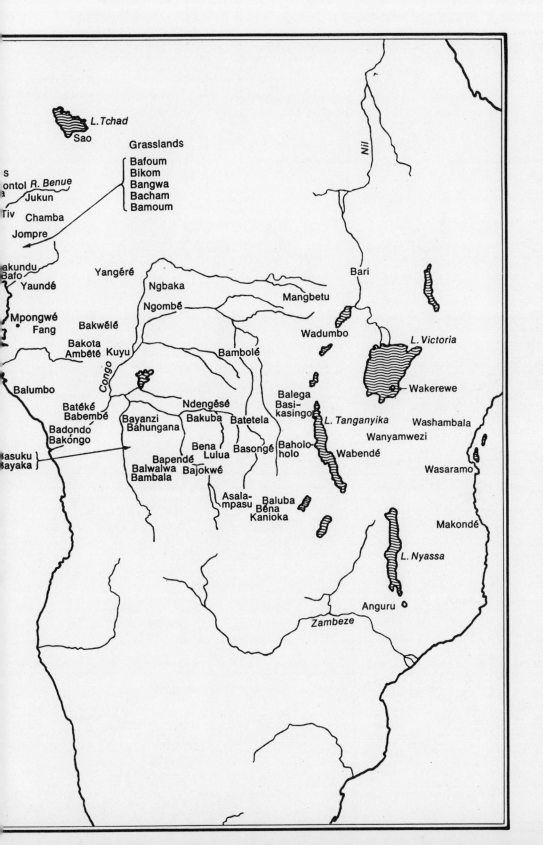

L. Tchad
Sao

Grasslands

Bafoum
Bikom
Bangwa
Bacham
Bamoum

s
ontol R. Benue
Jukun
Tiv    Chamba
Jompre

akundu
Bafo
Yaundé

Mpongwé
Fang

Bakota
Ambété   Kuyu

Balumbo

Batéké
Babembé
Badondo
Bakóngo

asuku
ayaka

Yangéré

Ngbaka

Ngombé

Bakwélé

Congo

Ndengésé

Bayanzi
Bahungana

Bakuba

Batetela

Bambolé

Bapendé
Balwalwa   Bajokwé
Bambala

Bena
Lulua

Basongé

Asala-
mpasu
Bena
Kanioka

Baluba

Bari

Mangbetu

Wadumbo

Balega
Basi-
kasingo

Baholo
holo

L. Victoria

Wakerewe

L. Tanganyika

Wabendé

Nil

Washambala

Wanyamwezi

Wasaramo

Makondé

L. Nyassa

Anguru

Zambeze

141

# Oceania

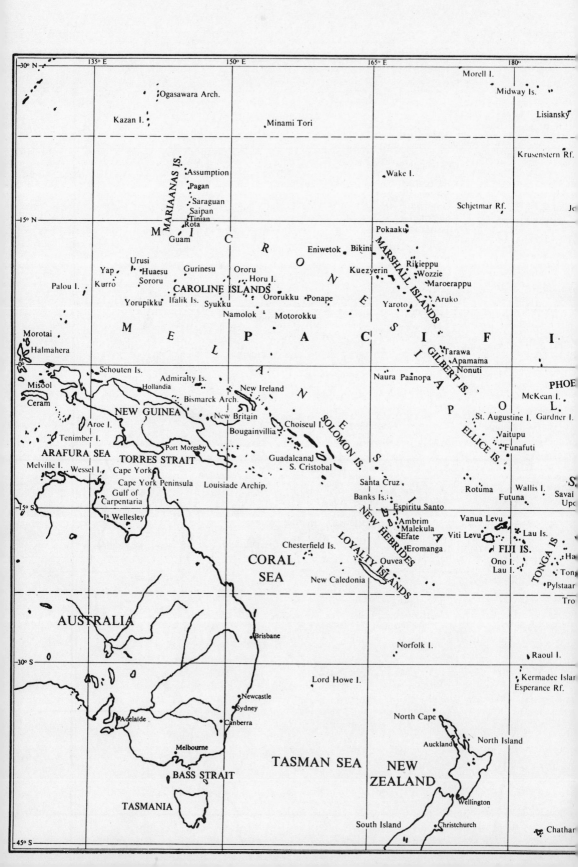

-30° N · 135° E · 150° E · 165° E · 180°

Morell I.

Midway Is.

Lisiansky

Ogasawara Arch.

Kazan I.

Minami Tori

Krusenstern Rf.

MARIAANAS IS.
Assumption
Pagan
Saraguan
Saipan
Tinian
Rota
Guam

Wake I.

Schjetmar Rf.

Jc

-15° N

M
I
C
R
O
N
E
S
I
A

Pokaaku

Eniwetok   Bikini

MARSHALL ISLANDS

Rikieppu
Wozzie
Maroerappu

Kuezyerin

Urusi
Yap   Huaesu   Gurinesu   Ororu
Kurro   Sororu        Horu I.
CAROLINE ISLANDS
Yorupikku   Ifalik Is.   Syukku   Ororukku   Ponape
Namolok   Motorokku

Aruko

Yaroto

Palou I.

Morotai
Halmahera

M   E   L   A   N   E   S   I   A

P   A   C   I   F   I

Schouten Is.
Admiralty Is.
Hollandia
Bismarck Arch.
New Ireland
New Britain

Tarawa
Apamama
Nonuti

GILBERT IS.

PHOE

Nauru Paanopa

McKean I.

St. Augustine I.   Gardner I.

ELLICE IS.

Vaitupu
Funafuti

Misool
Ceram

NEW GUINEA

Aroe I.
Tenimber I.

Port Moresby

Bougainvillia

Choiseul I.
SOLOMON IS.
Guadalcanal
S. Cristobal

L   O   I   A   P   O   L

Santa Cruz

Rotuma
Futuna

Wallis I.

S

Savai
Upo

ARAFURA SEA   TORRES STRAIT

Melville I.   Wessel I.
Cape York
Cape York Peninsula
Gulf of
Carpentaria
Is Wellesley

Louisiade Archip.

Banks Is.

Espiritu Santo

Vanua Levu

Lau Is.

-15° S

NEW HEBRIDES
Ambrim
Malekula
Efate
Eromanga

Viti Levu

FIJI IS.

TONGA IS.

Ha

Ono I.
Lau I.

Ton

Pylstaar

Chesterfield Is.

LOYALTY ISLANDS

Ouvea

New Caledonia

CORAL
SEA

AUSTRALIA

Brisbane

Norfolk I.

Raoul I.

Tro

-30° S

Lord Howe I.

Kermadec Islan
Esperance Rf.

Newcastle
Sydney
Adelaide
Canberra

North Cape

Auckland   North Island

Melbourne

TASMAN SEA

NEW
ZEALAND

BASS STRAIT

TASMANIA

South Island
Christchurch

Wellington

Chathar

-45° S

I. Guadalupe

CALIFORNIA

HAWAIIAN OR SANDWICH IS.

Necker I.

Niihau Kauai
Oahu
Maui
Hawaii

Revilla Gigado

Clipperton

Palmyra
Washington
Fanning O C E A N
Christmas I.

Jarvis I.

Malden
LINE ISLANDS
Strabuck I.

N E S I
Penrhyn I.

Hatutu
Nuku Hiva MARQUESAS IS
Hivaua
Adelaide Fahu Hiva

anger Is.
Humphrey I. Vostok I. Caroline I.
Flint I.
A

Suvarov I.
Puka Puka

Rangiroa Takaroa
Bellinghausen Bora-Bora Raroia TUAMOTU ARCHIPELAGO
Scilly I. Raiatea Toau Makemo Tatakoto
merston Tahiti Anaa Amanu
Aitutaki SOCIETY ISLES Marokau Parao Reao
Hervey Is. Nengonengo
Raratonga Amanu-Raro Pinaki Tureia
Maria I. Mururoa
COOK ARCHIP. Mangaia Moran
Rurutu AUSTRAL ISLANDS Gambier I.
Tubuai Vavitu Oneo I. Elisabeth I.
Pitcairn I. Ducie

Lancaster Rf. Easter Island
Rapa

Maria Theresa Rf.

0    500    1000    1500    2000 km

**New Guinea**

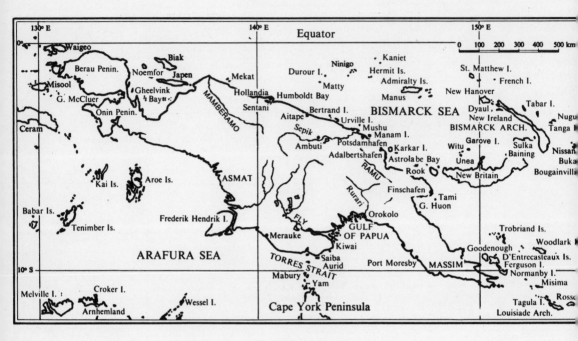

# Dictionary

# A

### Abelam

This people inhabiting the region of the Prince Alexander mountains on the left bank of the Sepik in New Guinea is known for its sculptures, basket-work masks, and in particular for the remarkable paintings on palm-leaves which decorate the large dwellings of the men, or the roof timbers.

### Acheulian

A cultural period of the Lower Paleolithic named after the site at Saint-Acheul (Somme). It followed the Abbevillian (after the village of Abbeville on the Somme), which provided the first hand-axes, flints crudely flaked by hammering on both sides. In this period, the technique of hammer-flaking improved, although there was no attempt at finer flaking or at polishing. Two types of tool or weapons are found: the almond-shaped hand-axe, with a base for gripping; and the oval hand-axe in which the whole perimeter was sharpened.

### Addaura

After the last war, the chance explosion of an abandoned ammunition dump at Monte Pellegrino revealed the existence of a fine set of rock engravings. Although belonging to the Lower Paleolithic period, the human and animal figures in this cave have little in common with Franco-Cantabrian art. They are, nevertheless, a transition stage between those of the Rhône valley and the Italian sites, in particular that of Romanelli. In addition to horses, bison and does, human figures are grouped around a strange scene, thought by some to depict "acrobats" dancing; by others, a ritual execution by auto-strangulation. The second interpretation seems more probable, but we may ask if this is a mythical scene with a didactic intention, or the straight-forward portrayal of some known event? The method of composition is severe, on a single plane, and the figures are superposed. The clear, curt incisions in the rock recall the colour drawing of the Spanish Levant; but the technique appears to be undeniably Saharan.

### Alpera

Discovered in 1910 in the province of Albacate, west of Almansa, the Alpera paintings are considered among the finest examples of eastern Spanish art.

The great Cueva Lieja frieze, with its numerous portraits of men and animals, is particularly full of life. The archers of Alpera show themselves here to have been an extremely energetic race.

## Altamira

While excavating the Altamira cave near Santander in the north of Spain in 1897, Marcelino S. de Santuola's attention was drawn by his little daughter to a collection of animals painted and engraved on the vault of a cave which she had just discovered. Convinced that these works, and those in the surrounding passages, were of great antiquity, Santuola immediately began a campaign which only Juan Vilanova y Piera in Spain and Piette in France supported. The International Congress for Prehistoric Archeology and Anthropology, which met in Madrid the following year, refused even to discuss the matter. It was not until Peyrony, Breuil and Capitan discovered Combarelles and Font-de-Gaume in 1901, that the question of Altamira's authenticity arose again. A year later, Emile Cartailhac, one of Santuola's most persistent adversaries, was prepared to admit in public that he had been wrong. The existence of prehistoric rock art was at last recognized. The Altamira cave in the Cantabrian mountains contains about a hundred polychrome figures, grouped on the ceiling of the hall near the entrance. Spread over a distance of fourteen metres, are twenty-five life-size animals, mostly bison, encircling horses, deer,

wild boar, anthropomorphic figures, signs and hands "in reserve". These paintings are often engraved, and take advantage of the natural formation of the walls to emphasize the moulding and vast bulk of their subjects. Most of the work is Middle Magdelenian, although a part, in simple outline, would appear contemporary with the Aurignacian.

## Ambrym

The population of this island in the Melanesian archipelago of the New Hebrides numbers about 3,000. They make sand drawings, and they carve monumental drums and statues "of rank" out of arborescent ferns, frequently in polychrome.

## Angles-sur-l'Anglin

In the sanctuary of Angles-sur-L'Anglin in the Vienne a collection of relief fragments, objects of personal adornment and domestic art were brought to light, as well as a large frieze of animal figures, and three deeply imprinted portraits of the female body. They have been classed as Middle Magdalenian. The composition is punctuated by a number of broken rings.

## Arcy-sur-Cure

This prehistoric sanctuary in the Yonne, of medium depth, contains a collection of wall engravings which go back to the Middle Paleolithic. The animal theme

147

proceeds from the entrance to the rear of the cave, accompanied by a quantity of signs.

### Arudy

A prehistoric site in the Basses Pyrenees, in which a number of decorated objects were discovered, perforated bones, spatulas, spear-throwers (see entry), and strange semicircular rods of reindeer antler figured with elaborate curvilinear relief.

### Ashanti

The Ashanti who inhabit the greater part of southern Ghana number about 800,000. During the last three centuries, they have exploited their considerable gold deposits, and mastered the art of working that metal. Apart from terracotta funerary objects, a few wooden objects, and cloth elaborately woven to a symbolic design, their entire artistic output is conditioned and inspired by gold. Jewellery, weights and measures, miniature fertility dolls, pendant masks are ingeniously smelted, chiselled and engraved. The wood of the royal throne is covered with incised gold leaf of geometric design. Ashanti society is monarchical and matriarchal.

### Asmat

A people notable for adapting their life to the swamp conditions in the southeast of western New Guinea. They paint their bodies, sculpt expressionist funeral masks, perforate canoe prows and large shields in heavy relief enhanced by polychrome painting.

### Astrolabe (Bay of)

In the south-east of Papua, it takes its name from the ship in which the French navigator, Dumont d'Urville (1790–1842) sailed there. Notable for fine statuary in the form of stakes encircling the men's dwellings, masks, engraved tortoiseshell armbands, circular polychrome shields, and "tapa" (see entry) blankets, decorated with signs.

### Atie

The Atiés inhabit the Adzopé region of the southern Ivory Coast, where they founded a matriarchal society. They sculpt female figures, stakes ornamented with symbolic mythical animals, and they work gold. Engraved drums, and an effigy coloured with leopard spots are brought out annually and worn on the head. On these occasions the participants paint their bodies, generally white.

## Aurignacian

A cultural period of the Upper Paleolithic named after the Aurignac stratum (Haute Garonne) dating from approximately 30,000. The first engravings and paintings on plaques appear (Belcayre, La Ferassie, Isturitz), animals' heads, sexual symbols and the first connections between animals and signs. Their stone tools included core and end-scrapers, blades, and gravers, many kinds of split-based spear-heads of tone or reindeer antler. The perforated bone also makes its appearance in the Aurignacian.

## Australes (Isles)

At the extreme south of the Polynesian archipelago, the Australes include the isles of Tubuai, Rurutu, Raivavac, Rimatura and Rapa — about 4,000 inhabitants in all. For the decoration of utilitarian and ceremonial objects, such as religious statues, engraving is the most eloquent form of expression.

## Azilian

A cultural period of the Mesolithic named after the Mas-d'Azil (Ariège) stratum, beginning at the close of the Upper Paleolithic (about 8,000). Still unversed in agriculture, its human species lived by hunting and fishing; they domesticated the dog. As in other Mesolithic cultures, its products are typified by microlithic tools (e.g., scrapers), and wide use was made of bone and reindeer antlers (double-headed harpoons). Certain Azilian sites contain a number of river pebbles engraved or painted in red ochre. Hachuring, spots and spirals were generally employed to form a symbol which, whatever its graphic variations, derived essentially from the human figure. The Azilian period also marked a break with Paleolithic wall art.

## Baga

The Bagas on the Guinea coast number about 40,000, and live in close cultural contact with their neighbours, the Nalus. Like them, they are farmers, and their society has a patriarchal orientation. Their ceremonies employ the same horizontal mask, the "Banda", whose plastic polychrome combines both human and animal elements, and represents those sea gods who are so important in the mythology of the Guinea coast peoples.

## Bakuba

In the central Congo, between the rivers Kasaï and Sankouru, the ancient Bakuba empire forms a federation of more than eighteen Bantu peoples. The Bukabas have traditionally inhabited the northern Oubangui, from the first millenium down to our era. Their heyday between 1600 and 1620 dates from after their installation in their present territory, as does their tradition of representing the king in effigy. But their art is not confined to sculpture; their engraving is elaborate, especially of cups, receptacles and wooden boxes, whose geometrical decoration derives from plaiting and its symbolism. Most of the mask types serve as support for the multi-coloured plaits of beads, cowries, shells and feathers, whose application is adapted to the polychrome composition. The Bakubas, numbering about 73,000, are farmers, but they have also greatly developed their handicrafts.

## Bakwele

Inhabiting the Sangha river in the Congo, the Bakwelés created masks in the form of a heart, with harmonious proportions, simple, unpretentious lines, and discreet colouring emphasizing a grave and reflective quality.

## Baluba

To the south-east of the Congo, stretching as far as the lake of Tanganyika, the vast Baluba empire contained a composite collection of Bantu peoples, of different origins, but sharing a homogeneous culture. This solidly based state had its heyday about two hundred years ago,

and its influence reeched as far as Rhodesia, in particular its matriarchal concept of society, and the sacred character of royalty. Although their art is notable for a variety of styles, the Balubas developed a highly individual form of statuary, whose character is also reflected in their masks. The northwestern Balubas sculpted masks with protuberances, entirely surrounded by a network of ribs or veins painted in white ochre.

## Bambara

Numbering about a million, the Bambara or Banmana, of Malinkian origin, founded in Mali a patriarchal society based on age-groups combined with degree of initiation. Agriculturists little influenced by Islam and deeply attached to their traditional religion, they spread as far as the Niger, on the Upper Volta and the Ivory Coast. Cultural organisations, in particular mask societies, are predominant in their social life. Each age group and caste is distinguished by a quantity of closely determined artistic activities. Thus, sculpture is the work of the smiths, entrusted with forging instruments with which they can communicate with cosmic myths, when soil fertility cults are celebrated.

## Bamilike

Inhabiting the grassy plains of the Cameroons, the Banilike, numbering about 500,000, comprise semi-Bantu agricultural populations who have cre-

ated an original statuary and a figurative decor in relief, to decorate the pillars and door-jambs of their dwellings. Their creative talents are also seen in the giant drums, and their expressive use of coloured beads on thrones and masks. But Banilike art gains its intensity and energy, particularly in their great dance masks, from the Bachams, living in the Bamenda.

## Bamoun

Settled in the Cameroonian savannah, possessing a stable political system, the Bamoun kingdom still possessed real art *ateliers* at the beginning of this century. In its capital, Foumban, masks with puffed cheeks and a variety of utilitarian objects, such as goblets, pipes and pieces of bronze, were fashioned; there was also a weaving industry. The Bamouns, who are semi-Bantua, also created a homogeneous art, in which carved thrones covered with multi-coloured beads seem some curious outgrowth of the Baroque.

## Bankanu

The Bankanu group belongs to the large Bakongo population, whose Bantu culture long withstood the influence of missionaries. Inhabiting the east of the

151

Southern Congo, the Bankanu sculpted large masks; but principally they painted fine bark tablets which frequently served as support for a figure in relief.

## Bantu

The Bantus are a collection of populations of very diverse ethnical origins; but the languages they speak belong to the same family. They inhabit the immense savannah of south equatorial Africa, and take the name semi-Bantu, when they overlap near the Guinea coast with the Paleonigritic cultures, whose origins are in the northern savannahs.

## Baoule

The Baoules form a fraction of the Akan ethnical complex (Ashanti, Agni, Baoule, Abron), who by the beginning of the eleventh century had already migrated south from the north of what is now Ghana in search of gold. Not long after 1700, Osei-Toutou succeeded in unifying the various groups of the Ashanti into one kingdom, of "The Golden Seat" — an altar-throne believed to have fallen from heaven into the lap of the country's founder. After his death in about 1730, there was rivalry between his two nephews, Opokou-Ware and Dako, the latter being killed in combat. His sister, the princess Abra Pokou, managed to escape west with her followers. Before establishing themselves sporadically between the Congo and up to Bandama on the Ivory Coast, the exodus of this people (mid-eighteenth century) gave rise

to a cycle of myths closely bound up with water gods. As well as a considerable statuary, the Baoules sculptured many masks, some polychrome, in particular of the buffalo and the ram, animals which both take part in fertility cults and appear on doors; and in the pendant gold masks made by lost wax casting. They regarded gold as a living metal equipped with a soul by the water spirits.

## Bariba

A population of northern Dahomey culturally and politically linked with the old kingdom of Gourma, which was a dependency of the Mossi empire. The Bariba engraved gourds, arms, wooden utensils, and worked leather, which was then decorated with coloured motifs.

## Basonge

South-east of Bakuba and near the Baluba, the Basonges erected a solidly based patriarchal society. In spite of their neighbours' influence, they continued to give their art a strongly personal flavour, by accentuating the angular nature of their statuary and — even more exaggerated — by the geometrical shapes of their masks. The sheer volume of the "Kalebue" masks, particularly the Bena-Mpassa in the region of the Lomani, is expressive, an effect enhanced by concentric coloured flanges.

## Bateke

Inhabiting the right bank of the Congo in the vicinity of Brazzaville, the Bateke are Bantu agriculturalists. A considerable part of their sculpture is concerned with the systematic production of statuettes, endowed with prophylactic qualities. They make great use of these "medicines" for offensive and defensive purposes. Flat, near-circular masks are also found in the Bakebe country, the decor finely chiselled and stylised, inspired by the human face, which is powerfully recreated by the sculptural manner of applying the colour.

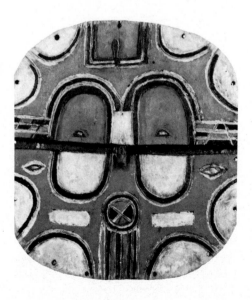

## Bayaka

In the south-west Congo, between Kouango and Kouilou, the Bayaka celebrate the cult of ancestor worship, and practise a highly refined mask art. Surmounted by animal or emblematic figures the masks, which represent a mythical event or some particular rank, are decorated with raffia, while their reflective, meditative expression is emphasized by the way the flat tints stand out. Polychrome bark tablets are placed on the walls of the dwellings used for initiation ceremonies.

## Belcayre

The site of Belcayre at Thonac in the Dordogne contained a flag-stone on which a ruminant is deeply engraved. A hundred metres further, a large block was found with broken rings and cup-shaped utensils incised on it. These works belong to the Aurignacian period.

## Benin

In the ancient Benin kingdom (12th–14th century A.D.), power was divided between the Oba, the political head, and the Oni, the religious head, who lived in the holy city of Ife. It was in Ife that the Benin artists learnt the lost-wax mould technique for casting bronze, which allowed an extremely expressive relief décor for written themes, as well as for depicting the surrounding space. This art reached

153

**Bobo-Fing,** Upper Volta
*Mask smeared with pigment*
Paris, Musée des arts africains et océaniens

its peak at the end of the 15th century, and then gradually declined into purely academic forms, notably in sculpture.

### Bernous

The Bernous cave near Bourdeilles in the Dordogne possesses what is undoubtedly one of the earliest series of cave art. It includes a mammoth, a rhinoceros and perhaps a bear, engraved in depth, with a wide if somehat stilted line. This probably belongs to the Aurignacian period.

### Bobo

Inhabiting the Upper Volta, the Bobo farmers can be divided into three groups: the Bobo-Fing or "Black" Bobos, the Bobo-Gbe or "White" Bobos, and the Bobo-Oule or "Red" Bobos. They celebrate the cult of ancestor worship and agrarian rites notable for the use of large

polychrome masks, on which geometrically cut heraldic motifs stand out. Extremely varied in form, as is the setting for the signs in their décor, these masks uphold the protecting spirit of the village, the Do, who is entrusted with control of natural forces when the time of sowing comes, or when, at the death of one of its members, the community is bereaved.

### Bourdeilles

The Fourneau-du-Diable at Bourdeilles in the Dordogne is a pile of rocks, the result no doubt of the collapse of a shelter. One block was found with black painted spots which may portray animals, and two other blocks carved in relief. One of these, about 60 centimetres long, depicts five members of the ox, and two of the deer family, two horses, and some indecipherable markings. The other, of lesser importance, is thought to depict a bear or a wild boar, and an ibex. All these reliefs are typical of the Solutrean period.

### Bozo

Settled in the Mali, living by fishing in the Niger and the Bani, the Bozos based their economy and culture on mythological traditions linking them closely with the Dogon. As with all Malinkian peoples, theirs was a patriarchal society, divided into castes. They engraved and painted signs expressing these symbols on the prows of their large canoes. They owned some fields on the river bank, and built up a society of masks connected with a ritual celebrating the mythical origins of agriculture.

## Breuil, Henri (1877-1961)

A prehistorian who, by thousands of surveys, unflagging attention to detail in interpretation, a faculty for synthesis and unfailing enthusiasm, completely mastered a field which, as he examined and discovered it over a period of fifty years, was constantly expanding. From 1901 on, after taking part in the discovery of Combarelles, Henri Breuil devoted his life to prehistorical investigation, travel and instruction. With more than 500 monographs, and innumerable classes and lectures, he attempted to reveal something of the humanity interred in the great Paleolithic sanctuaries, to discover the springs of their religion and art, even the way they thought, as expressed in their many creative activities. By establishing in 1934 a double cycle, Aurignaco-Périgordian and Solutreo-Magdalenian, he developed the first system of chronology capable of accounting for the succession of styles and cultures during the millennia of their evolution. He travelled all over the world, from Altamira to Lascaux, from the Spanish Levant to the Sahara, South Africa to the Arctic regions, to decipher the messages engraved or painted by mankind before the invention of writing. The sum of his researches is contained in his *Quatre cents siècles d'Art parietal* (Montignac, 1952), a book of fundamental importance, covering the various aspects of his work.

## Bronze Age

Succeeding the Neolithic and preceding the Iron Age, the Bronze Age shows an advance in methods of production (this does not necessarily occur in every new civilisation). Produced from the smelting of copper and alloyed with tin, a technique discovered in Asia, bronze was used for arms and tools. From the end of the fourth millennium, it was in use in Anatolia, Palestine, Mesopotamia, Egypt, and shortly after the third millennium in Greece and Crete. It was not introduced into the rest of Europe till after the second millennium. The Bronze Age is contemporary not only with the beginnings of metallurgy, but also with the invention of the wheel, the use of oxen for traction, the first writings in certain zones of the Mediterranean basin, the division of work into different handicrafts, the increase in commercial exchanges, and the rise of urban societies and great empires.

## Bruniquet

The Bruniquet cave in the Tarn-et-Garonne contained a quantity of engravings on small limestone plaques, shoulder-blades and reindeer antler, as well as objects decorated in relief, in particular spear-throwers and cleverly fashioned perforated bones (see entry). Apart from a few human figures and geometrical motifs, these animal figures are undoubtedly the most finished examples of Magdalenian domestic art.

155

## Cap-Blanc

The Cap-Blanc shelter at Marquay in the Dordogne has a monumental frieze about 12 yards long, parts of which are in highly accentuated relief. Seven horses, three oxen and two bison belonging to the Middle Magdalenian period are depicted.

## Capsian

One of the most important North African mesolithic cultures, deriving its name from the Tunisian site Capsa (now Gafsa), and dating from the end of the Upper Paleolithic. Its handicrafts are found beyond the Sahara, as far afield as Kenya, and include particularly tools formed from blades, and many microliths of geometric design.

## Caroline Islands

Before coming under American administration, this Micronesian archipelago was colonized in 1527 by the Portuguese, and then occupied by the Spaniards, the Germans and the Japanese. The population is about 35,000. Sculpture is rare, but the painted figures on the gables of the men's houses should be noted.

## Castillo

In the province of Santander near Puente Viesgo is a limestone peak in which several caves have been hollowed out. The most important, that of Castillo, possesses a number of wall paintings which belong to several Upper Paleolithic periods — digital tracings, coloured hands "in reserve", figures and engraved or painted signs. Animal paintings predominate, notably the bison, outlined with a black or red contour or, as at Altamira, in polychrome and modelled. A number of decorated objects have been classed as Middle Magdalenian.

## Ceremonial huts for Men

Immense huts, sometimes as much as 100 yards long, are found in Papua in the region of the river Sepik, where the men meet to discuss communal problems. They were a centre for the most important ceremonies.

## Champlevé

In engraving, a champlevé figure or motif is one in which the background is cut away, as opposed to an incised décor on a surface, in order to achieve an impression of volume. In carving wood, it entails removing these areas that will ultimately be white. The champlevé technique is part of the evolution away from incision, and towards relief work.

## Charco del Aqua Amarga

Discovered in 1913, the paintings in the gorge of Charco del Aqua Amarga near Alcanis in the province of Teruel, are rich in hunting scenes and warriors in animated movement, systematically repeated to produce a most lively effect. This method of writing is often found in Spanish Levantine art.

## Châtelperronian

A cultural period of the Upper Paleolithic, named after the discovery of a site at Châtelperron (Allier); it begins about 35,000 B.C. The Châtelperronian marks the transition from flake to blade tools: gravers, scrapers, drills. Bone objects are found throughout the period, as well as the first articles of personal adornment (the pendants of Arcy-sur-Cure), and the beginnings of decoration by regular or grouped incisions.

## Chefferie

This is the French word for a system by which political and religious authority was exercised in certain African and South Sea societies. Whether by election or heredity, based on the family, clan or tribe, Chefferie is a hierarchical order, a complex institution which always implies a close control by the men's assembly and the council of elders.

## Chimeneas

The Chimeneas cave has recently been discovered in the province of Santander near Puente Viesgo, in the massif which also contains the Castillo cave. Most of its paintings go back to Early Magdalenian.

## Cogul

Cogul in the province of Lerida is noted for its "dance of the women", a picture linking the figures of women to those of oxen and the goat family. One of the first sites to be discovered in the Spanish Levant, it was described as early as 1908. The flat monochrome tint of certain animals gives a perforated effect.

## Combarelles

The engravings in the Combarelles cave near Eyzies (Dordogne) had been mentioned by Pomarel to Capitan, Breuil and Peyrony, who studied them in 1901. Breuil started his surveys in 1903, a procedure which helped to end the arguments about the authenticity of previous discoveries. Three hundred engravings, ranging from approx. four inches to three feet in length, were found 60 yards from the entrance. The horses, bison, bears, reindeer, mammoths, ibex, bovids, stags, hinds, lions, wolves and anthropomorphic figures, are so interwoven that a rapid and comprehensive reading is impossible. A number of different methods of incision, often emphasized by the use of colour, were employed. A sanctuary of medium depth, its series of rock paintings date mostly from the Middle Magdalenian.

### Cook Islands

Also known as the Hervey Isles, were discovered by James Cook in 1775. The population is less than 2,000, in part originally from New Zealand, Tahiti and the Windward Isles. Engraving primarily but also some colour, distinguishes their sculpture, particularly in their ceremonial objects: spoons, howel, etc. The "tapa" (see entry) decorations are very varied.

### Cougnac

The Cougnac cave in the Lot dates from the Early Magdalenian; none of it is far from day light. It is remarkable for the way in which the figures are distributed according to the shape of the cave, and the compositions are joined to one another, by using the same group of signs throughout the cave.

### Cowries

Cowries are the shells of small molluscs fished for in the Indian Ocean and transported in quantities to Africa, where they were used for money or as objects of adornment. In the latter case, they adorn masks, statues, clothing, and are used in necklaces, bracelets, belts and costumes.

### Dan

Inhabiting the periphery of the western Ivory Coast, Guinea and eastern Liberia, the Dan and Guere peoples form a cultural whole, relatively homogeneous in the variety of social and religious activities. Dan art is well balanced, depicting the human face in a contemplative mood seldom found in forest peoples. The colour, which is used sparingly and always discreetly on masks, is also applied to the human face.

### Dating

The problem of dating archeological discoveries can be undertaken only by experts. The empiric approach has long maintained that the rougher the tool employed, the greater its age. This typological approach has since been replaced by the stratigraphical, based on geology and paleontology as much as on archaeology. This method enables a relative chronology of the remains found in a given stratum to be established. It also applies to the superimposed pictorial layers on a rock. It can reveal only sequences or identical periods of time, not the length of that time or its absolute date. We must await the more precise methods of dating by the discoveries of atomic science before we can talk of absolute dates; even here there is bound to be a margin of error. Several techniques are now employed: dendrochronology, or the analysis of growth circles in trees; geochronology, or the analysis of the varves deposited in ancient glacial lakes; the analysis of fossilized pollen, of argon and potassium in minerals, of the proportion of fluorine absorbed by bones and teeth; finally, analysis by the carbon 14 process. "During their lifetime, plants and animals absorb radio-active carbon from the atmosphere, a process which ceases with death; whereupon the radio-active carbon in their organisms disintegrates at a known speed. By measuring the amount of carbon 14 which remains in organic debris, charcoal, bones or cinders, the age can be assessed, as well as that of the archeological layer containing them, subject to a degree of probable error that may vary from a century to a thousand years." (D. Sonneville-Bordes. "L'Age de la Pierre". PUF. 1961.)

## Denguese

In the Congo north of Sankourou, the Denguese produced an original statuary

— and this in spite of the strong influence of their Bakuba neighbours in all domains of their social and cultural life. The statues were essentially commemorative, of their dead chieftains, including the head and torso, down to the prominently displayed sexual organ. The facial expression is grave, and the torso is cut or scarified with carefully composed hierarchical designs.

## Dogon

With a population of about 200,000, the Dogon inhabit the rocky region in the loop of the Niger, also Mali between Bandiagara and Hombori. They have strongly resisted all foreign cultural influences, maintaining the essential features of their traditional religious and social structure. In the cliff caves

159

arranged in cemeteries, they conserve ancient hard-wood sculptures, as grey as stone, effigies of men with upraised arms, or hermaphroditic creatures in theatrical postures — most of them more than two hundred years old. They take their name from the mythical Tellems, long thought to be the ancestors or predecessors of the Dogons; but they possess all the character of their statuary, from which they cannot be dissociated. These figures with upraised arms are also found in relief on shutters and doors, while the image of an ancestral pair, man and wife, is found again on wooden locks, although of a more geometrical and sculptural nature.

### Douala

Living in the mangrove swamps of the Cameroonian littoral, the Douala constructed canoes more than 20 yards long, capable of carrying about a hundred persons. On the prows of their craft, they carved a perforated and composite décor, usually in polychrome, in which the influence of European traders plays a part in the traditional motifs.

### Ebbou

The Ebbou cave in the Ardèche contains a series of engraved animal figures typical of the sanctuaries of the medium-depth Early Magdalenian.

### Ennedi

In the Ennedi mountains in the Chad Republic, a number of sites containing paintings have been discovered. They cover a period of five millennia, and the most recent are later than the 16th century of our era. Most of them deal with pastoral themes.

### Eyzies (The)

Eyzies-de-Tayac near Sarlat in the Dordogne is in the centre of a region which is extremely rich in prehistoric sites, containing work belonging to several periods of the Upper Paleolithic. The principal are: the La Mouthe cave, the Rey cave, the Poisson shelter in the Gorge-d'Enfer, the l'Oreille-d'Enfer cave, the Laugerie-Haute shelter, the Fournier shelter, the Dellus shelter; and the two most important, the caves of Combarelles and Font-de-Gaume.

## Fagg, Bernard (contemporary)

The English archaeologist and ethnologist, brother of William Fagg, is Assistant Keeper of the Ethnographical Department of the British Museum. Between 1944 and 1951 in Nigeria, near the villages of Jaba, Jemaa, Wamba and Makafo, he discovered terra-cotta sculptures dating back about five centuries before our era.

## Fali

Living in the Cameroons at the extreme end of the northern mountains of Adamaoua, not far from Lake Chad, the Fali, numbering about 36,000, have at various periods been driven into the mountains by the Peuls. Traditionally, they come from the east, a region near the Haoussa country, and their migrations go back to the 16th century. They have expressed their cosmogony, the events of their history, their mythical animals, in elaborate engravings seen on their wooden furniture, even in their architecture and interiors. This elaborate symbolism is repeated in the esoteric motifs of their mural paintings and engravings.

## Faure, Elie (1873-1937)

A pupil of Bergson and a general medical practitioner, he became an essayist and art-historian, and an indefatigable supporter of all the great contemporary social issues. He gave up his time to the Workers' Universities, addressing them in a course of lectures between 1905 and 1909 on the history of art. These were the basis for his celebrated "History of Art", the first volume of which appeared in 1909, the last in 1921. A complete edition of his work was re-edited by Jean-Jacques Pauvert in 1964.

## Ferrassi

The Ferassi shelter at Savigny-sur-Bugne in the Dordogne has revealed, in addition to the torso of a female statuette worked in reindeer antler, a number of stone blocks bearing traces of engravings, paintings and animal figures, some with deeply incised vulva. Most of them date back to the Aurignacian period.

## Fiji (Islands)

Situated west of the Tonga Islands, with a population of about 400,000, the Fijians were for a short time monarchist, but in 1870 were ceded to the British crown. It was here that the British made their first experiments in indirect administration. Most of the present day inhabitants are Indian coolies, imported for the growing of sugar-cane and the sugar refineries. Their pottery and wooden clubs are covered with incised decoration, whose regularity and high quality are revealed in "tapa" work (see entry).

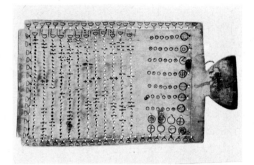

### Fon

Of Ewe origin, the Fons, numbering more than 800,000, occupy the whole southern part of Dahomey. By the 16th century of our era their society was monarchical and military, with its famous and redoubtable corps of Amazons. The many religious sects exercised a powerful influence through their priests on every social class, educating them ideologically during the long and periodic retreats it was customary to pass in the monasteries. Their polychrome reliefs illustrate principally historical or legendary events, and primeval myths, subjects also depicted in their wall paintings and hangings inspired by motifs from the royal palaces of Abomey.

### Font-de-Gaume

A few kilometres from Les Eyzies in the Dordogne, the Font-de-Gaume cave was inspected in 1901 by Peyrony; Breuil started his surveys here in 1903. The high quality of its works of art helped silence the doubts expressed about the authenticity of previous discoveries. The sanctuary is of medium depth, its painting ex-

tending along a narrow gallery 120 metres long, onto which open small rooms and lateral passages. About 200 figures have been identified, including bison, horses, mammoths, reindeer, oxen and ibex. These paintings are often associated with signs, and there are a number of superpositions, as in the great polychrome bison of the frieze traversed with small delicately engraved and painted mammoths. Most of the parietal works are typical of the Middle Magdalenian, but certain details may go back to the Aurignacian.

### Franco-Cantabrian (Art)

Essentially the parietal art of the sanctuaries in south-west France, the Pyrenees and the Cantabrian mountains. The caves of the Dordogne, the Charente, the Gironde and the Vienne are in the most northern part. More to the south are those of Herault, Aude, Gard and Ardèche, forming a distinct group on

their own. The Pyrenees and their Cantabrian extensions, with the Asturian caves on the Spanish side, and the Pyrenean ones on the French side (in which must be included those of the Lot) form the largest area. Owing to the number of sites, the importance of the discoveries, the relative ease with which they can be classified chronologically and topographically, Franco-Cantabrian is the only instance of parietal art which provides enough material for a coherent account of that art, with its aesthetic and cultural values.

### Frobenius, Leo (1873-1938)

German archaeologist and ethnologist. In 1910 he discovered at Ife in Nigeria sculptures in bronze and terra-cotta dating back to before the 13th century A.D. In 1925, he published with Obermaier a monograph on the rock carvings in the Saharan Atlas mountains; and in 1937, a selection with commentary of 2,500 surveys which he had conducted at Tassili and Fezzan.

### Futuna (Island)

Situated to the north-west of the Fiji Islands, it is attached to the Wallis Islands and has a population of 1,500. In the past, its traditional links were mostly with Samoa. Its "tapa" décor (see entry) is original and sparse.

### Gabillou (Le)

Near Mussidan in the Dordogne, the Gabillou cave contains engraved figures open to the light; and deaper, some painted ones. On one wall is a horned human figure associated with latticework signs. This "magician" may be a mythical creature. The sanctuary dates back to the beginning of the Magdalenian.

### Gargas

Near Aventignan in the Hautes-Pyrénées the Gargas cave was successfully prospected by Regnault and Cartailhac in 1906; then in 1907, by Cartailhac, Breuil and Neuville; to be surveyed in the following years by Breuil. One of the first

163

Gravettian sanctuaries whose paintings are open to the daylight, it is especially important on account of the number of its hands "in reserve", and the black, ochre and red imprints which are occasionally superposed. The absence of one or several finger-joints in certain hands has been interpreted as a ritual mutilation. Examination of these finger marks in the clay has revealed the first animal sketches.

## Gasulla

Discovered in the early thirties, the paintings of the Gasulla gorge near Ares del Maestre in the province of Castellon include very stylized battle or hunting scenes, evidence of a desire to recreate an event in stenographic composition. Also, there is a strange figuration which has been intepreted as the "execution" of a man by archers.

## Glaciation

A geological period determined by the precipitations and cooling of the climate, which causes ice some hundreds of metres thick extending over whole regions. In central Europe during the Pleistocene period there were four glaciation periods: the Günz, about 600,000 the Mindel, about 450,000; the Riss, about 200,000; and the Würm, about 80,000 B.C. Identified by the German geologists, Penck and Bruckner, who began their surveys in the Alpine valleys where the deposits are more easily observed, these glacial phases have made it possible to define corresponding glaciations in other regions of the world.

## Gourdan

A number of engravings have been found at Gourdan in the Upper Garonne — on stone, reindeer antlers and perforated bones (see entry), with animal motifs cut into them. They date mostly from the Magdalenian.

## Gouro

Owing to their geographical position, the Gouros always maintained close links with the Baoule, at least since the latter arrived on the Ivory Coast some two centuries ago. The art of the two peoples has much in common, owing to mutual influences and reciprocal assimilations. But the Gouros mask art is subtler, bordering on the precious, and their weaving, in which they use traditional motifs, more accomplished.

## Gravettian

A cultural period of the Upper Paleolithic beginning about 25,000 B.C., named after the tongue of land known as de la Gravette (Dordogne), containing many and varied stone implements. Compositions with symbolical themes were developed, associating and coupling animals with signs. Engraving and painting became more precise, as seen in the shelters of Labatut, Péchialet, Isturitz, Laugerie-Haute. The first hands "in reserve" appear in Pair-non-Pair, la Grèze,

Gargas. Most of the statuettes known as "Aurignacian Venuses" appear in the Gravettian period, at Lespugue, Brassempouy, the Ptaud shelter, Tursac, Willendorf, Kostienki, Dolni-Vestonice. Engraving evolves towards relief, as in the horned woman of Laussel.

### Grebo

Agriculturists of the Ivory Coast living in the forest zone of Cavally who ornamented the walls of their huts with engravings and paintings, drawing on a repertoire of geometrical motifs, animal and vegetable shapes.

### Grèze (La)

The Grèze cave at Marquay in the Dordogne contains deeply incised parietal engravings of animals — the remains, for example, of a relief representing a bison, which is evocative of the Cap-Blanc style. This is one of the first sanctuaries containing parietal works; it goes back to the Gravettian.

### Griaule, Marcel (1898-1956)

An ethnologist and professor at the Sorbonne who dedicated his life to the study of the Dogon civilization. One of the first to limit his field of research to a single population, he was not content with the exterior aspect of works of art, but wished to discover and understand the cultural complexity of an entire people. His monumental work, *Masques*

*dogon* (Paris, 1938), his interpretation of the original myths running through social and religious life in *Dieu d'Eau* (Paris 1948), his many articles on the symbolic and cosmological overtones of African negro art, have inspired disciples to consider what creative processes lie behind the external and material manifestations of a people. His book *Arts de l'Afrique noire* (Paris 1947), by revealing what goes on in the mind of the sculptor, has laid the foundation for this kind of synthesis.

### Guere

Inhabiting the forest areas of the western Ivory Coast, the Gueres formed with the Dan a cultural, social and religious entity. They created violently expressionist masks, combining the physical aspect of the human face with the myths of the past connected with it. These were essentially "landscape" masks, with corrugated surfaces, aggressive expressions, frequently tangled beards and patches of startling colour.

165

**Guiart,** Jean (born 1925)

Ethnologist and historian of the Pacific, director since 1957 of South Sea religious studies at the 5th section of l'Ecole Pratique des Hautes Etudes. A pupil of Maurice Leenhardt, he followed his steps in New Caledonia, where he classified the structure of traditional society in the Grande Terre and the Loyalty Isles. He also undertook several research expeditions to the New Hebridean archipelago, the Ambryn isles, and the isles of Malekula, where he traced the remains of the old culture. His revaluations of the sociological and religious structure of these societies for his articles in the *Histoire de l'Art* of the *Encyclopédie de la Pléiade* (Paris 1961), and his book *Océanie* (Paris 1963) reveal that there is much more to these peoples than the semimagic. semi-exotic legends popularly associated with them.

**Hausa**

Extending from the Niger to northern Nigeria (with a few settlements in Dahomey and Mali), the Hausa peoples have different origins, but share a common Hamitic language. Their present population is over three million. Deeply Moslem, their society was controlled on every level by their religion, personified in the Sultan of Sokoto. The Sultanates of Kano, Sokoto and Zaria had in the past founded pacific regimes, in accordance with these rulers' plans for economic expansion.

**Hawaii** (Archipelago of)

Known formerly as the Sandwich Islands, this Polynesian archipelago is today a state of the U.S.A. In the effigies of their war gods, as in their ceremonial capes

and coats, the use of colour, down and feather is brought to its highest pitch. Their sculpture recalls the art of New Zealand. The "tapa" (see entry) of the Hawaiian islands has a variety of colours, and finely printed geometrical motifs.

**Hominids**

A subdivision of the primates including man and his quaternary ancestors. To distinguish them from Pongids (large monkeys like the gorilla, chimpanzee, orang-utang and gibbon), they are still called Hominids. This is a generic term including, apart from *Homo sapiens*, anthropoid fossils such as the pithecanthropus of Java, the sinanthropus of China, the atlanthropus of north Africa and the Neanderthal man of Europe. These are fossils of the most archaic form of humanity known to us.

**Homo sapiens**

He appears in the Upper Paleolithic about 35,000 B.C. with the discovery in 1868 of Cro-Magnon man, named after a place thought to be in the present commune of Les Eyzies in the Dordogne. He is the direct ancestor of all types of present-day humanity. Starting in the Franco-Cantabrian area, his civilization was to extend rapidly through Siberia and Alaska as far as the American continent. He revolutionized tools and the nature of work, thereby developing his conscious creative activity.

**Humboldt** (Bay of)

Near the frontier dividing New Guinea in two. Here pottery and "tapa" (see entry) have been found, decorated with lively calligraphic motifs derived from animal figures.

**Huon** (Gulf of)

In eastern New Guinea, this region possesses statues, masks and reliefs whose surfaces and shapes are accentuated by the use of polychrome — which also enhances the geometrical rhythms of the incised decoration.

**Ife,** Nigeria
*Baked earth with incisions*
(before the 13th century)

**Senufo.** *Mask*

## Ideogram

A sign representing an idea or object without any reference to sound. In so far as it is figurative, it may also be regarded as hieroglyphic. It expresses a non-phonetic meaning.

## Ife

The religious centre of the Yoruba country in the south-west of Nigeria, where remarkable statues in terra-cotta and bronze dating back to before the 13th century have been found. The technique of casting bronze by the lost wax method was taught in Benin by artists from Ife.

## Initiation

Varying in duration, frequency and programme, initiation consists in a number of religious ceremonies and physical endurance tests which grant the initiate access to the adult community. This "birth" to man's life is accompanied by instruction and revelations of a social-cultural nature. Initiation can be completed in one single retreat, but also in several stages with rites which are part of the inner circle of initiation, making the different stages of life.

## Isturitz

The Isturitz cave in the Basses-Pyrénées reveals a large number of animal figurines worked in limestone, bone cuttings, and engraved or panelled blocks; also a relief five metres broad, engraved on a stalagmitic pillar, depicting a large reindeer and various animals which are vaguely identifiable. They date from the Aurignacian to the most recent Magdalenian.

## Kanigara

A New Guinea population established in the neighbourhood of Tambanum in the Sepik middle valley. Kanigara art includes pottery in the form of human figures, orators' stools with carved figurative décor, and large engraved and perforated wooden plaques. The Kanigaras also paint on the bark of areca palm trees compositions with symbolical themes derived from birds and the human face.

## Konkomba

This people inhabit the north of Togo. They produce engraved gourds, and decorate the interior walls of their huts with a series of human and animal figures, methodically grouped and accompanied by geometrical signs. Some of the latter reoccur in their complicated body scarification.

## Kono

The Konos inhabit the forest regions of Mount Nimba in Guinea, extending to Liberia and the Ivory Coast. Their social organization is based on seniority of promotion in the different stages of "poro" initiation, aimed at creating the socially perfect man. Masks often play a role in the religious and social life of the Konos, who also engrave and paint the walls of their huts with geometrical motifs accompanied by masked figures.

## Kouroumba

Living between the Dogon and the Mossi on the frontiers of Mali and the Upper Volta, the Kouroumbas are a people who, after a suitable period of mourning, celebrate the dispersion of their ancestors' spirits. For this ceremony, the priests attach to their head by means of a net a sculpture of polychrome geometric design representing an antelope. As far as is known, they have no other form of plastic expression.

## Krou

Inhabiting the south-east of Liberia and extending to the Ivory Coast, the Krou are courageous navigators. Their polychrome masks depict a crude and grotesque human face. The different designs with which they paint their bodies denote the various groups into which they are divided.

## Labastide

The Labastide cave in the Hautes-Pyrénées contains a series of parietal paintings and engravings formally and closely linked with figures in works of domestic art. They are in the remotest part of the sanctuary, and belong to the Middle Magdalenian.

## Labatut

The Labatut shelter at Sergeac in the Dordogne contains traces of painting on blocks which have become detached from the vault, and various stones covered with painted figures. Small black silhouettes, one of which is a stag, in the company of a large animal depicted in a red flat tint outlined in black, are painted on one of these stones. On another is a black hand "in reserve". Most of them are Gravettian.

## Lajoux, Jean-Dominique (contemporary)

Photographer and scenario-writer interested in Saharan ethnology and archeology. He took part in Henri Lhote's expedition to Tassili (1957), returning later alone to the same sites, where he spent three months in 1960 and 1961. He came home with a colour film and a remarkable series of photographs, *Merveilles de Tassili n'Ajjer* (Paris 1962). Using the most modern methods of research for his surveys, he showed that photography can faithfully reproduce every aspect of parietal painting.

## Laming-Emperaire, Annette (born 1917)

An instructor in prehistory at the Sorbonne, she has undertaken field-work in Chile, Brazil, Terre-de-Feu and France. Her writings show an appreciation of what modern research technique can achieve: *Découverte du Passé* (Paris 1952), and *L'Archéologie Prehistorique* (Paris 1963). Her most conclusive original contribution is however her book, *La signification de l'Art rupestre paléolithique* (Paris 1962), in which she does not hesitate to correct accepted premises based on magic and other totems.

## Lascaux

Discovered near Montignac in the Dordogne in 1940 by Ravidat and Marsal, the Lascaux cave has been surveyed since 1953 by Maurice Thaon and, later, Glory. This many-chambered cave is entered by the "Hall of the Bulls", whose walls and vault are covered entirely by animal figures: giant bulls powerfully outlined, masked or unmasked, tower above cows, stags, horses and a mysterious animal thought to be a unicorn. At the far end of this hall is the narrow exitless Painting Gallery, remarkable for the portrait of a cow bounding over a set of small horses, and a large lattice-work sign. There are also horses accompanied by bovine creatures, a stag dotted with black spots, two ibex confronting each other and separated by another large network sign. Superpositions abound, but without obliterating one another. This "passage" with its incised overlapping

**Lascaux**
*Black bull* (detail)
Side passage left wall

figures appears to be an introduction to the great collection in the Hall of Engravings where almost all the figures are horses, ibex, antelope and oxen, in lines grouped according to their species, but crossing and recrossing. It also contains certain signs which were long regarded as representing huts. On the left is the Great Gallery, decorated with a cornice used by the Lascaux artists, we may think, to depict the course of a river or stream in which a group of stags is swimming. Many paintings show bison accompanied by horses, and most of the others in the gallery have similar themes. The passage terminates with the Small Room of the Felines, whose signs have still to be deciphered. At the other end of the Hall of the Engravings is the Well, containing the famous scene of the dead man, of which interpretations are as numerous as they are contradictory. Although mineral oxides with an iron or

magnesium base may not provide much variety of colour, the Paleolithic painters, taking advantage of the natural colouring of the rocks, either to vary the "in reserve" theme, or to enhance a relief, achieved a variety of blacks, reds and yellows. Two colours used after the outline is drawn, bring the flat surface alive, and reveal the different planes. By varying tonality, an impression of the coat and fur of the animals is obtained. The colours were applied, it seems, either by the finger, a spatular or a wood-fibre brush; or by crushing the pigment on the rock. The latter technique appears to have been used for the bison, the wild oxen (shown with the same tone everywhere), and horses with tangled manes. But we are here in the realm of hypothesis. Breuil dated Lascaux between 24,000 and 19,000, at the zenith of the Aurignacian-Perigordian period. But after Leroi-Gourhan's chronology for paleolithic art, the experts are inclined to place it in the ancient Magdalenian, about 15,000. Moreover, two radio-carbon datings have given respectively 15,000 and 13,500.

### Laugerie-Basse

The shelter of Laugerie-Basse aux Eyzies in the Dordogne is near Laugerie-Haute on the Vezère. It is rich in engravings in bone and stone of a confused assortment of animals. A bison and a reindeer have been identified, deeply engraved in a block of stone. On another block, a bovine creature is painted in black and red, dotted with brown spots. Most of these works,

171

particularly the decorated objects, date from the Magdalenian.

### Laugerie-Haute

The Laugerie-Haute shelter is near Eyzies on the Vezère in the Dordogne. Apart from the many engravings and reliefs on blocks, fragments of the vault covered with red spots or black tracery have been found at the foot of the walls; also the remains of a rock relief of a reindeer, two horses (one measuring 1.75 metres in length) and a rearing bear. A broken ring is associated with the big horse. Most of the works are Gravettian.

### Laussel

The Laussel shelter at Marquay in the Dordogne, not far from Cap-Blanc, contains a number of blocks with engravings and reliefs. Most of the engravings are circular signs associated with cup-shaped vessels which are supposed to be vulvae (vagine); other cups are associated with what are perhaps phallic symbols. There are also stones, perforated or overloaded with rings. Apart from the many animals, the reliefs depict human-beings, such as the slender "archer", two steatopygic women,

a scene which may be of parturition or copulation; and finally, a naked female figure holding a bison's horn, the famous "Venus" on which traces of red can be discerned. This last is one of the masterpieces of paleolithic art, younger than Aurignacian, classified as in the Gravettian-Solutrean transition period, between approximately 25,000 and 18,000.

### Leenhardt, Maurice (1878-1954)

An ethnologist and protestant missionary who, by his personality and the originality of his views, stimulated the study of the South Seas civilization. A humanist and religious philosopher, he outlined in his comprehensive *Arts de l'Océanie* (Paris 1947) the aesthetic achievements of the South Seas.

**Leiris,** Michel (1901-    )

Ethnographer and writer in charge of research at the CNRS, attached to the Musée de l'Homme, he took part in the surrealist movement between 1924 and 1929, before turning to ethnography and becoming the secretary-archivist of the Dakar-Djibouti mission (the second expedition of 1931–33, under Marcel Griaule). From this long journey across Africa, he returned with a remarkably rich travel diary, *L'Afrique fantôme* (Gallimard, Paris 1934). He is a friend of Picasso, Miró and Giacometti, for whom he has written a number of texts. Although his ethnographic reports are scientifically accurate, he has a breadth of vision and culture, a power of synthesis, which have prevented him from being made the prisoner of mere facts — as his books show: *La Langue secrète des Dogon de Sanga* (Paris, 1948), *Les Nègres d'Afrique et les Arts sculpturaux* (UNESCO, 1935), *La Possession et ses Aspects théâtraux chez les Ethiopiens de Gondar* ("L'Homme", No. 1, Paris, 1958).

**Leroi-Gourhan,** André (born 1911)

Ethnologist and pre-historian, professor at the Sorbonne and director of the Prehistory research centre at the Musée de l'Homme, he revolutionized existing theories about the evolution of Paleolithic art. In particular, his new chronological system, by revising the norms established during the first half of this century, inaugurated a new phase in prehistorical research. In another connection, he emphasized the importance of composition in rupestral art, and advanced the knowledge of signs, of their symbolism and evolution.

**Lespugue**

A prehistoric site in the upper Garonne in which a small naked feminine statue was found. Sculpted in ivory, finely incised and polished, it has been described as a "Venus". This seems doubtful. Its beauty lies less in the symmetry and perfect proportions, than in its harmonious expression of femininity, the organic complexity and sculptural interpretation of a fecundity symbol. It is some time since this type of figurine has been described as an "Aurignacian Venus". They are now thought to have been made much later, and most of them, including this one, date back to the Gravettian-Solutrean transition period, approximately between 25,000 and 18,000.

**Levalloisian**

A cultural period of the last old Paleolithic and middle Paleolithic, so called after the geological layer of Levallois (Seine). The variety of the Levalloisian tools indicates the great progress made in the production of splinter blades. This technique depends on the preparation of a nucleus, the central part or kernel, from which splinters are knocked off in such a way that the correct sized tool is obtained. Large splinters with narrow blades are produced, as well as pointed implements for mounting on handles.

## The Levant (Spanish)

By this term we understand parietal art, generally paintings in shelters under rocks dispersed along the eastern shore of the Iberian peninsula. Distributed principally in the provinces of Lerida, Tarragona, Teruel, Castellan, Albacete, Murcia and Jaen, they are nearly all in monochrome, very occasionally in two colours. Most of them appear to belong to a culture which developed at the close of the upper Paleolithic and during the Mesolithic, perhaps from the traditions and myths of the Franco-Cantabrian civilization. But the variety of the fauna, the number of human-beings depicted and the group scenes (hunting with bows and arrows, war and dances) indicate that this is an original art. Moreover, by its schematic rhythm, its principle of syntactic composition, the art of the Spanish Levant is opposed radically to the organic structure of the great figurative themes of Franco-Cantabrian art.

## Levanzo

Some kilometres to the west of the Sicilian coast, the site of Levanzo in the Egadi isles contains a series of paintings and rock carvings well withdrawn from the light of day. They go back to the upper Paleolithic, but have little in common with the Franco-Cantabrian. This series of schematic figures painted summarily, derived from man and animal, is noteable for an emblematic sign related to that in the rocks of Bandiagara in Mali, and in which a transposition of the "Kanaga" mask of the present Dogons has been recognized.

## Levi-Strauss, Claude (1908-    )

A professor at the *Collège de France* and director of studies at the *Ecole pratique des hautes études*. Apart from his work on American civilizations, he is the author of *La Pensée sauvage* and *Tristes Tropiques*. He is one of the few scientists whose work has a comprehensive character, owing to his contention that ethnological discovery should be regarded as a philosophical experience.

## Lhote, Henri (1903-    )

He was attached to the *Musée de l'Homme*, and was in charge of research at the CNRS. From 1956 to 1957, he directed the study mission which brought back from Tassili n'Ajjer a large number of surveys — of which the more important elements were exhibited at the *Musée des arts figuratifs* in 1957–58. His book, *A la Découverte des Fresques de Tassili* (Paris 1958) contains his theories on the subject — on which he has also published more popular works.

## Limeuil

In the Dordogne, one of the Magdalenian sites which contain a quantity of engravings on small limestone blades. They represent animals and strange scenes, such as the one known as "funereal lamentations", which some observers have regarded as a parturition scene. Because of its abundant illustrations, Limeuil has long been regarded as a true *atelier* of prehistoric art. The method of engraving which is really more important than the engravings themselves, has not yet been identified.

## Lost Wax Mould Process

An ancient process of metal casting whose origins are still debated, and which has been practised in Africa for centuries. A figurine is first modelled in wax, then coated with clay which is allowed to harden in the sun. This is fired, so that the wax melts and can be poured out of the mould, which is refilled with molten metal. After cooling, the clay is broken, thereby freeing the metal figurine. This is then polished, engraved or chased, according to local tradition and whatever finish may be required.

## Lourdes

A prehistoric site in the Hautes-Pyrenées, in which strange, semi-circular wands from reindeer horns have been found, with elaborate curvilinear relief— for example, the engraving on a piece of shale of a bearded man with antlers and a horse's tail. This "magician" of Lourdes, a composite figure, is regarded increasingly as the symbol for some mythical creature.

## Madeleine (La)

The shelter of La Madeleine at Plazac in the Dordogne contains some very rare remains of parietal engravings which are difficult to decipher. Many of them, and the reliefs on stone, represent animals and rings. They belong to the Magdalenian period.

## Magdalenian

A cultural period of upper Paleolithic, so called after the geological layer of La Madeleine in the valley of the Vézère (Dordogne), in which three principal phases can be distinguished. In the old Magdalenian (about 15,000), the traces of Solutrean disappear, the assegais are of a different kind, while the reindeer antlers become the principal material for tools, arms, and for furnishing the interior of dwellings. Quantities of large wall compositions are found in the

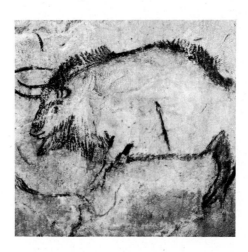

sanctuaries of Lascaux, Pech-Merle, Cougnac, Ebbou, and le Gabillou, all quite well illuminated by daylight, and containing the most abstract signs. In the middle Magdalenian (about 12,000) a considerable development in interior furnishing or dwelling equipment is to be seen in the propellants (see entry), perforated bones (see entry), polishing tools, objects of personal adornment, and spatulars covered with fine figurative or geometrical engravings (as in the semi-circular wands). Relief designs are found in sanctuaries open to the daylight, as at Cap-Blanc, Angles-sur-l'Anglin and La Madeleine; while in the sanctuaries more remote from daylight are quantities of paintings and engravings superimposed several times: as at Altamira, Font-de-Gaume, les Combarelles, Niaux, les Trois-Frères. In the late Magdalenian (about 10,000) a certain mannerism appears in the decoration of thin slabs and objects in general: as at La Madeleine, Teyjat, Limeuil. This tendency is found again, but exaggerated, in the last examples of parietal art, whose decay and degeneration is most marked. Magdalenian civilization was not able to survive the great climatic cataclysms which expelled the huge herds of reindeer and destroyed its economy.

## Magdeleine (La)

The cave of La Magdeleine at Penne in the Tarn is a sanctuary of the middle Magdalenian, whose parietal reliefs are close enough to the entry to be illuminated by daylight. These consist of a horse, and a little further on of two naked women, prostrate, facing one another. Beneath is the figure of what appears to be a bison. Each figure is about one metre long, and 70 cm. high.

## Maglemosian

Called after the geological layer of Maglemose on the Danish coast (See-land), where traces of human habitation were discovered in 1900, this is one of the most interesting mesolithic cultures in the nordic countries, While still using the heavy tools of the Paleolithic, it advanced the Magdalenian tradition of the microlith, adding the invention of the bent hook, the braided snare, the net and the drilling-brace, used for the decoration of certain objects. The Maglemosian technique of stippling spread well beyond the Baltic and Scandinavian to England and even France.

## Malanggan

Neo-Irish wooden sculpture with a complex structure owing to its polychrome and multiple perforations, presented in the form of a staff or mask. Each "Malanggan" is linked to a ritual cycle connected with the ancestor cult; its plastic themes are taken from a methology in which the animal plays a major part. It has a stabilizing power in economic and social life.

## Malekula

With its 12,000 inhabitants, this is one of the largest and most populated islands of the New Hebrides archipelago.

Except for vertical drums with deep engravings, the material most frequently used in its sculpture is the base of a bracken trunk. Exploiting the expressive quality of this material, the moulded coiffure of the heads is highly coloured, as are the statues of rank (see entry) and masks. The colour is more sombre on the posts sculpted to a human shape and in the funerary dummies.

## Mangbetu

In the huge forests of the northern Congo, the regions of Ouele and Mbomou, the Mangbetu founded a strictly hierarchical kingdom whose economy was based on agriculture. Although neighbours of matriarchal peoples, they developed the clearly patriarchal character of their society. The cranial deformation practised by the women is reflected in their statuary, as well as in their pottery and ivory work.

## Manon

Living in the boundary forest regions of Liberia, of Guinea and the Ivory Coast, the Manons are an agricultural people grouped in villages whose organization is based on the patriarchal system. Their social and cultural life is regulated by numerous institutions, of which the most important is the "poro", entrusted with the control of political and religious matters. They still make their clothes from vegetable fibres. Adornment and masks accompany tra-

ditional ceremonies. Facial or corporeal painting, generally in china clay, correspond with each degree of initiation.

## Maori

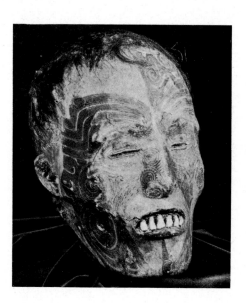

Maori art and society are the result of the many migrations which brought the Polynesians of the Cook Islands to New Zealand, the lands of the southern hemisphere and the Society Isles. Their art is characterized by the use of continuous spiral drawing, which enlivens their statues, architectural reliefs, utilitarian or ceremonial objects, and their deep facial tattooing.

## Marquess Isles (The)

A Polynesian archipelago, most of whose art is based on a strict graphic tradition which has not, however, impoverished it. The "tiki", the principal motif of their

177

themes (the image of a divine ancestor or a simple human stylization) appears in the engraved decoration of shell plaques, clubs, ceremonial canoe paddles, and in the complex meandering lines of their body tattooing.

### Marshall Isles

A Micronesian archipelago taking its name from its discoverer in 1788; its population has known Spanish, German, Japanese and American occupations. Coloured fibre materials are woven.

### Marsoulas

The cave of Marsoulas near Salies-du-Salat in the Haute-Garonne is a Magdalenian sanctuary of medium depth, whose wall paintings are based on a succession of different figurative themes linked by groups of signs. Some of these paintings, which are hachured by the use of an engraving technique, give the effect of moulding.

### Massin

A cultural zone so-called by the English ethnologist Seligman, including the eastern tip of New Guinea and the archipelagos of Entrecasteaux, Louisiade, Trobrians and Woodlark. The limestone spatulars, assegais, shields and masks are used to support the engraved decoration, primarily based on human features or bird shapes. This decoration recalls the rhythms of the spiral reliefs ornamenting the prows of the Trobriand canoes.

### Melanesia

A division of the South Seas which is more ethnographic than geographic, including New Guinea, the Bismarck

archipelago, the Solomon Isles, the New Hebrides, New Caledonia and their dependencies. These volcanic islands are covered with semi-tropical vegetation and inhabited by innumerable species of birds, which are found in the Melanesian iconography and symbolism. The pig, an imported animal, is a symbol of riches and, as such, appears in many social ceremonies. Melanesian dwelling areas differ in various regions. In New Guinea particularly the large huts of the men are used for celebrating cults; in these, their statuary and polychrome painting attain their highest expression.

## Meroe

Capital of the second Ethiopian kingdom (700–300 B.C.), its ruins extend along the western bank of the Nile in the Egyptian Sudan. But remains have been found well beyond this, as far as Khartoum, the extreme limit of Egyptian influence in Africa. In addition to Egyptian heiroglyphiçs, a Meroitic writing has been discovered derived from them; also various fragments of Greek inscriptions. North of Khartoum the habit of working in iron has existed since 400 B.C., and sites for exploiting it were found in the neighbourhood of Lake Chad.

## Mesolithic

An intermediary period between Paleolithic and Neolithic, about 8,000 B.C., characterized by the use of microlithic tools. Apart from hunting and fishing, the first means of transport and the domestication of the dog appear. In Europe, mesolithic cultures were undoubtedly contemporary with agricultural and pastoral civilizations in northern Africa and Asia Minor. The geometrical motifs engraved or painted in ochre on the pebbles at Mas-d'Azil (Ariège), and the decorations punched with the Maglemose (Denmark) drill, are important examples of Mesolithic art, to which are probably connected, if only partly, the paintings of the Spanish Levant, northern Africa, the Sahara, south Australia and the arctic regions.

## Micronesia

Under the term Micronesia are grouped a quantity of coral isles and archipelagos dotted across the Pacific between Indonesia and the Philippines in the west, Melanesia in the south, and Polynesia in the east. They include the Carolines, the Mariana islands, the Marshals, the Gilberts and their dependencies. In Micronesia, the Polynesian cultural tradition has recently undergone Malaysian influence. Plastic art is rare and confined to the Carolines; but the engraving and plaiting are rich in geometrical design.

## Minateda

The site of Minateda in the province of Albacete was discovered in 1914. In his quest for a chronology for the art of eastern Spain, Breuil believed that there were thirteen different periods. There is one composition in which human, animal or composite figures are shown on a common background, and often drawn to different scales. The big central ox has several different surfaces to his body, all painted with a technique more akin to engraving.

## Monod, Theodore (contemporary)

Professor at the *Musée national d'histoire naturelle*, and director of the *Institut Français d'Afrique noire* (IFAN) at Dakar, Theodore Monod began his productive career in the Sahara as a young man. He accompanied the

Augiéras-Draper mission (1927–28) to Hoggar on the Niger, and excavated a human fossil at Asselar (classified today as Neolithic). From 1930–39, he travelled in Mauretania, to Tanezrouf in the Adrar of the Iforas and Tibesti, more than 4,000 kilometres by camel. On his last Mauretanian excursion in 1954–55, he travelled 900 kilometres in under two months, the greatest distance until the time covered from one watering point to another. Botany, zoology, anthropology, oceanography, ethnology and other scientific studies are the subjects of his writings on the Sahara and Central Africa.

### Moors

A western Saharan population extending from south Morocco in the north to the Senegal and Mali in the south. The Moors (about 600,000) describe themselves as El-Beidane, "the Whites". In former times they were redoubtable warriors and ardent Musselmen, undertaking religious missions in western Africa. They are a race of camel shepherds and caravan dwellers; they breed cattle in the Sudan where, as at Oualata, they occasionally settle. Their art is essentially graphic, as expressed in engraving on wood or metal, leather work, and monochrome mural decoration in the houses of Oualata.

### Mouthiers

The shelter of the Chaire-à-Calvin at Mouthiers in the Charente revealed

small slabs with confused and indecipherable engravings — for example, a relief 2.50 metres long, representing two oxen and two horses. It was buried in the soil and bears traces of colour. It dates from the end of the Solutrean.

### Mpongwe

In the Gabon, in the basin of the Ogon, the Mpongwes and Balumbos created different variants of the same kind of mask, with a white face and coiled hair, all supposed to be female apparitions. The Mpongwes are one of the oldest peoples of the Gabon.

## Nago

The farmers of Nago, long dominated by the Fons, live in the frontier areas of the Dahomey coast. They are the most western representatives of the Yorubas who occupy a large part of southern Nigeria. The masks of their secret societies and their posts, sculpted with mythical figures, are decorated in lively polychrome.

## Nalou

The Nalous living in the boundary regions of Guinea are farmers with a patriarchal society. They number about 15,000. Their social-religious institutions influence their art, as can be seen at the time of the wearing of the "banda" masks. These are a synthetic sculpture based on zoomorphic elements, much adapted, and generally of aquatic origin. The most decipherable of these masks, in strong polychrome, combine human features with crocodile or antelope bodies.

## Neanderthal (Man of)

Taking his name from the geological layer discovered in 1856 near Düsseldorf, Neanderthal man belongs to the most recent form of Paleanthropics, whose civilization overlaps the middle Paleolithic. He lived more than 40,000 years before our era. He perfected tools, the use of fire, cave habitations; he organ-ized the first individual or collective burial places. He disappears at the beginning of the upper Paleolithic, leaving to *homo sapiens* a quantity of technical skills of inestimable value.

## Neolithic

The age of new or polished stone. The term serves today to describe the period during which the first technical revolution of humanity took place, the invention of agriculture — about 7,000 in the near east, 5,000 in central Europe, 4,000 in western Europe, 3,000 in America, and 2,000 in China. Man has suddenly become productive, practising stock-rearing, pottery, weaving. He settles and builds cities, founds the first empires: Egyptian, Mesopotamian, those of the Indus. The parietal art of the Sahara, north Africa and the Arctic continued through the Neolithic period, while that of south Africa and Australia has been practised until relatively recently.

## New Brittany

Off the north coast of eastern New Guinea, the island of New Brittany (the New Pomerania of the Germans) has more than 100,000 inhabitants. In the north, in the Gazelle peninsula, two peoples are known for their artistic production. The Sulkas sculpt the prows of canoes with painted décor, and make masks in weaved fibre, insubstantial in weight, lively in colour and protuberant shapes. They also make polychrome shields. The Baining use "tapa" (see entry) for their masks. Generally, the vegetable tissue is stretched on a frame, a support for a composite polychrome décor based on triangles and concentric circles.

## New Caledonia

The Melanesian archipelago discovered by Cook in 1724, with a population, the Kanakas, of 72,500. Apart from an abundant statuary, and masks bordering on caricature, New Caledonian art is based primarily on relief and engraving. The decoration of the frames is deeply engraved, composed of broken lines of superposed curves, in the form of ovals, lozenges and stars; it is generally surmounted by a human figure. This decoration is again seen in the wooden beams of the houses and their exterior posts. Lastly, a number of pieces of engraved bamboo show scenes of agricultural or ceremonial life, revealing the first contacts with Europeans.

## New Guinea

To the north of Australia, from which it is separated by the Coral and Arafoura seas and the strait of Torres, New Guinea is, after Greenland, the biggest island in the world (771,000 sq. km.). The climate is extremely humid, and a part is covered by almost impenetrable equatorial forest. It is inhabited by peoples distinguished from one another as much by their social, economic and religious life as by their artistic pro-

duction. Polychrome votive tablets come from the gulf of Papua, in a "tapa" (see entry) decorated with the designs of Lake Sentani. In the south-west, the Asmats produce shields with coloured relief. In the valley of Sepik, the ceremonial dwellings are decorated with monumental paintings. In Massim, the reliefs are perforated. All these varied productions share one feature — the use of curves and counter-curves, interminable spirals, the line always coiling back on itself, tying itself and untying itself as it were, like some weird, exhuberant vegetable growth — yet in its rhythmical way always remaining true to life.

## New Hebrides

A volcanic archipelago in the Pacific between New Caldeonia and the Fiji Isles, with a population of about 65,000. The central and northern parts belong to the Melanesian artistic group, but the south is clearly Polynesian. For their sculpture they generally choose as material the base of a bracken trunk, a surface of hard, fine needle-points from which they extract the full expression. This statuary, which is found notably at Ambryn and in the south of Malekula, is enhanced by the use of a violent polychrome.

## New Ireland

The 38,000 inhabitants of this island in the Bismarck archipelago are an important element in South Sea art. Thanks to their highly evolved social-cultural institutions, their contribution is one of the richest in the region. They produce brightly coloured "tapa" masks (see entry), sometimes similar to those of the Bainings in New Guinea, and polished, engraved and perforated shells. Their art is essentially that of the funeral ritual cycles, as seen in the polymorphous expressions of the "Malanggan" (see entry).

## New Zealand

To the south-east of Australia, New Zealand consists of two large South Sea isles, with a population of 2,400,000. As a result of successive emigrations from the Cook Isles, Australia and the Society Isles, the New Zealand maoris have a Polynesian origin — witness the different forms of their art, particularly in the graphic décor of their statues, as well as in their utilitarian or ritual material. This décor depends on a rhythmical curving line, in continual convolutions, rounding back on itself, without which the figures would be lifeless, no more than a piece of geometrical virtuosity.

## Niaux

The paintings in the caves of Niaux near Tarascon-sur-Ariège (Ariège) had been known to inquisitive tourists since the 18th century; but they were not "discovered" until 1906 by Mollard, to be surveyed in 1908 and 1909 by Breuil and Cartailhac. This is a deep sanctuary, whose first painted signs appear 611 metres from the entry, after a long corridor and a huge cavern with a lake in it. More corridors and stalactite halls

must be passed through before arriving at the famous *Salon Noir*, which contains unadorned but highly accomplished line drawings of animals, bison, horses, ibex, cervines, all hachured and outlined in clear, forceful black. Some of the bison — on whom other animals are often superposed, sharing part of the same line — are depicted as wounded by red and black arrows. Engravings in the clay soil add to the interest of the cave. Niaux is classified as middle Magdalenian.

183

# O

## Oualata

Isolated at the south-western extremity of Mauritania, this Moorish village of the western Sahara was an intellectual centre which, with its savants, schools and libraries, attracted many foreigners up to the 18th century, before being abandoned in favour of Timbuctoo. These connections could not fail to influence the society and art of the Oualata Musselmen, who live by cattle-breeding and sparse cultivation at the foot of the rock to which their village clings. The mural decoration, mostly in the interiors, is the handiwork of women, and consists of huge monochrome compositions which, in the words of Odette de Puigaudeau, recall "the ideogram, representing in a very stylized way only those parts of the body considered essential for the intended expression". This expression is clearly sexual, but we do not know what the symbols really mean. Their place in certain parts of the dwelling, particularly in the matrimonial bed-chamber, and for anything connected with the female, would indicate that they symbolize a fecundity cult.

initiation ceremonies are accompanied by facial painting.

## Oubi

An Ivory Coast population living in the forest on the borders of the Cavally, who engrave and paint mythical figures with geometrical and zoomorphic signs on the walls of their dwellings. Their

## Painting of the Body

The painting of the body (like the dance with which it is intimately connected), is one of the most ephemeral manifestations of man's artistic activities. It is met in Africa, the South Seas and Australia, where it is always individual and expressive, applied in innumerable ways, always adapted to the shape and size of the body. The coloured substance, of vegetable, mineral or animal origin, may cover the entire body, or be limited to certain parts, the breast or face, for example. The motifs may be traditional, and more than one colour may be used. Some of these variegated effects on the body transform the wearer into what is, virtually, a mobile mask — proper to the dance, where the mask finds its correct employment.

### Pair-non-Pair

The parietal engravings in the cave of Pair-non-Pair at Marcamps in the Gironde were discovered in 1896 by Daleau, who had seen them in passing, earlier, in 1883. They were surveyed by Breuil and Mary E. Boyle in 1934, 35 and 36. Characteristic of the period extending from the Gravettian to the beginning of the Solutrean, they emphasize for the first time the curvilinear quality in the backs of animals — a pictorial feature which, whether engraved or painted, was to feature increasingly as Franco-Cantabrian art evolved.

### Palau (Isles)

The isle of Palau (real name Babelthuap), and the two hundred islands included under that name, belong to the Micronesian archipelago of the Carolines, with a population not exceeding 9,000. They were discovered in 1543 by Villalobos.

### Paleolithic

The age of ancient or cut stone which is divided into three principal phases: the old Paleolithic, which covers the first three glaciations; the middle, and the upper, Paleolithic, which cover respectively the first and second halves of the fourth glaciation. In the old Paleolithic, beginning about 500,000, the first stone implements were produced — first, simple split pebbles (pebble culture); then, stone splinters, some with two faces, characteristic of the different

185

cultures of that period (Clactonian, Abbevillian, Acheulean), in which the early anthropoids moved. During the middle Paleolithic, starting about 100,000 the early anthropoids elaborated tools from the splinters. In about 40,000, Neanderthal man began to fashion the first bone objects and carry out the first burials (in the Mousterian-Levalloisian civilization). In the upper Paleolithic, beginning about 35,000, *homo sapiens* arrives and human cultural evolution accelerates. He invented art, means of propulsion, and perfected the cutting of bone and flint (blade production). This cultural period, which is subdivided into the Châtelperronian, Aurignacian, Gravettian, Solutrean, Magdalenian (see these entries) is also known as the age of the reindeer.

### Papua (Gulf of)

On the marshy deltas of the rivers Fly and Purari in New Guinea, the region known as the Papuan gulf is inhabited by a people who, linguistically and culturally, can be compared only with certain Melanesian peoples. They have something in common with the aboriginese of Australia and Tasmania, qualities acquired no doubt through the intermediary of the island peoples in the strait of Torres. Beside their "tapa" masks, their engraved and painted bark belts, the art of this region is distinguished by votive tablets and plaques of various sizes, stylistically homogeneous, but adapted according to the village and different forms of ritual. Destined to receive the spirit of an ancestor or an aquatic spirit, they can be used as masks, or rhombs which are spun on their axis, emitting an eerie throbbing sound supposed to come from mythical beings, or the spirits of the dead. The décor of their works of art is incised, in flat tints, segmented or hachured, with circles, ovals and stars, designs inspired by the human face or body.

### Parietal (Art)

This term includes all aesthetic productions, paintings, engravings, reliefs, found on vaults or rock walls. It is also known as rock art.

### Parpallo (El)

In a region where the artists of the Spanish Levant have left much evidence of creative activity. The shelter of El Parpallo near Casares in the province of Valence still possesses several thousand small slabs engraved or painted with animal figures. As at Limeuil, this was regarded as an *atelier* of prehistoric art. Although the works overlap a large part of the Paleolithic, most of them belong to the end of the Solutrean.

### Péchialet

The cave of Péchialet in the Dordogne is known principally for an engraving on shale depicting a bear between two men. Some commentators regard this as a hunting scene, a bear attacking one of the men; others regard it as a magic dance.

**El Pendo**
Province of Santander, Spain
*Engraved perforated bone*
*See page 188*

## Pech-Merle

At Cabrerets in the Lot, the cave of Peche-Merle was prospected in 1922 by David and Dutertre, then by Lemazi who made the surveys. Besides the human and animal figures traced by finger in the clay, this sanctuary near the daylight contains paintings of mammoths, the ox family, bisons, and one of the most elaborate parietal compositions in the old Magdalenian — two spotted horses traced in black, surrounded by a pointillist effect, and hands "in reserve"

## Perforated Bones

Owing to their shape and the expressive quality of the engraved décor or relief, perforated bone objects of the upper Palaeolithic were long thought to be sceptres of office, emblems of power or magical instruments — an opinion endorsed by their phallic shape. It seems more likely that they were used for straightening arrows, identical with the implements used by eskimos today.

## Peul

The origin of the Peuls is uncertain. Certain authors contend that they came from eastern Africa; others, from Egypt, passing through north Africa en route, so that their meeting with the paleonigritic peoples would have taken place in Senegal. They appear to derive from a civilization of nomadic eastern Hamitic shepherds, before they split into a number of groups which crossed western Africa as far as the Cameroons. Today, they are relatively crossbred, and most of them have been converted to Islam, while conserving their social caste system. Some are still nomadic, herding their wandering flocks, in particular the Bororo Peuls on the Niger, in Mali and the Cameroons; others are permanently settled, such as the Foula (or Foulbe — in the singular, Poullo) who, while continuing to breed cattle, have gradually been transformed into chiefs of the aboriginal farmers in the mountains of Fouta-Djalon.

## Pictography

From the Latin root "to paint", and the Greek "to trace, to write", pictography is, according to Marcel Cohen, to be found "in the many examples of proto-writing which transmit a meaning through a fragment of figured discourse, without its having been decomposed into words, that is without there being any effective connection with a known language". Pictography renders visible what can be expressed by word of mouth.

## Pindal

In the province of the Asturias near the village of Pimiango, the Pindal cave contains paintings thought to date from the middle Magdalenian. Elephants are drawn with loose brush-strokes in red, one of them bearing a red mark in the form of a heart. Nearer the entry is a lozenge shaped fish, an engraved bison, and another outlined in red, with signs and points in black and red.

## Pleistocene

The first part of the quaternary era, during which the glaciations took place. It is also known as the glacial epoch, or of the flood. During the Pleistocene, man appeared on earth and began developing his creative activities. The geological period in which we live today is called the Holocene.

## Polynesia

A division of the South Seas area which is more ethnographic than geographic. It contains a vast assortment of islands spread across the Pacific from Australia to America: the Fijis, the Tonga, the Samoa, the Ellis, the Phoenix, the Cook, the Australs, the Marquess, the Society, the Confederacy, the archipelago of Tuamotu and, at the extremity, New Zealand and the Hawaiis. The Polynesians were daring mariners, and are thought to have come from India in canoes with outriggers, after a long sojourn on the way in Indonesia. The local economic resources of these people are poor. In some parts stone sculpture has replaced the wooden variety; but it is the "tapa" (see entry) which furnishes Polynesia with its most original and varied means of aesthetic expression.

## Portel (Le)

Near Varilhes in the Ariège, the cave of Portel was discovered in 1908 by Drs. Jeannel and Fauveau; the surveys were carried out by Breuil and Vezian. Access is difficult: the cave includes several halls and galleries with paintings, most of which go back to the middle Magdalenian. Reindeer are painted in red, horses are spotted or outlined with shallow relief in black or red. Two bison, powerfully drawn in black, face one another. On the walls are a number of traces of bear-claws and some engravings, notably a bison and a horse wounded by an arrow. This last association is surprising, because elsewhere in the cave horses and bisons are segregated in separate galleries.

## Predmost

A prehistoric site in Moldavia, Czechoslovakia, where the bones of more than a thousand mammoths and various household articles have been unearthed. This collection has enabled the broad lines of the Predmostian, an upper Paleolithic culture, to be established. It developed in central and eastern Europe at a time contemporary approximately with the Aurignacian and the Franco-Cantabrian Magdalenian. Predmostian sites in the USSR have revealed the remains of half-buried dwellings.

# R

## Propellant

A kind of arm-like lever, generally made of reindeer antlers, the assegai-propellant is the first mechanism invented by Paleolithic man; it enabled the hunter to project his weapon with increased velocity. Figurative reliefs in the dwellings, with similar shapes, would indicate that these were among the masterpieces of Magdalenian art.

## Puigaudeau, Odette (contemporary)

An ethnographer who, in the course of several journeys in Mauretania, studied the mural decoration and handicrafts of the Moors of Oualata — in particular the position in the house of the symbolic motifs and furniture.

## Reindeer (Age of)

A term sometimes used to denote the upper Paleolithic. By the end of the last glaciation, most of the animal species had succumbed — but not the reindeer, whose large herds were to furnish man, through hunting, with a most important element for his economy. Traces of reindeer during the glaciations have been found in the east, centre and west of Europe, as far as the Cantabrian mountains and Catalonia, even on the French riviera. These animals advanced down to the neighbourhood of Trieste, then roamed north of the Danube and Black Sea, before leaving for Siberia and Greenland, their present habitat. It is interesting to note that the reindeer's place in Paleolithic art is — relative to that of the other species — unimportant; he appears seldom in the parietal compositions, in which horses and bison predominate.

189

## Roc-de-Sers (Le)

The geological layer of Roc-de-Sers in the Charente revealed important reliefs depicting, noteably, the ox family and the ibex, which are thought to date from the Solutrean. Those discovered last, in 1950, were still on their natural plinth, and disposed in a rectilinear frieze, which invalidates the hypothesis that these semi-circular sanctuaries were later overturned. The reliefs were apparently executed flush with the rock.

## Rouffignac

Visited from the 18th century onward, the Rouffignac cave at Miremont in the Dordogne did not reveal its paintings until 1956, thanks to the researches by Nougier and Robert. The sanctuary is deep, typical of the middle Magdalenian, with its great ordered ranks of mammoths, bisons, ibex and horses, from which the cervines and bulls appear to have been excluded. But the rhinoceri are among the finest in Paleolithic art; nowhere else in the Franco-Cantabrian region are there such a large collection of mammoths.

# S

## Sahara

Although the problem of dating has not been resolved, and the chronology adopted for prehistoric Europe is difficult to apply here, because of the absence of household *objets d'art*, or systematic excavations at the foot of walls, north Africa and the Sahara do possess a rough means of classification for their discoveries taken as a whole. Based on

the hypothetical superposition of different styles, it has provided some explanation for the quantities of parietal figures discovered; but it is inadequate and inexact for dating an art which has recently been augmented, and of which a part is now thought to be as recent as the period we call antiquity. But in the principal two dimensions established by Théodore Monod, the Precameline and the Cameline, four great periods for the engravings can be identified; that of the Bubale; of the cattle herdsmen; of the horse and cart; and of the camel.
In the great north African mountain mass of the Atlas, a large number of

animal and human figures have been found engraved, sometimes painted, generally in the neighbourhood of watering-points. For the central Sahara, the sites in the volcanic massif of Haggar, today inhabited by the Touaregs, possess various rock engravings or paintings contemporary with the Neolithic. The incised lean figures at Tefedest can be contrasted with the paintings of Mertoutek, in which women whose hair is arranged in the form of a crest or comb are superimposed on large flocks of cattle. Striving for a flat tint, the artists have taken advantage of the chromatic effects of ochre, whether yellow, blackish-brown, brown or red. In Mali, the parietal art of the Adrars of Iforas may belong to a neolithic tradition; a marked style producing an attenuated, vegetable-like appearance for both humans and animals would indicate the use of signs and symbols in their painting. On the Niger in the southernmost zone of the Sahara, the partly volcanic, mountainous massif of the Air, are walls engraved with schematic figures derived from man and animals, and independent of one another; several of these may well go back to the Neolithic. Lastly, in the northern region of Chad, the mountainous and volcanic massifs of Tibesti and Ennedi are a reservoir of rock art, whose origins must be sought as far back as the Paleolithic. The sites of Gonoa and Gira-Gira at Tibesti are notable for the variety of their engraving techniques and themes, the firmness and freedom of their figures. The Ennedi paintings depict scenes of pastoral life.

### Samoa

There are some 121,000 inhabitants in this Polynesian archipelago, which was first referred to in 1722 by the Dutchman, Rogeveen. Its art takes the form principally of motifs and compositions in "tapa" (see entry).

### Santa Cruz (Isles)

Attached to the Salomons but regarded as belonging to the northern prolongation of the New Hebrides, the isles of Santa Cruz were discovered by Carteret in 1767. The French navigator La Pérouse was shipwrecked here in 1788. More important than the sculpture or engraving, is the ingenious plaiting of coloured fibres in harmonious compositions.

### Sao

A collection of peoples who, from the 9th to the 16th century, inhabited the middle area of Chad, and the extreme north of the Cameroons, before being decimated or converted to Islam. The Sao — meaning "men" probably — have left on the emplacements of their villages a large number of effigies and ceramics or bronze objects connected for the most part with an ancestor cult. The human figures in particular serve as support for a series of engraved signs, which may refer to the resumption of corporal scarification, or the graphic transposition of a complete religious symbolism.

## Scalariforme

A term by which certain "abstract" signs which accompany parietal paintings and engravings has long been described. Executed in outline or in dots, it was thought that they were stairs or ladders; but it appears today that they are, for the most part, connected with sexual symbols, and indicate in stylized form masculine and feminine figures.

## Scarification

An incision of indeterminate depth in the skin, a custom fairly general throughout Africa. Distinctive, religious or simply decorative, scarifications are made in well-defined parts of the body, and generally during some ceremonial gathering. They enable persons of the same tribe to recognize one another, and mark the passing from one degree of initiation to another. They satisfy a traditional regard for the body as an aesthetic object.

## Sect (Member of)

Someone who professes a partisan faith in a doctrine, and a system of life elaborated and controlled by a sect. Religious sects have played an important part in certain African societies, particularly in Dahomey, in the old kingdom of the Fons. Strictly subordinated to the authority of the priests and strongly hierarchical, they were entrusted with the ideological education of their members during the long, periodic retreats under strict discipline in the convents. Corporal scarifications indicated the degree of initiation at any given moment.

## Senghor, Léopold Sédar (born 1906)

A poet and Senegalais politician. Apart from his own poems (*Chants d'Ombre, Hosties Noires, Ethiopiques,* Editions du Seuil), he is the author of an *Anthologie de la Nouvelle Poesie nègre et malgache de Langue Française* (PUF), with a preface by Jean-Paul Sartre. His address to the First International Congress of Coloured Writers and Artists (Paris 1956) appeared in *Présence Africaine* (June–November 1956), under the title *L'Esprit de la Civilisation ou les Lois de la Culture negro-africaine.*

**Senufo,** Ivory Coast
*Door with engraved decoration*
Paris, Musée des arts africains et océaniens

## Senoufo

These are Pacific farmers who inhabit the damp savannah of the northern Ivory coast, and the boundary regions of Mali, and the upper Volta. The Senoufos (population today, over a million) have been relatively successful in preserving their traditional institutions. Intervening at different levels of a basically heirachical

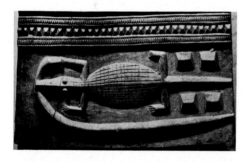

society, the "lo" (an elaborate system of initiation, and organizer of social life) fulfills a function at once religious and political. It determines the rules of conduct for certain rituals and stimulates that part of their artistic activity concerned with the liturgical equipment for their sanctuaries and initiation enclosures. The statuary used in the "lo" ceremonies consists of human effigies representing a supernatural entity, and emblematic animals connected with some deity. Among these emblematic animals, the most expressive is that of the "porpianong", a large bird with outspread wings, a kind of hornbill equipped with a long beak twisted back on the belly of a pregnant woman. Apart from their abundant production of expressive figurines made by the wax mould process (see entry), and their fine woven cloth, the Senoufos revealed their creative ability in the décor for the reliefs of shutters and doors.

## Sentani (Lake of)

Dominating Humboldt bay, in the north-west of western New Guinea. In the neighbourhood, bronze axe-heads have been found, indicating an antique connection with the Bronze Age of south-eastern Asia. According to a local muth, these axe-heads come from the west, their centre being in the Sepik. Their engraved décor is still found among the inhabitants of this area, at the approaches to the lake. The posts and roof timbers of the men's ceremonial dwellings, constructed on piles, are hollowed, moulded and perforated; here are curvilinear motifs derived from the lizard or man, figuring on oval plates, the bodies of drums and the double books of New Guinea furnishing, even on the ritual stuffs of "tapa". In all this, they reveal linear incisiveness, without ever abandoning their traditional elaborate spiral designs.

## Sepik

The region of Sepik (the principal river of New Guinea, whose valley is marshy along its entire course) is one of the shrines of the South Sea creative genius, for long considered stylistically unique. The art of Sepik is polychrome, and if it possesses a certain homogeneity in inspiration and plasticity, its themes vary throughout the region which it

193

influences. At present, eight principal
centres can be identified, although all
are closely related and many exchanges
take place between them. The Washkuks,
in the loop of the middle Sepik, paint a
curvilinear stylization of the human face,
which they insert in scalloping, in
spirits, in suns, on the open envelope of
palm leaves. The choice of this support
is to be found moreover throughout the
Sepik region, on the interior walls as well
as the exteriors of the great ceremonial
dwellings of the men. In the neighbourhood of Maprik, the Abelams paint
heirarchical figures with lively flat tints
on this material. The Chambuli who live
near the lake of the same name, deploy
their concentric rhythms, starting from
the eyes in the paintings, or from their

polychrome masks, influences which are
to be found among their neighbours the
Iatmüles. The cowrie masks of the
Iatmüles seem to have influenced the
wicker masks of the Kambringis in the
middle loop of the Sepik, who are
known for their pottery roof tiling. In
the neighbourhood of Tambanum, the
Kanigaras of the middle Sepik also
constructed roofs in polychrome terra-
cotta, and varied the concentric circle
design in their masks by the use of
cowries. These cowries, combined with
fragments of spiral shell, are set in a
vegetable gum which is applied to the
woven armature in certain masks of the
Mundugumor who inhabit the river
Yuat, a tributary of the Sepik. Along the
lower course of this river, vegetable
painted panels depict human figures,
stylized according to their sexual attributes. Their shape and appearance is
adapted to the florid form of the
decoration, which appears to have
something in common with the design of
certain Australian paintings on bark.
Lastly, here and there on the Sepik
estuary, great shields with anthropomorphic decorations engraven in chalk
spirals are found. They recall the graphic
composition in the votive plaques of
Papua.

**Society** (Isles of)

A volcanic Polynesian archipelago whose
principal island is Tahiti, and from
which successive migrations have set out
in the direction of New Zealand. About
25,000 inhabitants.

## Solomon (Isles)

With ten large islands and dozens of smaller ones, extending in the arc of a circle from the north of the New Hebrides to New Guinea, the Solomons (110,000 inhabitants) are one of the most important Melanesian archipe-

lagos. They were discovered in 1567 by the Spaniard Alvaro de Mendana de Neira. Although the mask is unknown here, they possess a large body of statuary, notable for its spare linear simplicity. Apart from this, however, decoration in the form of incrustation is frequent — as in their great canoes covered with mother-of-pearl, and particularly in their oval shields, veritable mosaics of incrustation. But it is not as free in style as that of the figured motifs on certain shells, or the engraved white-washed motifs transposed almost into signs, with which their dance shields seem to vibrate.

## Solutrean

A cultural period of the upper Paleolithic, so-called after the site of Solutré (Saône-et-Loire), beginning about 18,000. The evolution of painting appears to have marked time during the Solutrean, while engraving, in technique as in expression, flourished, culminating in the relief, e.g., Roc-de-Sers, Bourdeilles. Parallel with this, tools reached a rare perfection, characterized by their delicate finish; certain blades are 30 cm. long, and only a few millimetres thick.

## Songhai

The Songhais of the Niger were founders of a powerful empire which, in the 16th century, was the principal rival of Mali. They developed stable social and religious institutions; they produced fine woven blankets with geometrical motifs, and their pottery was painted in ochre, one remarkable design being sets of rhythmically varied triangles.

## South Africa

In the extreme south of the African continent, in a region containing one of the oldest populations, a homogeneous civilization long preserved from any European influence, are a quantity of rocks, painted and engraved, dating from upper Paleolithic times down to a relatively recent date. This South African civilization based on hunting and gathering, essentially Paleolithic in its economy, culture and art, has survived down to our own times. There is no doubt that the Bushmen, living apart in the salty savannah and the half-desert zones of the Kalahari, are the last feeble descendants of the African stone

195

age. Their pictorial subjects are taken for the most part from two great periods of their history. One, the older, is pacific, reflecting the thoughts and myths of the hunters; the other, more recent, is animated, depicting the opposition put up by a people who defended their hunting reserves against the invading Bantus — and who then had to stand impotently by, watching the arrival of the Boers (Dutch for "peasants"), who settled chiefly in the Transvaal and the Orange Free State, before their defeat in 1902 by the British. In this last period, the mythical element gradually disappears, accompanied by a decline in artistic expression. Most of the Rhodesian and South African sites have been examined and tentatively classified, but they cannot be dated in terms of the evolution of stone tools; so that the present classification is purely hypothetical. But a serious study of the Bushmen's oral tradition has, in certain cases, enabled us to substitute for the "magic" interpretation ascribed to the works of their presumed ancestors an analysis of their mythical content; we can therefore understand them, and appreciate their sculptural quality, better. The relation between Bushman rock art and that of the pastoral civilizations of the Sahara and North Africa — even with the paintings of the Spanish Levant — has still to be defined. Carried out before our chronological reckoning begins, they may well have been adapted in their turn to the image of the myth they portray. They were executed millenia ago, among a hunting community, by the direct ancestors of the present-day Bushmen. We are unlikely today to come upon anything more than adapted versions of the works themselves — a flicker of the last Bushmen, before they left for the depths of the Kalahari desert, where their principal artistic activity was confined to engraving and painting ostrich eggs for water carrying.

## Statues of Rank

They correspond to each of the ranks in the New Hebridean social hierarchy. The ranks are not hereditary, nor do they mark the degree of initiation; they are acquired in the course of public ceremonies, for which payment was made in pigs, the traditional source of wealth. Generally cut in the trunk of bracken, more importance is attached to the stylization of the human face than to that of the body.

## Tami (Isle of)

This little island in the gulf of Huon, eastern New Guinea, possesses sculptural art of uneven quality, which is frequently coloured. The wooden or "tapa" masks have regular features, which are symmetrically enlivened by polychrome décor. The same symmetry is seen in the composition of the engraved and white-washed motives which decorate the portable drums, plates and wooden utensils. These motifs, in which the triangle and the circle are associated and find expression everywhere, derive from a geometric stylization of man and bird.

## Tapa

Called "siapo" by the Polynesians (the most ingenious experimenters in this field), "tapa" is a vegetable tissue obtained from the inner side of the bark of a mulberry tree. The bark is collected from young plants and placed to soak in water until it ferments. It is then hammered with a wooden bat which

stretches it into irregular bands, sometimes twice as long as the original. The same hammering technique is employed for closing the holes resulting from the operation and soldering the bands together, as for inlaying the texture with fragments of coloured tapa for decoration. Other methods for decorating the tapa exist: dyeing; tracing with more or less conventional motifs; dry or colour pressing; stamping. Tapa, which is made by the women, was developed into an incomparable means of pictorial expression.

## Tassili n'Ajjer

The great plateaux surrounding the Hoggar massif possess a quantity of walls which have been painted and engraved for several millenia. The rock engravings of animals and hunters are thought to be of Neolithic origin; the paintings more recent. They were first noted in 1909; although they have been carefully studied none has told us anything of the meaning of these frequently monumental mural compositions, nor of the mythology which inspired them. The most elaborate parietal paintings are found on the sites of Sefar, Jabbaren, Inaouanrhat and Tin Tazarift.

## Tattooing

There are two methods. The Marquessian consists in causing a series of corporal perforations with mallet-blows on a comb coated with a pigment of

197

oily soot; repetition of this induces a flat tint or a band of dark colour. The New Zealand method is by incision of varying depths with a cutting instrument.

### Tectiforme

This term has long been used for certain abstract "signs" which accompany Paleolithic wall paintings or engravings. Composed of parallel intersecting strokes, grouped in chevrons or bundles, these signs were interpreted anecdotically in terms of the animals surrounding them, as if they were "realist" portraits of snares, or huts whose roofs were covered with faggots and dried grass. In fact, we are now almost certain that they derive from a very developed stylization of frequently associated masculine and feminine figures, with a sexual symbolism.

### Teyjat

The cave of Teyjat in the Dordogne is typical of the decay of parietal art in the sanctuaries after the beginning of the late Magdalenian period. They are no more than fine incisions, always exploiting the same old process. Only the engravings on bone, independent of the technical skill, still reveal a graphic sense of colour and rhythmical design.

### Tibesti

To the north of Chad, in the mountains and volcanic massifs of the Tibesti, engravings have been found at an altitude of 1,300 metres; the site of Goura contains particularly fine animal figures. Portraits of huge rhinoceri, elephants with crinkled ears and striped trunks, are deeply hollowed in the soft rock, with continuous broad supple lines which take advantage of the surface excrescences; they are contrasted with the more nervous drawing of the giraffes, frail creatures with which they are often coupled. At Gira Gira and at Gonoa, there are few paintings of the ox family, and these are dominated by the defaced engraving of an ox with horns in the form of a lyre, of which only the upper part has been found. On the other hand, human figures are numerous, of a most stylized kind. At Gonoa, two are impressive for their size, and in the graphic firmness of their incision. In both examples, the man is naked, seemingly masked, his movement accentuating his curvature. One is brandishing a shield and a bow, the other a club or a stone axe. The movement of the second endows him with a feeling of immense, almost mythical, power. This marching man of Gonoa seems to be setting out to conquer the world.

## Tjurunja

Spread in large numbers across central Australia, "Tjutungs" are engraved plaques of wood or shale, oblong or circular, of varying dimensions. Each clan possesses its own, and they cannot be viewed by women or non-initiated persons; they are hidden in places chosen for the cult, and are periodically rubbed with ochre or grease. Their engraved décor is developed from concentric circles and parallel lines representing a rhythmical episode. They are read by following the tracing of the incisions with the finger, the commentary of the reader being punctuated by the chorus of the initiates.

## Tonga

This Polynesian archipelago, partly coral, partly volcanic, was the centre, in spite of its extent, of an important maritime empire which has managed to preserve a relative independance down to our own times. Its warlike expeditions went in its hey-day as far afield as the Ellis Isles, Rotuma, Samoa, and Fiji. Its art is poor, but wooden ivory statues clothed in vegetable tissues and archaic potteries representing gods have been found. Its only decoration is the "tapa", in the use of which it shows real inventive power, as much in the themes chosen as in the composition.

## Totemism

A body of beliefs about the totem, a term derived from the word "ototeman" borrowed from a dialect of the north American Indians, by which ethnologists designated the mystical bond uniting a human group to an animal, a plant or a natural phenomenon. Totemism, whose function is "classificatory", symbolizes the clans which differ among themselves socially, and in what they have in common — each participating organically, whatever may be the category granted as its share, in the elaboration of the universe.

## Trobriands (Isles of)

This archipelago is a prolongation of the eastern tip of New Guinea, part of the cultural region known as Massim which includes the archipelago of Entrecasteaux, Louisade and Woodlark. The prows of canoes and certain shields are

199

completely overlaid with decoration modelled with a spiral and perforated relief, whose rhythms vary in a Baroque manner. This reappears in the engraved whitened ornament of the chalk spatular whose most decipherable motifs are about humans, animals, or more especially birds. It is the last, incidentally, which appears to inspire the development in volutes of the décor on certain shields and canoe prows.

### Trois-Frères (The)

In the Tuc d'Audoubert at Montesquieu-Avantés in the Ariège, the cave of the Trois-Frères was discovered in 1916 by Bégouen and his three sons. Breuil began the surveys in 1921, and continued them from 1930 to 1940. This deep sanctuary with its uneven relief contains galleries

with heavily incised engravings leading to the famous hall of the "Magician". This anthropo-zoomorphic person who dominates three panels — dedicated respectively to bison, reindeer and horses — and who was long considered "the master of the animals", "the god of the chase and fecundity", appears increasingly to us as a composite creation, a plastic synthesis entrusted with transmitting the power of the myth. Most of the parietal works here date from the middle Magdalenian; the engravings go back to the Aurignacian and the Gravettian.

### Tuareg

A nomadic people of the central Sahara organized in hierarchical castes, whose main centres are — the mountainous massifs of Hoggar, Tassili n'Ajjer, the Adrar of Iforas, the Air, and the area within the loop of the Niger. The Touaregs numbering about 350,000 are Berbers who originally lived as camel shepherds. They still carry on a nomadic life, but their economy as they approach the Niger now depends on the breeding of sheep, goats and oxen. As in most nomadic Saharan societies, Touareg art is produced by an artisan caste, the Enadens, who specialize in the production of objects or the decoration of leather, wood or metal engraving. They accompany the Touaregs in their changes of abode, but tend to settle and found artisan centres — as at Agades on the Niger, which produces all the material equipment, and that for their cults,

required in their nomadic life. They train technicians and create styles.

### Valltorta

Between Albocacer and Tirig in the province of Castellan, shelters beneath the rock in the gorge of Valltorta possess the greatest number of parietal paintings in the whole of the Spanish Levant. The discovery dates from 1917. It was thought that in certain of the leaping archers, sartorial details, hair styles, masks and finery, could be identified.

### Villepin

The decorated objects found at Villepin in the Dordogne bear witness to an expressive decline in engraving. In fact engraving, occupied with artifice and virtuosity, had lost its freedom and all its meaning. This improverishment of technique as well as of subject is typical of the end of Magdalenian culture.

## Wallis (Islands)

Discovered in 1767 by an English Captain of the same name, this Polynesian Archipelago has around 6,000 inhabitants. The magnificent "Tapa" of the Wallis Islands often combine different techniques of engraving motifs on vegetable or wooden moulds.

## Washkuk

Population of the Middle-Sepik valley near Ambuti, whose artistic activities are principally seen in the mural decoration of the men's ceremonial huts. The paintings are done on a vegetable base, usually the open envelope of the lower leaves of a Palm tree, then integrated into the skeleton structure of posts and beams, engraved and often coloured. This polychrome art, whose spiral, circular, lozenge-shaped motifs are drawn from the human figure, is sometimes similar to the tree fern sculpture of Ambrym.

with some fertility cult, this figurine hewn out of limestone is no longer considered Aurignacian. It has just been re-dated as much later. The majority of works of this kind, indeed, are contemporary with the Gravetto-Solutrian transition between 25,000 and 18,000.

## Willendorf

Prehistoric Austrian station where a considerable amount of tools were found which proved the wide diffusion of Paleolithic industries across Europe. But Willendorf is best known for its "Aurignacian Venus", a nude female Steatopygous statuette with pronounced sexual characteristics, the head buried in a bee hive hair do. Probably linked

## Witu (Islands)

Small Melanesian Archipelago south west of New Britain, of around 4,000 inhabitants.
"Tapa" masks whose form is created for a geometric tracing of vivid colours and wooden masks which are firmly inscribed with weak colour patterns, constitute the main polychrome expression of the Witu islands' art.

## Wobe

Peopling the western forests of the Ivory Coast, the Wobe are part of the complex culture formed by the Dan and the Guere. More rough even than those of the Guere, their masks give rein to the expressionism of their form and colours. According to B. Holas the Wobe recognize having copied the strongest masks of the Guere. Their body paintings mark the end of initiatory retreats.

## Yap (Island)

Micronesian Island, part of the Archipelago of the Carolines, where a kind of plaiting of coloured fibres is practised.

## Yoruba

With over five million people this is one of the strongest peoples of Africa and its concentration in south west Nigeria does not prevent them from extending to the interior of Dahomey, to Togo and to Ghana. Yoruban mythology is very complex and entirely dominated by the God Olorun. Only the Olisha, the protective Goddesses, several hundred in number, are abundantly represented in the statuary or provided for in the signs of recognition. The masks are generally consecrated to the cult of the dead. Polychrome art is frequently seen in the sculpture and engraving which, on the great drums of the secret Ogboni society — political leaders — uses relief to show mythological scenes between the interlacings.

Printed in Italy

# Bibliography

## 1. Pre-History

H. G. Bandi and J. Maringer: *L'Art préhistorique* Basle and Paris 1952.

Georges Bataille: *Lascaux ou la Naissance de l'Art*, Geneva 1955.

Henri Breuil: *Quatre Cents Siècles d'Art pariétal*, Montignac 1952.

H. Breuil and R. Lantier: *Les Hommes de la Pierre ancienne*, Paris 1959.

Henri Breuil: *Les Roches peintes d'Afrique australe*, Paris 1954.

P. Graziozi: *L'Arte dell'antica Eta della Pietra*, Florence 1956.

Jean-Dominique Lajoux: *Merveilles du Tassili n'Ajjer*, Paris 1962.

A. Laming-Emperaire: *La Signification de l'Art rupestre paléolithique*, Paris 1962.

A. Laming-Emperaire: *L'Archéologie préhistorique*, Paris 1963.

A. Leroi-Gourhan: *Les Hommes de la Préhistoire. Les Chasseurs*, Paris 1955.

A. Leroi-Gourhan: *Les Religions de la Préhistoire*, Paris 1964.

A. Leroi-Gourhan: *Histoire de l'Art*, Vol. 1 and *Histoire universelle*, Vol. I de l'Encyclopédie de la Pléiade, Paris 1961.

G. H. Luquet: *L'Art et la Religion des Hommes fossiles*, Paris 1926.

Théodore Monod: *L'Adrar Ahnet*, Paris 1932.

Louis-René Nougier: *La Géographie humaine préhistorique*, Paris 1959.

## 2. Oceania

Gilbert Archey: *Sculpture and Design: an Outline of Maori Art*, Auckland 1955.

Tibor Bodrogi: *L'Art de l'Océanie*, Budapest and Paris 1961.

A. Bühler, T. Barrow and C. P. Mountford: *Océanie et Australie*, Paris 1962.

A. P. Elkin and R. and C. Berndt: *Art in Arnhem Land*, London and Melbourne 1950.

Jean Guiart: *L'Art autochtone de Nouvelle-Calédonie*. Noumea 1953.

Jean Guiart: *Histoire de l'Art*, Vol. 1 de l'Encyclopedie de la Pleiade, Paris 1961.

Jean Guiart: *Océanie*, Paris 1963.

Karel Kupka: *Un Art à l'Etat brut*, Lausanne 1962.

Maurice Leenhardt: *Notes d'Ethnologie néo-calédonienne*, Paris 1930.

Maurice Leenhardt: *Gens de la Grande Terre*, Paris 1937.

Maurice Leenhardt: *Arts de l'Océanie*, Paris 1947.

G. H. Luquet: *L'Art néo-calédonien*, Paris 1926.

Ch. P. Mountford: *Art, Myth and Symbolism*, Melbourne 1956.

## 3. Africa

H. Baumann and D. Westermann: *Les Peuples et les Civilisations de l'Afrique*, Paris 1948.

Germaine Dieterlen: *Essai sur la Religion bambara*, Paris 1951.

Leo Frobenius: *Histoire de la Civilisation africaine*, Paris 1936.

Marcel Griaule: *Masques dogon*, Paris 1938.

Marcel Griaule: *Arts de l'Afrique noire*, Paris 1947.

Marcel Griaule: *Dieu d'Eau*, Paris 1948.

M. J. Herskovits: *The Background of African Art*, Evanston 1945.

Bohumil Holas: *Les Masques kono*, Paris 1952.

Bohumil Holas: *Le Culte de Zié*, Dakar 1955.

Bohumil Holas: *Les Sénoufo*, Paris 1957.

C. Kjersmeier: *Centres de Style de la Sculpture nègre africaine*, Paris 1935-1958.

Jean-Paul Lebeuf: *Les Civilisations du Tchad*, Paris 1950.

Jean-Paul Lebeuf: *L'Habitation des Fali*, Paris 1961.

Michel Leiras: *L'Afrique fantôme*, Paris 1934.

Michel Leiris: *Les Nègres d'Afrique et les Arts Sculpturaux*, Paris 1954.

F. Olbrechts: *Plastiek van Kongo*, Brussels 1946.

Presence Africaine: *L'Art nègre*, Nos. 10-11, Paris 1951 (see especially the articles of Marcel Griaule, William Fagg and J. P. Lebeuf).

# List of illustrations

# Dictionary

Prehistoric Painting

This first volume in the series *History of
Painting* was printed and bound by
Officine Grafiche Arnoldo Mondadori
in Verona

The text was
composed in Times 10 point type and the
first and third parts were printed on machine
coated paper and second part on blue
cartridge paper.

The cover and lay-out of the inside pages
were designed by Jean-Marie Clerc of
Editions Rencontre.